A Southern Baptist Dialogue

Calvinism

A Southern Baptist Dialogue

Calvinism

E. RAY CLENDENEN
& BRAD J. WAGGONER
EDITORS

NASHVILLE, TENNESSEE

Printed in the United States of America

1 2 3 4 5 6 7 8 9 10 11 12 • 16 15 14 13 12 11 10 09 08
VP

Contents

Theological Stereotypes

Election and Calling

Working Together to Make Christ Known

Abbreviations

BHH	*Baptist History and Heritage*
BFM 2000	Baptist Faith and Message 2000
CTJ	*Calvin Theological Journal*
FJ	*Founders Journal*
GOTR	*Greek Orthodox Theological Review*
GTJ	*Grace Theological Journal*
HCSB	Holman Christian Standard Bible
JBC	*Journal of Biblical Counseling*
JETS	*Journal of the Evangelical Theological Society*
LCC	The Library of Christian Classics. Philadelphia, 1953–
Lumpkin	W. L. Lumpkin, *Baptist Confessions of Faith.* Rev. ed. Judson, 1969
MJT	*Midwestern Journal of Theology*
NAMB	North American Mission Board
NASB	New American Standard Bible
NICNT	New International Commentary on the New Testament
NIDOTTE	*New International Dictionary of Old Testament Theology and Exegesis,* ed. W. A. VanGemeren
NKJV	New King James Version
Presb	*Presbyterion*
OED	Oxford English Dictionary
SBC	Southern Baptist Convention
SBJT	*The Southern Baptist Journal of Theology*
SwJT	*Southwestern Journal of Theology*
WTJ	*Westminster Theological Journal*

Preface

The good news is that this book is another substantive step in the direction of understanding God's Word and wrestling with the implications of that understanding for local church ministry. Due to over two decades of our denomination's focus on the doctrine of inerrancy, coupled with all the related foundational beliefs that we hold dear, today we are debating matters like Calvinism instead of liberal ideas like whether or not Jesus actually rose from the dead. This is good.

I (Brad) enrolled in seminary in 1979 when theological compromise was far more pervasive than most grass roots Southern Baptists realized. Years later I developed several close friendships with people who were students in some of our more compromised institutions. I was appalled to hear what was claimed and argued and propagated as "truth" in the classrooms of those schools. If I had known then that today we would be debating *Calvinism*, I would have gotten on my knees and thanked God (as I do) that the nature of the debate would become so much healthier. My praise would not have been based on any personal zeal for Calvinism, but on the recognition that we would no longer be fighting over whether or not the Bible is trustworthy.

The bad news is that the current debate regarding Calvinism is not as healthy as it needs to be. There is a lot of misunderstanding related to many of the issues. There is a fair amount of misrepresentation on both sides of the debate. To make matters worse, the tone of the debate is often characterized by arrogance, intellectual elitism, snobbery, or simplistic flame throwing. Too often the number of "points" one claims to hold or not to hold is used as the test of orthodoxy or fellowship. Too often friendships are destroyed and peace in many of our churches is shattered by the way this debate is handled.

The reality is that the issues surrounding Calvinism are not going away. As Ed Stetzer will chronicle in his chapter, the number of leaders who embrace five-point Calvinism is growing. Therefore it is essential that we handle this debate with integrity and with love. We must not drag our churches into the mud to fight about words (2 Tim 2:14).

Early in 2007, with concern for the local church, Dr. Danny Akin, Dr. Tom Ascol, Dr. Thom Rainer, and I met to brainstorm how we could facilitate a healthy dialogue related to the issue of Calvinism. By the way, only one of us considers himself a five-point Calvinist, so this was never approached from the perspective of promoting Calvinism. Rather, we wanted to promote honest, God-honoring debate and analysis.

The result of this brainstorming was the decision to schedule a forum at the Ridgecrest Conference Center in the fall of 2007 to provide a healthy context for discussion and dialogue. Five reputable Calvinistic scholars were selected to represent various issues from the Reformed point of view and five reputable non-Calvinists were selected to represent alternate points of view. The chapters of this book began as addresses in the plenary sessions at Ridgecrest plus a chapter by Ed Stetzer which adds significant research related to the degree and magnitude of Calvinism within our denomination.

Our prayer and hope are that this book will advance our understanding of the issues surrounding Calvinism and will promote ongoing godly dialogue. The manner in which we handle this and other points of contention will significantly impact our churches. May God bless our efforts to understand His Word, to edify His church, and to share the gospel around the world.

I (Ray) can only add my gratitude to God that this book (and the conference where it originated) represents an unalterable commitment to the gospel. Every contributor is driven by zeal to bring to a lost world "the light of the knowledge of God's glory in the face of Jesus Christ" (2 Cor 4:6 HCSB). The authors are all driven above all by a passion to see the powerful, unadulterated gospel set free in the world, to have innumerable men and women finding life in Christ, and that His church in this generation might be the healthy, effective instrument in His hands to display His glory. It is in that commitment that we can all have one mind, one love, "sharing the same feelings, focusing on one goal" (Phil 2:2).

Brad Waggoner and E. Ray Clendenen, editors

A Southern Baptist Dialogue

Calvinism

The Current Climate

Calvinism, Evangelism, and SBC Leadership

Ed Stetzer
Director, LifeWay Research and Resident Missiologist
Nashville, Tennessee

THIS REPORT ANALYZES AND COMPARES data from two recent surveys—LifeWay's 2006 Calvinism Study and the NAMB's Center for Missional Research 2007 New Minister's Study. Drawing from these two sources, we get a good view of the proportion of Calvinist pastors and/or church staff in SBC churches and how Calvinist doctrine influences several factors related to evangelism.

Although opinions abound about Calvinist doctrine, little empirical data is available that analyzes how a belief in irresistible grace and election influences evangelism in the local church. By comparing LifeWay's 2006 Calvinism Study and the NAMB's New Minister's Study, my hope is that we can use specific data to answer the general question: Do churches with Calvinist leadership remain committed to evangelism?

Here is a summary of the findings of these two studies:

- Calvinism is a growing influence among Southern Baptist leaders with about 10 percent affirming the five points of Calvinism. However, when we look at recent SBC seminary graduates who now serve as church pastors, nearly 30 percent identify themselves as Calvinists.
- Congregations led by Calvinists tend to show a smaller attendance and typically baptize fewer people each year. The data doesn't explain why these churches are smaller.
- Even though churches with Calvinist leadership baptize fewer people each year, their baptism *rate* is virtually identical to churches led by non-Calvinists. The baptism rate is the percentage of annual baptisms relative to the total average worship attendance, a statistic used to measure evangelistic vitality.
- Both Calvinistic and non-Calvinistic leaders believe local congregations should be involved in sponsoring missions and planting new churches. The two studies showed 95 percent of

both leadership types affirmed the necessity of missions and church planting.

- Recent graduates who are Calvinistic report that they conduct personal evangelism at a slightly higher rate than their non-Calvinistic peers.

The protocols related to these studies are provided at the end of this chapter; however, some specific findings are reported in the following graphic illustrations.

Preaching about Calvinism

Starting with the 2006 LifeWay Calvinism Study, about 10 percent of SBC pastors say they are five-point Calvinists whereas nearly half of SBC pastors (47%) address the issue of Calvinism from the pulpit several times a year or more.

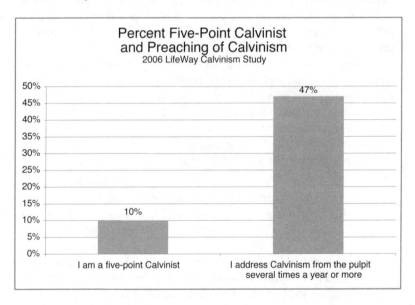

These results reveal that pastoral leaders who identify themselves as Calvinists are the minority. Even though nearly half of SBC pastors surveyed say they preach on issues related to Calvinism, this is not terribly surprising considering the issue is present in some form whenever the salvation message is explained or presented. All in all, however, Calvinism is not widespread throughout the Southern Baptist Convention.

The 2007 NAMB New Minister's Study indicates a fairly substantial increase in those who agree they are five-point Calvinists compared to those in the LifeWay study who say they are Calvinists. In fact, 27 percent of seminary graduates serving currently in SBC church leadership roles strongly or somewhat agree with the statement, "I am a five-point Calvinist." However, it is difficult to make a direct comparison between the two studies since the 2007 NAMB New Minister's Study includes any seminary graduate between 1998 and 2004 who is serving at any level of church staff leadership. The LifeWay Calvinism study only looked at SBC senior or lead pastors.

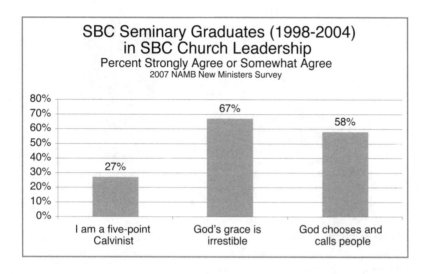

Among the recent seminary graduates serving in SBC church leadership, a majority of them agree specifically with two tenets often associated with Calvinism:

- God's grace is irresistible (67%).
- God chooses and calls people (58%).

A cautionary note at this point: Church leaders who are not Calvinists in the formal sense could still believe in either of these statements.

Clearly Calvinism appears on the rise among recent seminary graduates compared to SBC pastors as a whole, particularly when the NAMB study is compared to the 2006 LifeWay Calvinism Study. In order to obtain a better comparison between the two studies, it is helpful to limit the 2007 NAMB New Minister's Study to only those who are senior or lead pastors of SBC churches. This better aligns with the LifeWay study of pastors. By doing this, the combined studies reveal a 19 percentage point difference between recent seminary graduates who say they are five-point Calvinists against SBC pastors as a whole.

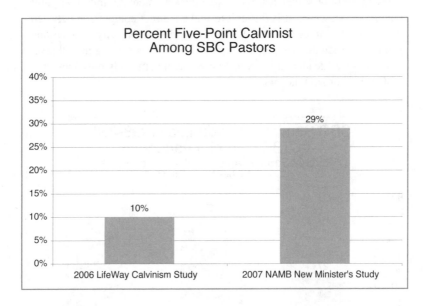

These results confirm that Calvinism is on the rise among recent seminary graduates of SBC seminaries; however, it is still far from a majority of recent graduates now serving as pastors.

Is the Rise of Calvinism a Generational Effect?

If more SBC church leaders identify themselves as Calvinists, is this because younger leaders are more likely to embrace the tenets of Calvinism, or is it because Calvinism is now emphasized more in seminary education than it was in the past?

By looking at the generational peers of SBC seminary graduates,

- We can see that younger leaders identify themselves as five-point Calvinists slightly more that older leaders. When we compare leaders born from 1945 through 1975 with leaders born in or after 1976, we can see the increase toward Calvinism is between 20 and 30 percent.

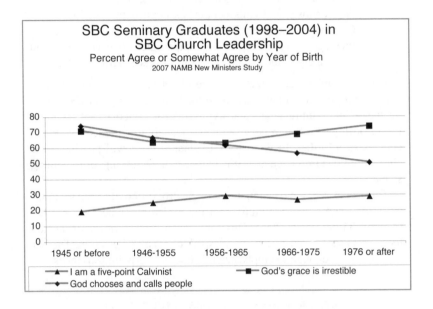

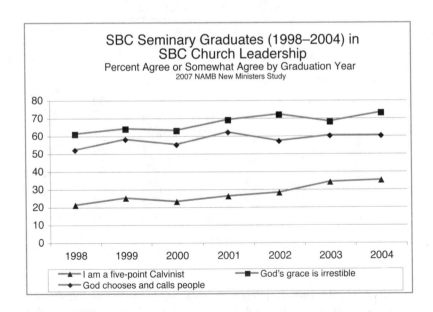

- At the same time, there is a steady decline of those who believe God chooses and calls people (as defined by election within Calvinistic doctrine). The NAMB study gives a further mixed message by revealing, among leaders born between 1946 and 1965, a dip in those who agree God's grace is irresistible.

It is difficult to determine if an age effect is at work here. It does appear that younger cohorts are more likely to be five-point Calvinists, but the belief in central tenets of Calvinist doctrine fluctuate substantially for all birth peers. If a trend for younger leaders to embrace Calvinism does exist, a further breakdown by graduation year will provide some clues about this trend, whether it is increasing, decreasing, or remaining stable.

There does seem to be an increase in the proportion of seminary graduates who agree with Calvinist doctrine, up from 21 percent in 1998 to about 34 percent in 2004. This same seven-year period indicates an increase in those who believe in irresistible grace and election. The bar chart below is enough to emphasize this rise in five-point Calvinists.

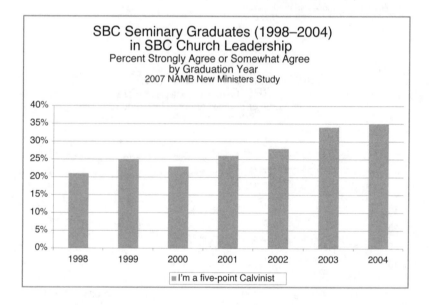

If we add the 2006 LifeWay Calvinism Study to the trend analysis, the proportion of Calvinist solo or senior pastors is consistent through those born in 1975. Because a random sample was used, the small proportion of pastors under age 32 does not allow for accurate comparison

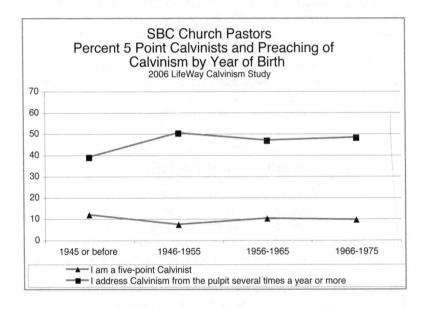

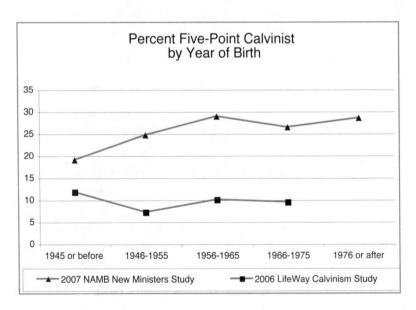

to older ages. Between 7 and 11 percent of pastors claim to be five-point Calvinists across these older age groups. The proportion of pastors addressing the subject of Calvinism from the pulpit does increase by generational peers over time.

Calvinist pastors are still very much in the minority despite the upward trend among seminary graduates, and at the current growth rates it will take some time before Calvinist-led churches approach an equal or majority status within the Southern Baptist Convention.

Seminaries Most Likely to Produce Calvinist Pastors

The NAMB and LifeWay studies also reveal a transition is taking place among Southern Baptist seminaries with a new order for which institutions are more likely to produce Calvinist leaders. The NAMB study indicates that since 1998 Southern Seminary produced the largest relative proportion of Calvinist pastors with Midwestern in the second position. The LifeWay study, one year older than NAMB's, indicates Golden Gate as the seminary producing, on a relative scale, the most Calvinist leaders with Southeastern in the second slot.[1] However, in some cases, the samples are too small to draw definitive conclusions. Therefore, we have only listed the order, not the amount, by seminary.

2007 NAMB NEW MINISTERS	2006 LIFEWAY CALVINISM
Southern	Golden Gate
Midwestern	Southeastern
Golden Gate	New Orleans
Southwestern	Southwestern
New Orleans	Midwestern
Southeastern	Southern

The LifeWay study indicates less difference in the seminary rankings among all pastors included in the study. The greater difference is revealed when looking at recent seminary graduates. In other words, more recent graduates from certain schools (particularly and in order, Southern, Midwestern, and Golden Gate) were more Calvinistic than the

---

[1] Note that the NAMB study represents recent seminary graduates and is therefore representative of the current state of Calvinist-producing leadership by seminary. But the Lifeway study represents all SBC seminary-trained pastors and so reflects seminary training in the past several decades as a whole.

other schools and more Calvinistic than the sample of all graduates in the LifeWay study.

Does Calvinistic Leadership Lead to Less Evangelism?

Many people assume that Calvinist pastors, because of their belief in God's election, are less likely to share their faith regularly than non-Calvinist leaders. Yet this idea is not supported by the data in these studies. The number of Calvinist leaders who share their faith weekly is similar to the amount of non-Calvinist leaders who engage in weekly evangelism. This percentage remained consistent even when Calvinist leaders agreed with statements, such as:

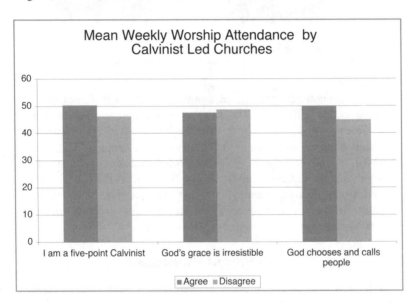

- I am a five point Calvinist.
- God's grace is irresistible.
- God chooses and calls people.

As noted at the beginning of this chapter, the mean weekly attendance is substantially higher among churches led by non-Calvinist pastors: 28 percent higher in the NAMB study and 8 percent higher in LifeWay's study. In general, Calvinist pastors lead smaller churches.

21

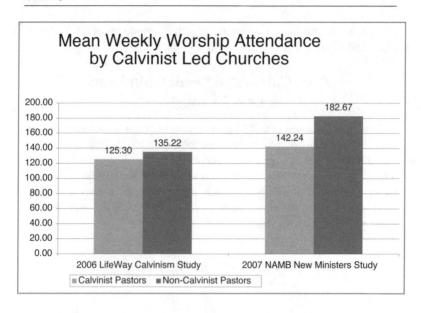

Mean Weekly Worship Attendance by Calvinist Led Churches

On a side note, congregational size between the two studies reveals a recognizable difference. The LifeWay study demonstrates a much lower mean worship attendance than the NAMB study. The LifeWay attendance figures are based on the Annual Church Profile (ACP), while NAMB's attendance figures are self-reported by the respondents. The LifeWay sample represents all SBC churches whereas the NAMB study includes only churches employing recent SBC seminary students. The smallest SBC churches who could not afford a full-time staff member would be less represented in the NAMB study.

Number of Baptisms

Baptisms tend to give a better indication of a congregation's commitment to evangelism; the number of yearly baptisms reveals whether a church is actually reaching the lost instead of just moving believers around. In the NAMB study, congregations led by non-Calvinist leaders baptized 30 percent more than Calvinist led congregations. This is similar to the higher worship attendance figures for the same group. On the other hand, the LifeWay study indicates Calvinist congregations baptize essentially the same number of people as non-Calvinist-led congregations.

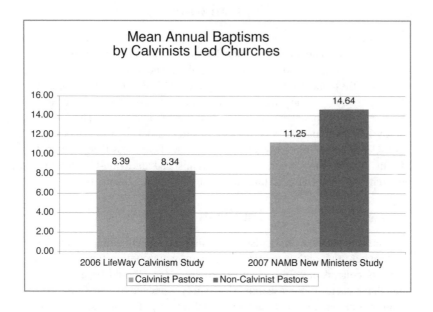

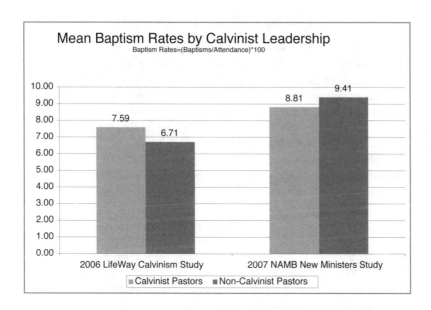

Baptism Rates

An even better measurement of a congregation's commitment to evangelism is the baptism *rate*, which looks at how many baptisms occur every year for each 100 in average worship attendance.

Using these measures, the LifeWay and NAMB studies provide conflicting results. In the LifeWay study Calvinist-led churches appear to have a higher baptism rate than non-Calvinist led churches. The NAMB study indicates just the reverse. The difference between Calvinists and non-Calvinists within these surveys is small, always less than 1 percent. From this we can conclude that Calvinist-led and non-Calvinist-led churches evidence similar rates through their annual baptisms.

Implications

Data such as this can be used and misused. Already, after the conference where this data was presented, many were quoting (and misquoting) its conclusions. Important information here should be addressed, and that calls for more research. More study is needed on *why* Calvinistic churches are smaller and baptize fewer, yet they still have similar baptism rates.

Failing to Engage Lostness

Regardless of who has better numbers, both Calvinist-led and non-Calvinist-led congregations in the SBC are failing to reach lost people in North America. Theological discussions, such as the ones about Calvinism, are important, but my fear is that many churches love their traditions or love theological debates more than they love the lost. Should we be compelled to debate or compelled to be on mission? Our mission is to tell the lost about Jesus Christ; God calls us to act as agents of reconciliation between God and man. Our goal is not to win a theological debate; rather, it is to keep our eyes on the prize for which we were called heavenward—the high calling of Christ.

Summary

Research cited reveals several important items regarding Calvinism among SBC church leaders:

- Churches with Calvinist leaders are still a small minority in the Southern Baptist Convention.

- Even though Calvinism is on the rise among recent seminary graduates, it will take years to approach any equality with non-Calvinist-led congregations.
- Calvinist-led churches are generally smaller in worship attendance and annual baptisms than non-Calvinist led churches.
- Annual baptism rates indicate little difference between Calvinist-led and non-Calvinist-led churches.

2006 LifeWay Study Protocols

The data reported in this chapter is part of an ongoing project by LifeWay Research toward understanding the theological and evangelistic implications of Calvinism on SBC congregations. Using a random sample of Southern Baptist churches, LifeWay Research conducted telephone interviews with 413 senior or lead pastors during August 2006 regarding their opinions and attitudes surrounding Calvinism. This sample provides for a margin of error of +4.8 percent at the 95 percent confidence interval.

Key questions asked during the interview included:

- Do you consider yourself a five-point Calvinist? (yes, no, don't know)
- How frequently do you address Calvinism from the pulpit? (Would you say you address it more than once a month, once a month, less than once a month but several times a year, or once a year or less?)
- Respondents were also asked if they had attended seminary and, if so, what seminary they had attended.
- They were also asked for their age. This enabled us to calculate their year of birth and conduct trend analysis.

Critical to the results reported in this chapter is the capacity to link Annual Church Profile data (including baptisms, worship attendance, etc.) to the church of each pastor surveyed. This enabled patterns of SBC churches to be understood in the context of Calvinist pastors versus non-Calvinist pastors.

2007 NAMB New Minister's Study Protocols

In late 2006, all 1998–2004 masters-level seminary graduates from Golden Gate, New Orleans, Midwestern, Southeastern, Southwestern, and the Canadian Southern Baptist Seminary were invited to complete an online survey regarding their experiences in seminary and their current opinions and beliefs. Southern Seminary declined to participate, thus a limited subset of Southern graduates was available for the study. Although more than 2,000 seminary graduates completed the survey, 1,234 respondents indicated that they were serving currently as pastors or staff members at an SBC church. Within this group, 527 serve as senior or solo pastor of a congregation. Whenever comparisons are made between the NAMB and LifeWay surveys, this later "pastor only" group represents the NAMB data.

The number of respondents by seminary are: Golden Gate (N=270), New Orleans (N=287), Midwestern (N=148), Southeastern (N=403), Southwestern (N=978), Canadian Southern Baptist Seminary (N=11), Southern Seminary (N=52).

Several key questions germane to this report on Calvinism were asked during the interview. Each of the questions asked for the respondent's level of agreement: strongly agree, somewhat agree, somewhat disagree, strongly disagree, and don't know.

Some of these statements included:

- I am a five-point Calvinist.
- God is the true evangelist; and when He calls someone to Himself, His grace is irresistible.
- People do not choose to become Christians; God chooses and calls people who then respond to Him.
- I give a verbal presentation of the gospel (outside of church) at least once a week.

Responses for this report were collapsed into two categories: (1) agreement, which includes those stating strongly agree and somewhat agree, and (2) disagreement, which includes strongly disagree and somewhat disagree.

Respondents were also asked their age, seminary of graduation, and year of graduation. As in the LifeWay survey, this enables trend analysis of the direction for Calvinism over time.

Additionally, respondents were asked about their annual number of baptisms in the last reporting period and their average weekend worship attendance. Although these data may be softer than Annual Church Profile numbers, these responses will still enable us to understand the relationship of Calvinist-led churches on these important variables.

A Southern Baptist Dialogue

Calvinism
The Historical Record

Southern Baptists and Calvinism: A Historical Look

David S. Dockery
President, Union University
Jackson, Tennessee

LET US THINK TOGETHER IN THIS CHAPTER about our heritage, our history, and the traditions that have shaped Southern Baptist life. Many of those traditions are wonderful, and we need to hold on to that which is good (1 Thess 5:21). Not everything that is a part of our history is something we want to reclaim and carry forward, yet many aspects of it are good and helpful. We need to carry forward the good for the cause of Christ, for the advancement of His kingdom, and for His glory.

We will consider the historical record relating to Southern Baptists and Calvinism. You might get the impression from the little booklet by Fisher Humphreys, *God So Loved the World*, that Calvinism has had a minimal influence on Southern Baptist life. From Tom Nettles's *By His Grace and for His Glory*, you would think that Calvinism has shaped almost every aspect of Southern Baptist life or certainly has been a major influence.

Our question then for this chapter is, Are Southern Baptists Calvinists, or have Southern Baptists been Calvinists? And the answer is yes and no. If you ask our Wesleyan and Arminian friends, they say yes without hesitation, for the dividing line for them is the issue of eternal security. Anyone who holds to eternal security from their perspective is a Calvinist of some type, which covers almost everyone in every aspect of Southern Baptist life today. On the other hand, if by that question we mean, Are the majority of Southern Baptists or have the majority of Southern Baptists been consistent, five-point Calvinists? I think the answer is no. While our chapter focuses on Baptist history, we cannot neglect the biblical teaching on this important subject.

The Bible clearly affirms the sovereignty of God. The Bible affirms the responsibility of men and women, and the Bible affirms both the sovereignty of God and the responsibility of men and women together. We must find ways to hold together these important truths without neglecting either. Our question, however, is not to look at Baptist history in general or to look just at church history in general but to think particularly about God's sovereignty and human responsibility as they have been interpreted throughout church history and primarily in Baptist life. Baptists always have had differences over the issue of how to understand God's sovereign initiative in salvation and the importance of human responsibility, and the present situation is no exception. We offer this brief historical overview to help us understand these complex issues from a historical perspective.

Historical Overview

The Early Church

The early church fathers generally adhered to a belief in which the role and activity of the human will were deemed highly significant in the process of bringing about salvation. An example of the strong emphasis placed on the human response is found in Cyprian (200–258), bishop of Carthage, who maintained that, although salvation can be obtained only by an act of God's grace, this was conditioned by the relative worthiness of those for whom intercession is made by the saints. Most of the early church fathers were not as extreme as Cyprian, but most gave emphasis to the human response as opposed to seeing election as the unconditional, sovereign work of God. The two great schools of theological thought and biblical interpretation in the third, fourth, and fifth centuries, the Alexandrian and Antiochene schools, were no exception. The Antiochenes tended to magnify the human element in salvation more than did the platonically influenced Alexandrians.

The debate peaked in the early fifth century with the divergent positions expressed by Pelagius, a British monk who was active in Rome about 383–410, and by Augustine of Hippo. Pelagius's doctrine of salvation was grounded in human freedom. Electing grace, he maintained, is offered equally to all because God is no respecter of persons. For Pelagius, election really was equated with the revelation of God's law through reason, instructing men and women in what they should do and holding out eternal sanctions. By electing grace, he meant an infused grace that made it possible to live without sin. The theology of Augustine of Hippo (354–430) provided an approach that was different from Pelagius.

Augustine maintained that humans still have a free will; however, because of the fall of Adam this will is unable by itself to do good or to come to God. The right use of free will is dependent wholly on God's choice and His grace. Augustine affirmed that the source of salvation is God's eternal decree, which is unchangeable. Election is in accord with God's foreknowledge, and both those who are saved and those who are lost are so predetermined. At the Synod of Carthage (418), Augustine's theology was declared orthodox, while Pelagius was decried a heretic. A modified form of Pelagius's theology known as semi-Pelagianism developed in the fifth century. It affirmed divine election while ascribing to the human will a share in conversion. This position was condemned by the Council of Orange (529), who concluded that election is totally of God and that only through grace can believers ask for grace.

The Medieval Period

The medieval church generally taught a mediating position similar to semi-Pelagianism. A representative of those stressing human action was Peter Abelard (1079–1142), who denied that election was totally of God and affirmed that human free choice is by itself capable of good. The most Augustinian advocate of this period was Bernard of Clairvaux (1090–1153), whom we best know as the author of the hymn, "Jesus, the Very Thought of Thee." He confessed that, first, one cannot have forgiveness of sins apart from God's mercy. Second, one can perform no good work unless God gives it; and finally God's elect cannot merit eternal life by any works, for eternal life is a freely offered gift of God. The greatest theologian of this time was Thomas Aquinas (1225–1274). He advocated a quasi-Augustinianism, affirming God's free, electing grace while making a real place for human response.

The Reformation

The greatest renewal of Augustinianism came during the sixteenth-century Reformation with Martin Luther, Ulrich Zwingli, and John Calvin. In contrast to Desiderius Erasmus (1446–1536), who emphasized the primacy of human reason over the sovereignty of God, Martin Luther (1483–1546) strongly affirmed God's unconditional work of election. Luther did not deny that people on occasion do seek and ask for the grace of God, yet even this seeking or asking is the gift of grace, not of humans eliciting grace. Luther is best known for his view of justification by faith, but he was fully persuaded that the beginning of salvation must be attributed to God's free, electing grace.

The fullest articulation of the doctrine of election was expounded by John Calvin (1509–1564), who brought together biblical doctrine systematically in a way that no other Reformer before him had done. Calvin held that God does not graciously accept us because He sees our change for the better, as if conversion were the basis of forgiveness. God comes into our lives, taking us just as we are out of His mercy. Electing grace is by no means offered by God to be rejected or accepted as it may seem good to us. On the contrary, that same grace alone inclines our hearts to follow its movement and produces in us the choice as much as the will. Luther and Calvin, as with the other Reformers, were insistent that electing grace is not simply an offer to be rejected by men and women at will, but it is a change of the inner being so that people are effectually led to believe the gospel.

In order to think about the issue of Calvinism, we need to take a more focused look at John Calvin, who was born in 1509. He was a second-generation Reformer. When Martin Luther nailed the ninety-five theses to the church door in Wittenberg, Calvin was eight years old. We know little about Calvin's conversion, whereas Luther's conversion is well-known. Calvin's conversion was more like Lydia's in Acts 16, where we read that God opened her heart and she believed the Gospel. Calvin, around the age of 20, claimed that by a sudden conversion God subdued his heart to teachability. In 1536 Calvin found himself in the city of Basel, a refugee from religious persecution in France. At the age of 27, he published a little book that he called *Institutes of the Christian Religion.* It was a brilliant, systematic introduction to Protestant theology. Calvin hoped that it would be a key to open a way for all the children of God into a good and right understanding of Holy Scripture. Over the next 23 years Calvin edited, revised, and expanded this work numerous times. By 1559, it had become a four-book edition of the first great systematic theology in the history of the church. The basic outline followed the Apostles' Creed.

Book 1 is about the knowledge of God, His general revelation in creation, His special revelation, the Bible, and His concern for all people through His providential care. Book 2 focuses on the person and work of Jesus Christ, His atoning death on the cross, which is God's remedy for sin and the guilt of humanity. Book 3 explores the work of the Holy Spirit in salvation, particularly in the life of prayer, the mystery of predestination and Christian hope in the resurrection. When Calvin penned early editions, the issues of predestination and election were treated in book 1, but in his final editions it was explained in book 3. No longer was it treated as a matter of philosophical speculation about the decrees of God but instead had become a response of worship and theological reflection on God's work of salvation. This approach recognizes that God has saved believers who now respond in thanksgiving to this work of grace. Book 4 is about the church. Calvin had clear ideas about the organization of the visible church, its officers, sacraments, and responsibilities in the world. Calvin saw the church as a dynamic presence in the world, responsible not only for religious activities but also for giving shape and direction to every aspect of culture and life. Our culture has changed considerably, yet Calvin has much to teach us about how we should think about the work of Christ in the world.

Calvin died on May 27, 1564, and at his own request he was buried in an unmarked grave. His life's goal was to be a faithful servant of the Word of God. No doubt he would have agreed with one of his spiritual descendants, John Robinson (1576–1625), the pastor of the pilgrim fathers: "I have followed Calvin no further than he has followed Christ. For the Lord has yet more truth and light to break forth from His Holy Word." If people go to Geneva today expecting to find the tomb or grave of Calvin, they will not find it. They will find only a marker on the street where he lived, which tells us the dates of his life.

At the University of Leiden, in Holland, Jacob Arminius (1559–1609), who was a moderate Calvinist, developed between 1603 and 1609 what has become known as Arminianism. It was intended as an alternative to the teachings of John Calvin and highlighted the issues of general atonement, conditional election, universal offer of salvation, and an emphasis on God's mercy. The Arminians challenged the prevailing Calvinist stream in Holland at that time. About a decade later the Calvinists came together to examine the teachings of the Arminians and rejected them, putting together what has become known as the five points of Calvinism. These five points cannot be found in Calvin's *Institutes* but were developed about 50 years after Calvin. At the Synod of Dort (1618–1619) we find the articulation of the five points of total depravity, unconditional election, particular redemption, irresistible grace, and the perseverance of the saints. The Synod actually put them in this order: unconditional election, particular redemption, total depravity, irresistible grace, and perseverance of the saints. We have put them in the order of the tulip because it was done in Holland, the flower of Holland, which allows us to recall more easily: T-totally depravity, U-unconditional election, L-limited atonement (better known as particular redemption), I-irresistible grace, P-perseverance of the saints. We now turn our attention to the influence of Calvinism in Baptist life and thought.

Baptist Life and Thought

Early Baptists

At this same time, in 1609, the early Baptists under John Smyth and Thomas Helwys gathered together a group committed to the New Testament, its teachings about congregationalism, and believer's baptism. At this time the General Baptists were birthed. About 30 years later a completely different group called Particular Baptists developed in London and put together the First and Second London Confessions between the 1640s and 1670s. By 1644, England had seven Particular Baptist churches, and by 1689 most Baptists in England were Particular Baptists. General Baptists tended to ebb and flow. Many of them fell into a heresy of *deism*[1] or *rationalism*.[2] But by the end of the seventeenth century, England had large numbers of Particular Baptists.

Baptist churches were started in America in Rhode Island during the mid-seventeenth century. The Philadelphia Confession, which became the theological framework for early Baptists in America, was developed in 1707, about 70 years after the founding of the first Baptist church in this country. The Philadelphia Confession, the first important confessional statement for Baptists in America, was largely a restatement of the Second London Confession. Baptists early on in this country were Calvinists, and the early confessions expounded these convictions. But now we must fast-forward our survey to focus on Southern Baptists.

Southern Baptists

Today Southern Baptists comprise more than 16 million church members in all 50 states of the United States, making it the largest evangelical denomination in this country. The SBC has tended to exist separately from the rest of American Christianity because of its inability to separate from Southern culture, its parochialism, and its self-sufficiency, though there are some indicators that these things are beginning to change. For almost three decades the Southern Baptist Convention has been embroiled in controversy regarding theological issues and denominational polity. We now find ourselves asking important questions about our identity, our heritage, our future, who we are, and where we are going.

Out of this controversy at least four things have happened: (1) a refocus on the Bible and its authority, (2) a reemphasis on theology, (3) an attempt to reclaim and to understand our heritage, and (4) a beginning of conversations with evangelicals outside of Southern Baptist life. We have looked for help and renewal from the broader evangelical world. Those four things that have brought us to this particular point in the early years of the twenty-first century where we are asking the questions that are being addressed in this book. The official sesquicentennial history of the Southern Baptist Convention, written by Jesse Fletcher in 1994 (page 323), quoted comments that I had made in an address at the

---

[1] This is the view that God created the universe and left it to run on its own according to the "laws of nature."

[2] This is the view that human reason is sufficient to attain knowledge.

Institute for the Study of American Protestantism. I predicted the rise of Calvinism in Southern Baptist life in the twenty-first century. Many could see that while recovering the Baptist doctrine of the truthfulness of Scripture (1979–present) some would reconnect to nineteenth-century Baptist leaders not only to reaffirm their commitments to the inspiration of the Bible but also to be introduced to the soteriological commitments of such men as Richard Furman, J. L. Dagg, Basil Manly Sr., Basil Manly Jr., John A. Broadus, James P. Boyce, W. B. Johnson, J. M. Frost, not to mention William Carey, Andrew Fuller, Charles Spurgeon, and Adoniram Judson. It seems impossible to imagine that a convention asked to reappropriate the commitments of Basil Manly Jr. and B. H. Carroll on Scripture could do so without rediscovering their soteriological commitments as well.

Certainly it is a long way from 1845 in Augusta, Georgia to where we are today; but Southern Baptists came together at that time largely because of a lack of interest among American Baptists for missions in the South and also from the questions about who could send missionaries and who could be a missionary. Southern Baptists trace their roots to two groups of Baptists in the South. One is the so-called Charleston Tradition, characterized by confessional theology, strong support for education, quasi-liturgical worship, and order. The other is the Sandy Creek tradition with somewhat different emphases and practices.

The Sandy Creek Association was formed about a decade after the founding of the Charleston Association in 1742. Sandy Creek, led by Daniel Marshall and Shubal Stearns, can be characterized by revivalism, suspicion of educated ministry, and Spirit-led worship. The early years of the Convention, including the founding faculty at Southern Seminary were largely shaped by the Charleston Tradition. The grass roots, however, then as now, had much more in common with Sandy Creek. Those two important concepts have to be held together. We cannot just look at who the leaders were to understand Southern Baptists, even though we recognize that those leaders and the early writing theologians are our primary sources for understanding our heritage.

John L. Dagg

Southern Baptists' first writing theologian was John L. Dagg (1794–1884). His *Manual of Theology* is still worth reading today. He taught at Mercer University for many years. He stood in the reformed tradition of earlier Baptists theologians such as Bunyan, Keach, Gill, Fuller, and Backus. Almost all of Dagg's theology was a study in the grace of God. He was a consistent Calvinist, and the early Southern

Baptists who read theology were shaped and influenced by Dagg's consistent Calvinism.

James P. Boyce

The founder of Southern Baptist Theological Seminary, James Boyce (1827–1888), was the second writing theologian. He was greatly influenced not only by the Charleston Association and tradition there but also by his education at Princeton. Impacted by Charles Hodge and the legacy of Francis Turretin, Boyce brought his Princeton-influenced understanding to his theological work at Southern Seminary in 1859 and expanded that influence until his death in 1888.

Boyce was hardly different from the other members of the founding faculty. He represented the teaching of Basil Manly Jr., John Broadus, and William Williams. All four of the founders claimed a heritage connecting them to the Second London Confession, to the Philadelphia Confession, and to the Charleston Tradition, and this heritage is found in Boyce's *Abstract of Systematic Theology*. It was often said that the young men were generally Arminians when they came to the seminary, but few went through Boyce's course in theology without being converted to his strong Calvinistic views. Just as we see changes taking place among those who have been recently educated at our Southern Baptist seminaries, so apparently that also was the story of the young men who came to Southern Seminary during the last decades of the nineteenth century.

J. M. Frost and Others

As the nineteenth century concluded, Southern Baptists founded the Sunday School Board (now LifeWay Christian Resources). In 1891, J. M. Frost was named the first president or secretary of the Sunday School Board. At the turn of the century, he put together a small multiauthored volume called, *Baptist: Why and Why Not*. Frost took the lead in this influential work, but F. H. Kerfoot, who also taught theology at Southern Seminary between the Boyce and Mullins' eras, also was a major contributor, and T. T. Eaton, longtime faculty member at Union University, made a significant contribution. All of these contributors shared basic theological commitments influenced by the Philadelphia Confession and the Charleston Tradition.

B. H. Carroll

As the Southern Baptist Convention expanded westward, a giant named B. H. Carroll (1843–1914) stepped onto the scene. Carroll was the pastor of First Baptist Church Waco, founded the Department of

Theology at Baylor University, and was the founder of Southwestern Seminary in 1908, where he taught and served as president from 1908 to 1914. In his book *Baptists and their Doctrines*, Carroll claimed that regeneration is an action which precedes faith, an important mark of consistent Calvinism. So the founder of Southwestern Seminary as well as the founders of Southern Seminary were shaped by the influences of Calvinism.

E. Y. Mullins

At this particular time, in the early years of the twentieth century, a change began to take place in Southern Baptist life, pictured by E. Y. Mullins (1860–1928), the fourth president of Southern Seminary and the most influential Baptist thinker in the early part of the twentieth century. Mullins, in his book *Baptist Beliefs,* claimed that Arminianism overlooked certain essential truths about God in its strong championing of human freedom. On the other hand, Calvinism ran to extremes in some of its conclusions in its earnest desire to safeguard the truth of God's sovereignty. We are learning to discard both names, he claimed, and adhere more closely to the Scriptures while retaining the truth in both systems.

Mullins was not neutral in these matters. He was what most would call a modified Calvinist or an Amyraldian.[3] In his book *Baptist Beliefs,* he noted that grace always persuades and convinces and makes us willing to come, however mysterious it may be in its actions upon our hearts. He observed that God chooses us and we choose God, but God's choice of us is prior and more important. God saves primarily because He has chosen man but also through man's choice of God. God guides, controls, and wills the glorious outcome of our salvation. Mullins was shaped by the Calvinist theology of Boyce and Kerfoot and worked out of that tradition, even while he focused on the importance of Christian experience. E. Y. Mullins, even with new initiatives, nevertheless worked out of this modified Calvinist tradition. His influence was great not only in the early years of the twentieth century but for decades after his death. What he was doing at Southern Seminary, W. T. Conner (1877–1952) was doing at Southwestern Seminary in almost the same way.

W. T. Conner

In Conner's books *Christian Doctrine* and *The Gospel of Redemption*, he affirmed his belief in election but rejected limited atonement and

---

[3] This view derives its name from the French pastor and professor Moses Amyraut (1596–1664). His modified Calvinism taught that God decreed the salvation of all men, conditioned on their repentance and belief.

irresistible grace. Election for Conner was definable in terms of God's purpose, but he refused to focus on the discussion of God's decree. His work was more influential west than east of the Mississippi River. With Conner teaching at Southwestern Seminary for four decades and Mullins at Southern Seminary during the first 30 years of the twentieth century, a new trajectory developed that shaped Southern Baptist life for many generations. Though J. M. Frost, F. H. Kerfoot, and J. B. Tidwell (at Baylor University) followed a Calvinistic theology similar to but not as strict as Dagg and Boyce, the two great theologians in Southern Baptist life in the first 50 years of the twentieth century, Mullins and Conner, emphasized human experience, human response, and soul competency and redirected the conversation among Southern Baptists. Southern Baptist thought moved from a hermeneutic of divine sovereignty with Boyce, Broadus, and Manly to one of personal revelation and experience with Mullins and to a lesser degree with Conner, which brings us to the 1950s.

Herschel H. Hobbs

By 1950, Southern Baptists had become a programmatic people. From 1954 to 1979 the SBC was on the road to becoming yet another mainline Protestant denomination—by this time the largest Protestant denomination in the country, surpassing United Methodists. With the exception of great men like Curtis Vaughan, James Leo Garrett Jr., and others, most leaders at this time were embarrassed by the SBC's revivalistic heritage and even more by the Calvinistic aspects of the Charleston Tradition. They wanted nothing to do with it; they wanted to get rid of it any way they could. The SBC attempted to reenvision itself, largely ignoring the nineteenth-century roots of the Southern Baptist Convention.

The spokesperson for the Southern Baptist Convention in many ways at this time was the centrist Herschel Hobbs (1907–1995). He would not have been one of those trying to lead Southern Baptists to become another liberal mainline denomination. Such would be an unfair assessment of Herschel Hobbs. In his writings, *What Baptists Believe* in 1964 and the Baptist Faith and Message in 1971, which amplified the work of the Baptist Faith and Message Committee that he led in 1963, Hobbs led Southern Baptists in the middle and latter years of the twentieth century toward a modified understanding of predestination and foreknowledge. He believed that God affirmed every free human choice in such a way that the choices are not predetermined. He maintained that God chose to limit His sovereignty so that men and women could either accept or reject God's salvific order in Christ. Hobbs was almost a thoroughgoing Arminian who believed in eternal security, but he was also a thoroughgoing biblicist. He influenced Southern Baptists during this period more than any other person. For 28 years he wrote the adult Sunday school lesson for every Sunday school teacher in Southern Baptist life.

So the middle of the twentieth century saw the Arminianizing of the SBC. What Hobbs was doing in a popular way was happening at the seminaries with Dale Moody and Frank Stagg. Both Moody and Stagg rejected not only the tenets of Calvinism but other evangelical teachings as well. Stagg's influence was perhaps greater than other Baptist educators at the time because he shaped two seminaries, New Orleans and Southern. He was probably the leading liberal of the day. Moody poked fun at Calvinism, saying something like this: "Number six, you're in a fix. Number seven, you're on your way to heaven, because God has decreed that all sixes go to hell and all sevens go to heaven." Through the influence of Dale Moody, Frank Stagg, and others, who rejected almost every tenet of Calvinism and reformulated an understanding of election, Southern Baptist theology changed greatly during the 1950s, 1960s, 1970s, and thereafter.

W. A. Criswell

One different voice in Southern Baptist life was W. A. Criswell (1909–2002), the notable pastor of First Baptist Church, Dallas. Criswell's legacy is best characterized by his thoroughgoing commitments to biblical inerrancy, expositional preaching, premillennial eschatology, and a deeper-life, revivalistic approach to Christian life and ministry. We cannot neglect his influence in any area of Baptist life in the middle decades of the twentieth century. While rejecting particular or limited atonement, Criswell affirmed the other traditional four points of Calvinism, at least as he would define them. Either God acts to bring about salvation, or else there is no hope. Criswell could influence a congregation with his amazing ability to speak. On special occasions he was the greatest preacher Southern Baptists have ever known, and he shaped a new generation; he was the grandfather of the conservative resurgence.

Other Shaping Influences

We find ourselves now the heirs of this tradition with its winding roads from 1845 or before until the present, a tradition influenced by the Philadelphia Confession of 1707, the Charleston Confession of 1742, the Abstract of Principles of 1858, the modified, more lenient Calvinist Confession from New Hampshire in 1833, and the Baptist Faith and Message (1925, 1963, 2000). Southern Baptists have been influenced by various traditions, and even Landmarkists such as T. T. Eaton (a five-point Calvinist) and J. M. Pendleton (a four-point Calvinist). Southern

Baptists in the early years of the twenty-first century are shaped by a renewed commitment to the Bible, by a new emphasis on theology, and by reclaiming our roots. We also should not neglect the influence the evangelical world has had on us over the last two decades. Men like Francis Schaeffer, Carl Henry, J. I. Packer, Millard Erickson, John Piper, and Don Carson have had a towering and shaping influence, especially on younger Southern Baptists. We now find various groups represented in the Southern Baptist Convention, including fundamentalists, revivalists, evangelicals, and Calvinists. Many people continue to misunderstand the differences among these groups, seeing all Southern Baptist conservatives as the same or wanting to find just one tradition that has shaped us; but that is a misreading of who Southern Baptists are now and who Southern Baptists have been.

The consistent Calvinists tend to be rejected by fundamentalists and revivalists. The contemporary church types are more and more detached from, if not apathetic toward, convention matters. The evangelicals are disappointed because of the lack of unity. The Calvinists feel the rejection, and those in the younger generation are at times frustrated and confused. At this critical time we need to understand who Southern Baptists are, where we have been, and where we are going. By and large we don't understand our heritage, our history, our theological identity, or the distinctives of the various traditions. It is time for us to be reintroduced to Furman, Manly, Broadus, Johnson, Frost, Mullins, Carroll, Conner, Moon, and Armstrong. We hardly know Lee, Rogers, Hobbs, and Criswell. Southern Baptists are at once both beneficiaries and victims of tradition. Thus we need to test the traditions and hold on to the truth (1 Thess. 5:21).

We are beneficiaries who have received nurturing truth and wisdom from God's faithfulness in past generations. We are victims who now take for granted things that possibly or probably need to be questioned. Southern Baptists are beneficiaries of good, wise, and sound traditions as well as victims of poor, unwise, and unsound traditions. The Bible must be the last word as we sift through and evaluate both our traditions and our challenges.

We must acknowledge that the ultimate danger to the gospel lies not in the nuances of our differences but in the rising tides of liberalism, neopaganism, and postmodernism that threaten to swamp Southern Baptist identity in cultural accommodation. We need to look for common ground with those who share commitments to biblical authority, to the gospel, and to Baptist congregationalism. With Luther Rice, who in 1814 founded the Triennial Convention, "Let us not become bitter against those who view this matter (the doctrine of election) in a different light, nor treat them in a supercilious manner. Let us be gentle towards all, for who has made us to differ from what we once were? Who has removed the scales from our eyes?"[4] Similarly, let us hear Charles Spurgeon:

> I have endeavored, in my ministry, to preach to you,
> not a part of the truth, but the whole counsel of God;
> but I cannot harmonize it, nor am I anxious to do so.
> I am sure all truth is harmonious, and to my ear the
> harmony is clear enough; but I cannot give you a com-
> plete score of the music, or mark the harmonies of the
> gamut. I must leave the Chief Musician to do that.[5]

Perhaps we can find a model of cooperation in the eighteenth-century awakenings with George Whitefield and John Wesley, who were close friends. Whitefield was a consistent Calvinist; Wesley, a consistent Arminian. They both affirmed the sovereignty of God. They differed over their understanding of how to define original sin and total depravity. Whitefield affirmed unconditional election; Wesley rejected it. Whitefield believed in particular atonement; Wesley did not. Whitefield held to irresistible grace; Wesley emphasized prevenient grace for all. Whitefield was convinced of the perseverance of the saints; Wesley was not. Yet they were best friends, colleagues, colaborers for the cause of the gospel. We can learn lessons here in the bridge-building effort, finding ways to advance the gospel and the cause of Christ.

Perhaps we can all agree with John Leland, the champion of religious liberty in Virginia. He claimed Baptists are people who hold to the sovereignty of God and the promiscuous preaching of the gospel. Let us also hear the words of Iain Murray, a Calvinist, who warns that when Calvinism ceases to be evangelistic, when it becomes more concerned with theory than with the salvation of men and women, when acceptance of doctrines seems to become more important than acceptance of Christ, then it is a system going to seed and will invariably lose its attractive power.

One Gospel:
Toward a Southern Baptist Consensus

Let those who have differing convictions about these matters grasp hands. We need not compromise our own convictions. We need to seek

---

[4] Cited in Timothy George, "Promoting Renewal, Not Tribalism," in *Christianity Today* (June 17, 1996): 25.

[5] Cited in Timothy George, *Amazing Grace: God's Initiative—Our Response*. Leader's Guide (Nashville: LifeWay, 2000), 156.

togetherness for the right reasons; we need to remember that doctrinal matters are important. We need to know how to distinguish between primary and secondary matters of faith. We need to pray for guidance and illumination from the Holy Spirit when we have theological disagreements; and we need to be humble, not arrogant, when dealing with differences and controversies. We need to find a core around which we can come together.

We must recognize that there is a need for boundaries to say that some things do not fit in Baptist life. We need to say that hyper-Calvinism (involving the rejection or neglect of evangelism and missions) does not fit. We need to say that consistent Arminianism (involving the rejection of eternal security) does not fit. Pelagianism, open theism, and process theology do not belong. We need to recognize that there can be errors on both sides of the Calvinist question. We can learn from the mistakes of the past and recognize our Baptists distinctives, recommitting ourselves to biblical authority and the Baptist understanding of the church.

We must recognize that Calvinism is not necessarily a key Baptist distinctive; it is not a primary doctrine. We can join hands as Calvinists, as modified Calvinists, as lenient Calvinists, as modified Arminians, working together to advance the cause of the gospel. It is time to recognize that a variety of perspectives can be found and have been found in Baptist life.

Faithful and earnest followers of Christ have viewed these important matters differently. Some have chosen to stress the human response and the importance of human free agency. Others have maintained the priority of God's sovereignty and divine initiative. That all Christians will ever fully agree on an answer to this question this side of heaven is doubtful. However, we can seek to stress common areas of agreement from which we can develop a shared consensus. We can agree that God is the author and the finisher of our salvation. We can all affirm that we love Him because He first loved us; and like the model of Wesley and Whitefield before us who worked together with great appreciation, we need a new respect for one another while having different perspectives on this matter. We likewise can acknowledge our differences without breaking fellowship, while recommitting to our collaborative efforts for the cause of the gospel.

Let us not be sidetracked by secondary or tertiary matters where we might have disagreements. Instead, let us focus on primary matters where we seek to frame our message by biblical, historical, and theological understandings. We affirm that our evangelistic proclamation is shaped by the truth that God has created men and women in His image. Humans have sinned and are separated and alienated from God without any hope apart from salvific grace. In grace God takes the initiative in bringing sinners to Christ through the proclamation of the gospel message and the human response of faith. As a result of God's grace, believers experience salvation from sin, which involves conversion to God. All of salvation is from God, yet recipients of this salvation must respond in faith and commitment. The Bible expresses these truths in various ways but underscores throughout that God is the author and finisher of our salvation (Heb 12:2).

Therefore, we recognize the importance of means. We all need to agree, like William Carey 215 years ago, on the need and priority to go and proclaim the gospel, to send missionaries, to plant churches, to recognize that the work of the Spirit takes place through His Word and through prayer. We need to emphasize that sinners must respond to the gospel because God saves only believers. Even as we have seen a conservative resurgence over the last three decades, it is now time for us to pray for and work together for a Great Commission resurgence. We pray for God's guidance, grace, and blessing in our teaching and doctrinal discussions.

In conclusion, as we seek to build a theological consensus around the gospel for the good of our work together, let us ever be humble, and not arrogant, when dealing with these sacred matters. Moreover, we commit ourselves afresh to the good news of salvation by faith in Christ. We heartily confess and gladly affirm that Jesus Christ, as the God-man, has fully revealed God to men and women. Having lived a sinless life, Christ, as our substitute, died a death for the sins of the world. Having been raised from the dead, He now sits exalted at God's right hand, a position of honor and exaltation, exercising His rule and dominion. In Jesus Christ we place our trust and hope, offering our thanksgiving, praise, and worship for the gift of salvation He has provided for us by grace through faith (Eph 2:8–9). In this gospel, the one true gospel, we place our hope and ground our unity for service together. And we proclaim this gospel to the world to disciple the nations, with confidence in the promise that Christ will be with us even to the end of the age (Matt 28:18–20).

Sources

Berkouwer, G. C. *Man: The Image of God.* Grand Rapids: Eerdmans, 1962.

_____. *The Person of Christ.* Grand Rapids: Eerdmans, 1955.

Bloesch, Donald. *Christian Foundations.* Downers Grove: InterVarsity, 1992–2004.

_____. *Essentials of Evangelical Theology*. 2 vols. San Francisco: Harper and Row, 1978–79.

Bogue, Carl W. *Jonathan Edwards and the Covenant of Grace*. Cherry Hill, NJ: Mack, 1975.

Boyce, James P. *Abstract of Systematic Theology*. Philadelphia: American Baptist Publication Society, 1887.

Brunner, Emil. *The Doctrine of Creation and Redemption*. Philadelphia: Westminster, 1952.

Carnell, E. J. *The Case for Orthodox Theology*. Philadelphia: Westminster, 1959.

Carroll, B. H. *Baptists and Their Doctrines*. New York: Revell, 1913.

Conner, W. T. *Christian Doctrine*. Nashville: Broadman, 1937.

Conyers, A. J. *The Eclipse of Heaven*. Downers Grove: InterVarsity, 1997.

Cranfield, C. E. B. *The Epistle to the Romans*. Edinburgh: T & T Clark, 1975.

Criswell, W. A. *Great Doctrines of the Bible*. 6 vols. Grand Rapids: Zondervan, 1982–1986.

Dagg, John L. *A Manual of Theology*. Charleston: Southern Baptist Publication Society, 1857.

Denney, James. *The Death of Christ*. New York: Armstrong, 1903.

Dockery, David S. *Southern Baptist Consensus and Renewal: A Biblical, Historical, and Theological Proposal*. Nashville: B&H Publishing Group, 2008.

Edwards, Jonathan. *Religious Affections*. New Haven: Yale, 1959.

Erickson, Millard J. *Christian Theology*. 3 vols. Grand Rapids: Baker, 1986.

_____. *Does It Matter That I'm Saved?* Grand Rapids: Baker, 1996.

_____. *The Word Became Flesh*. Grand Rapids: Baker, 1991.

Fletcher, Jesse C. *The Southern Baptist Convention: A Sesquicentennial History, 1845–1995*. Nashville: Broadman & Holman, 1994.

Frost, J. M. *Baptist: Why and Why Not*. Nashville: Sunday School Board, 1900.

Forsythe, P. T. *The Cruciality of the Cross*. London: Independent Press, 1948.

_____. *The Justification of God*. London: Independent Press, 1948.

Garrett, James Leo, Jr. *Systematic Theology*. 2 vols. Grand Rapids: Eerdmans, 1990–1995.

George, Timothy, and David S. Dockery. *Theologians of the Baptist Tradition*. Nashville: Broadman & Holman, 2001.

Guinness, Os. *The Dust of Death*. Downers Grove: InterVarsity, 1973.

Harris, Murray J. *From Grave to Glory*. Grand Rapids: Zondervan, 1990.

Henry, Carl F. H. *God, Revelation, and Authority*. Vol 2. Waco: Word, 1976.

_____. *The Identity of Jesus*. Nashville: Broadman & Holman, 1992.

_____. *Jesus of Nazareth: Savior and Lord*. Grand Rapids: Eerdmans, 1966.

Himmelfarb, Gertrude. *One Nation, Two Cultures*. New York: Knopf, 1999.

Hobbs, H. H. *The Baptist Faith and Message*. Nashville: Convention, 1971.

Husbands, Mark, and D. J. Treier. *Justification*. Downers Grove: InterVarsity, 2004.

Hughes, R. Kent. *Ephesians*. Wheaton: Crossway, 1990.

Hunt, Boyd. *Redeemed*. Nashville: Broadman & Holman, 1993.

Lewis, C. S. *Mere Christianity*. New York: MacMillan, 1955.

Luther, Martin. *Bondage of the Will*. Westwood, NJ: Revell, 1957.

McGrath, Alister E. *Evangelicalism and the Future of Christianity*. Downers Grove: InterVarsity, 1995.

Morris, Leon. *The Cross in the New Testament*. Grand Rapids: Eerdmans, 1965.

Mullins, E. Y. *Baptist Beliefs*. Louisville: Baptist World Publishing, 1912.

_____. *The Christian Religion in Its Doctrinal Expression*. Philadelphia: Judson, 1917.

Oden, Thomas C. *The Transforming Power of Grace*. Nashville: Abingdon, 1993.

Orr, James. *The Christian View of God and the World*. Grand Rapids: Eerdmans, reprint 1948.

Packer, J. I. *Keep in Step with the Spirit*. Old Tappan: Revell, 1984.

_____ and Thomas C. Oden. *One Faith*. Downers Grove: InterVarsity, 2004.

Poe, Harry L. *See No Evil: The Existence of Sin in an Age of Relativism*. Grand Rapids: Kregel, 2004

_____. *The Gospel and Its Meaning*. Grand Rapids: Zondervan, 1996.

Ryrie, Charles C. *The Grace of God*. Chicago: Moody, 1963.

Schaeffer, Francis. *Escape from Reason*. Downers Grove: InterVarsity, 1972.

Smith, David L. *With Willful Intent: A Theology of Sin*. Wheaton: Bridge Point, 1994.

Stott, John R. W. *God's New Society*. Downers Grove: InterVarsity, 1979.

_____. *Guarding the Truth*. Downers Grove: InterVarsity, 1996.

_____. *The Cross of Christ*. Downers Grove: InterVarsity, 1986.

Strong, A. H. *Systematic Theology*. Valley Forge: Judson, 1907.

Tozer, A. W. *The Divine Conquest*. Harrisburg, PA: Christian Publications, 1950.

_____. *The Knowledge of the Holy*. New York: Harper, 1961.

Thielicke, Helmut. *The Evangelical Faith*. Grand Rapids: Eerdmans, 1977.

Warfield, Benjamin B. *The Plan of Salvation*. Grand Rapids: Eerdmans, reprint 1975.

Wells, David F. *The Person of Christ*. Westchester, IL: Crossway, 1984.

Wesley, John. *Standard Sermons*. Vol. 1. London: Epworth, reprint 1935.

A Historical View of the Doctrinal Importance of Calvinism among Baptists

Tom J. Nettles
Professor of Historical Theology
The Southern Baptist Theological Seminary
Louisville, Kentucky

SOUTHERN BAPTISTS WERE THE PRODUCT of a complex of dynamics at work among Baptist Calvinists. The influence of Arminians was either completely rejected, in most cases, or severely muted, in some cases. The connective tissues of Calvinism, easily traceable because of their clearly partitioned distinctives, go back at least as far as John Spilsbery who wrote in 1643, "I believe God out of the counsel of his will, did, before he made the world, elect and choose some certain number of his foreseen fallen creatures, and appointed them to eternal life in his Son, for the glory of his grace: which number so elected shall be saved, come to glory, and the rest left in sin to glorify his justice."[1] This same confessional conviction can be seen as distinctly operative in Roger Williams, John Clarke, Obadiah Holmes, and William Screven, who urged the First Baptist Church of Charleston, South Carolina, to "take care that the person be orthodox in faith, and of blameless life, and does own the confession of faith put forth by our brethren in London in 1689."[2]

---

[1] John Spilsbery, *A Treatise Concerning the Lawfull Subject of Baptisme* (London: 1643), 44.

[2] David Benedict, *A General History of the Baptist Denomination in America*, 2 vols. (1813; Reprint edition, Freeport, NY: Books for Libraries Press, 1971), 2:123. The Confession of Faith of 1689 followed the text of a confession adopted in 1677 by a meeting of Calvinistic Baptist pastors in London. William Collins and Nehemiah Coxe, pastors of Petty France Church in London, presented this confession to that meeting having used the Westminster Confession of Faith as its basis. In 1689, representatives from 107 churches met in London, after the Act of Toleration issued under William and Mary, to discuss the status of the Particular Baptist churches as well as to express their "thankfulness to God" for his special providence in "raising up our present King William, to be a blessed Instrument, in his Hand, to deliver us from Popery and Arbitrary Power." At that meeting the representatives also affirmed their approval of the 1677 Confession which

The Philadelphia Association retained these convictions by adopting the 1689 Confession as its own and judging theological orthodoxy in its light for two centuries. As an example, the church planter John Gano wrote in 1784 in his exposition of the doctrine of "Effectual Calling" in an associational circular letter: "They are such as God hath chosen and predestinated both to grace and glory, elected and set apart in Christ, as redeemed by his blood, although by nature children of wrath even as others. . . . This is an holy, heavenly, and, consequently, an high calling."

As the Separate Baptists converged with the Regular Particular Baptists, they brought not only a First Great Awakening experiential zeal along with them but a fully compatible theological position as they covenanted under the influence of Shubal Stearns to uphold "particular election of grace by predestination of God in Christ, effectual calling by the Holy Ghost; free justification through the imputed righteousness of Christ."[3] Daniel Marshall, Stearns's brother-in-law, followed his lead in developing a confession for the Baptist church at Kiokee, Georgia, when he wrote,

> According to God's appointment in his word, we do hereby in his name and strength covenant and promise to keep up and defend all the articles of Faith, according to God's word, such as the great doctrine of election, effectual calling, particular redemption, justification by the imputed righteousness of Christ alone, sanctification by the Spirit of God, Believers Baptism by Immersion, the saints absolute final perseverance in Grace.[4]

Daniel Marshall's son, Abraham Marshall, founded the Georgia Baptist Association and gained the adoption of an abstract of doctrine in 1790, believing it was his duty to do so since it was "impossible to have communion where there is no union." The abstract affirmed the "imputation of Adam's sin to his posterity" and the "corruption of human nature and the impotency of man to recover himself by his own free will-ability." They asserted their belief in the "everlasting love of God

---

thus became known as the 1689 Confession and also as the Second London Confession. (Joseph Ivimey, *History of the English Baptists* 4 vols. [London, 1811–1830], 3:332, 336). This Confession gained wide popularity in Baptist life among Calvinistic Baptists on both sides of the Atlantic as seen in the quoted opinion of Screven as well as the adoption of the Confession by the Philadelphia Association in 1742, having been used even prior to that in rendering theological judgments in answer to the several queries by member churches, and the Charleston Association in 1767 and many of the associations affiliated with them in Christian fellowship.

[3] Robert A. Baker, ed., *A Baptist Sourcebook* (Nashville: Broadman Press, 1966), 18.

[4] Thomas Ray, *Daniel and Abraham Marshall: Pioneer Baptist Evangelists in the South* (Springfield, IL: Particular Baptist Press, 2006), 244.

to his people, and the eternal election of a definite number of the human race, to grace and glory" through a covenant of redemption "between the Father and the Son, before the world began, in which their salvation is secure, and that they in particular are redeemed." Those so elected in Christ in this eternal covenant, "will be effectually called, regenerated, converted, sanctified, and supported by the spirit and power of God, so that they shall persevere in grace, and not one of them be finally lost."[5]

The Charleston Association in its adoption of the 1689 Confession and in the preaching of such men as Oliver Hart, Richard Furman, and Basil Manly Sr. bequeathed the same theology to James P. Boyce. In his analysis of the doctrine of perseverance of the saints, Boyce wrote:

> This doctrine is inseparably associated with the other doctrines of grace which we have found taught in God's word. So true is this, that they are universally accepted, or rejected together. The perseverance of the saints is a part of every Calvinistic confession. . . . All the evidence, therefore, of the truth of the doctrines already examined, may be presented in favour of this which is a necessary inference from them. In like manner, all the independent proof of this doctrine confirms the separate doctrines, and the system of doctrine, with which it is associated.[6]

Boyce's conviction at this point challenges the contemporary position of many Baptists who still maintain a doctrine of perseverance but separate it from the rest of the system of which it is intrinsically a part.

Southern Baptists of the nineteenth century would have confirmed the "Defence of Calvinism" on the part of Charles Spurgeon who argued by query:

> What is the heresy of Rome, but the addition of something to the perfect merits of Jesus Christ . . . ? And what is the heresy of Arminianism but the addition of something to the work of the Redeemer? Every heresy, if brought to the touchstone, will discover itself here. I have my own private opinion that there is no such thing as preaching Christ and Him crucified, unless we preach what nowadays is called Calvinism. It is a nickname to call it Calvinism; Calvinism is the gospel, and nothing else. I do not believe we can preach

---

[5] Ibid., 247–48.

[6] J. P. Boyce, *Abstract of Systematic Theology* (Cape Coral, FL: Founders Press, 2006; first published 1887), 428.

the gospel, if we do not preach justification by faith without works, nor unless we preach the sovereignty of God in His dispensation of grace; nor unless we exalt the electing, unchangeable, eternal, immutable, conquering love of Jehovah; nor do I think we can preach the gospel, unless we base it upon the special and particular redemption of His elect and chosen people which Christ wrought out upon the cross; nor can I comprehend a gospel which lets saints fall away after they are called.[7]

Perhaps Spurgeon's insistence that Calvinism pure and simple is the gospel will seem hyperbolic to some, but Spurgeon's intent was to emphasize that the grace-centeredness and God-centeredness of Calvinism embraced both the merited condemnation of sinful humanity in the whole as well as the utter freeness of divine grace for sinners more thoroughly and completely than any other historically developed view of salvation. Saving grace arrives on sinful planet Earth by Christ's incarnation and by the sovereign operations of the Spirit on elect individuals by the same degree of utter freedom. Neither human merit nor human initiative will give rise to God's saving act or its fruition in the experience of any individual. Other systems may excite preaching that contains a sufficiency of gospel truth to bring about evangelical repentance and faith, but this occurs only when the compromised elements of their systems are out of view.

While Spurgeon never changed his position on the corrupting influence of non-Calvinist doctrine, he also knew that some theological movements were even more sinister. He believed that "Arminianism has usually been the route by which the older dissenters have traveled downward to Socinianism," and that Calvinism had a "conservative force" for retention of vital truth; nevertheless, he professed to care "far more for the central evangelical truths" than for Calvinism as a system.[8] Spurgeon stood against a change within the Baptist Union that not only pressed away the doctrines of grace but also compromised on other cardinal issues of revealed faith such as the deity of Christ, substitutionary atonement, the inerrancy of Scripture, the entire system of imputation, and the personality of the Holy Spirit.

Perhaps in a day when we are seeking a consensus, we should remind ourselves that Calvinists have stood for more than just their distinguishing doctrines but have held steadfastly to other doctrines that are essential for

---

[7] Charles Spurgeon, *Autobiography,* 2 vols. (Edinburgh: Banner of Truth Trust, 1962, 1973), 1:168.

[8] Charles Spurgeon, *Sword and Trowel* (April, 1887), 196.

the health of Baptist churches in our day. On this basis one would hope to press for an agreement that Calvinism has within it a core of doctrinal beliefs not unique to Calvinism but nevertheless essential for the vitality of the witness of every Baptist church. At the same time, one could argue that these commonly held core affirmations are more consistently attested within the Calvinist system, and thus a decline in Calvinism will mean a decline in overall health of the churches. What follows are eight examples of these core doctrines.

1. The Baptist Calvinist historically has been a consistent advocate of the divine inspiration of Scripture. A large number of cogent defenses of the inerrancy of Scripture have been written by Calvinists. Some would say that these are among the most profound ever produced in Christian literature. Outside Baptist life one would merely have to call to mind the affirmations of John Calvin,[9] Francis Turretin,[10] John Owen,[11] Charles Hodge,[12] B. B. Warfield,[13] J. Gresham Machen,[14] J. I. Packer,[15] and the late James Montgomery Boice to learn gratitude for the profundity of their grasp of this doctrine and its intrinsic importance for Christian faith.

Within Baptist life such Calvinists as John Spilsbery, Benjamin Keach, John Gill, Andrew Fuller, Charles Spurgeon, John L. Dagg, and John A. Broadus wrote specific defenses of biblical inspiration and inerrancy at critical junctures in the historical progress of Baptist witness to a variety of skeptics and unbelievers. Spilsbery bound himself to the witness of Scripture in setting forth a biblical church order believing that the apostles served as "unerring Oracles of God, and the infallible mouth of Christ," so that to all the churches their "testimony was unquestionable."[16] Benjamin Keach defended the immediate inspiration

---

[9] John Calvin, *Institutes of the Christian Religion*, Book 1, chapters vi-x.

[10] Francis Turretin, *Institutes of Elenctic Theology*, 3 vols. trans. George Musgrave Giger, ed. James T. Dennison, Jr. (Philipsburg, NJ: P&R Publishing, 1992) 1:55–167.

[11] John Owen, *Works of John Owen*, 16 vols. {Edinburgh: The Banner of Truth Trust, 1968), 16:296–345.

[12] Charles Hodge, *Systematic Theology*, 3 vols. (New York: Charles Scribner & Company, 1872), 1:151–191.

[13] Benjamin Breckenridge Warfield, *The Works of Benjamin Breckenridge Warfield*, 10 vols. (Grand Rapids: Baker, 1981), 1:3–456, entitled *Revelation and Inspiration*. Warfield's contribution astounds the imagination. The variety of his articles on different aspects of the issue of Holy Scripture combined with the historical, theological, and exegetical scholarship along with striking literary value and memorable analogies make his contribution to this issue virtually unsurpassed in Christian literature.

[14] J. Gresham Machen, *Christianity and Liberalism* (Grand Rapids, Eerdmans), 1923.

[15] J. I. Packer, *Fundamentalism and the Word of God* (Grand Rapids: Eerdmans, 1958), 41–114; idem, *God Has Spoken* (London: Hodder and Stoughton, 1965), *passim*.

[16] John Spilsbery, *Gods Ordinance, The Saints Privilege* (London, Printed by M. Simmons for Benjamin Allen, 1646), 2, 3.

of the Bible as "every part of it the genuine dictate of the Holy Ghost" that is "contained most exactly and most purely in the Originals."[17] John L. Dagg wrote that

> a careful examination of the inspired word has not only served to repel the charge [of inconsistency] by reconciling the apparent discrepancies, but it has added new proof that the Scriptures were written by undesigning and honest men without any collusion, and that there is perfect harmony in their statements, even when apparently most discordant.[18]

John Broadus, who called Calvinism an "exalted system of Pauline truth," agreed with Dagg not only in his Calvinism but also in his confidence in Scripture, affirming that "most cases of apparent disagreement in the inspired writings have been explained, and we may be sure that all could be explained if we had fuller information." He based this confidence on his biblically taught conviction that "the inspired writers learned many things by observation or inquiry, but they were preserved by the Holy Spirit from error, whether in learning or in writing these things."[19]

Charles Spurgeon, the aforementioned Calvinist, withstood in solitary splendor the destructive ravages of modernism in the Baptist Union of England and fought against the broadening attitude of acceptance of such doctrinal diversity. For his courage and his defense of an inerrant Bible, he was rewarded with disdain and censure by the Baptists who should have embraced him as singularly faithful in his calling as a shepherd. "We who believe the Holy Scripture to be the inspired truth of God," Spurgeon believed, "cannot have fellowship with those who deny the authority from which we derive all our teaching."[20]

In *The Bible Doctrine of Inspiration* Basil Manly Jr., the author of the Abstract of Principles that serves as the confessional standard for faculties at Southern and Southeastern Seminaries, presented a strong defense of biblical inspiration that affirms the error-free character of the biblical text. Manly distinguished between revelation, inspiration, and illumination in a helpful way and also showed how God designed different kinds of outcomes from the variety of His superintending activities

---

[17] Cited in L. Russ Bush and Tom J. Nettles, *Baptists and the Bible* (Nashville: Broadman & Holman, 1999), 79, 80.

[18] John L. Dagg, *Manual of Theology* (Charleston: The Southern Baptist Publication Society, 1857), 34.

[19] John A. Broadus, *A Catechism of Bible Teaching* (Nashville: Sunday School Board of the Southern Baptist Convention and Philadelphia; American Baptist Publication Society, 1892), 15, 16.

[20] Charles Spurgeon, *Sword and Trowel* (November, 1887), 559.

in the world. While we *connect* God's operations in providence both in nature and in human affairs; His grace in redemption; His distribution of talent, strength, and wisdom among persons; and His work in producing an inspired volume, we also *distinguish* between the designed outcomes of each of these divine activities. Manly showed that whereas these other activities were not intended to produce infallible truth, the divine activity of inspiration did intend it and, in fact, accomplished its intention with no violation of human personality. He defended plenary inspiration with this understanding: "The Bible as a whole is the Word of God, so that in every part of Scripture there is both infallible truth and divine authority." [21]

Calvinism provides a more consistent rationale for inerrancy than other theological systems. One of the most often repeated objections to the divine inspiration of Scripture is that its assumption of perfect divine control of the process runs roughshod over human freedom. Virtually every defender of inerrancy has to discuss the relation between inspiration and human freedom. The writers must be robots or automatons, so the objection goes, in order to produce an error-free text. Apart from such a dictatorial process, given the limitations imposed by sin and creatureliness, an a priori expectation is that the human author will make some slip along the way. The Calvinist system, however, has no tension between the freeness of human personality and verbal inspiration. God's particular providence over all events includes every choice of every moral creature without diminishing the free moral agency of the creature. Through the use of a variety of means, God controls the entire complex of events in every sphere of His created order "according to the counsel of his own will" (Eph 1:11). In the same way that God's sovereignty brings about the fulfillment of His prophecies according to His decree with no violation of human freedom, so He inspired Scripture both as to authority and truthful content, that is, in a plenary way, without suspending the individual personality traits of every biblical writer. This view, called "compatibilism" in the wide-ranging debates on this issue, was fully affirmed by Basil Manly when he wrote, "Yet this human personality of theirs [that is, the apostles] is not in the slightest degree incompatible with their utterance being at the same time the message of God."[22]

2. The Baptist Calvinist historically has been a consistent advocate of a fully Trinitarian theology. Calvinistic Baptists have been among the most ardent defenders of the doctrine of the Trinity. Benjamin Keach in his exposition of the Covenant of Redemption noted strongly, "In this

---

[21] Basil Manly Jr., *The Bible Doctrine of Inspiration* (New York: A. C. Armstrong & Son, 1888), 59.
[22] Ibid., 173.

Covenant there is a clear Revelation or Manifestation of the Three Persons in the Deity, and their Glory doth equally and jointly shine forth."[23]

John Gill viewed the relation between the doctrine of the Trinity and the doctrines of grace in a similar way to Keach, stating, "The three divine persons are to be discerned most clearly in all the works of grace." He showed how this is true in the work of Christ as Mediator, and the truths of justification, adoption, regeneration, and future glorification. Gill, in fact, so strongly believed this infinitely important practical application of the doctrine that he stated:

> The doctrine of the Trinity is often represented as a speculative point, of no great moment whether it is believed or not, too mysterious and curious to be pryed into, and that it had better be let alone than meddled with; but, alas! It enters into the whole of our salvation, and all the parts of it; into all the doctrines of the gospel, and into the experience of the saints; there is no doing without it.[24]

In his treatise *The Doctrine of the Trinity Stated and Vindicated,* Gill pointed to the doctrine of the eternal generation of the Son as the foundation of the doctrine of the Trinity.[25] He reiterated this argument in *A Dissertation Concerning the Eternal Sonship of Christ* where he drew the calm but resolute conclusion that the doctrine is a "matter of such moment and importance, being a fundamental doctrine of the Christian religion, and indeed what distinguishes it from all other religions, for those of Pagans, Jews and Mahometans. . . . That is peculiar to the Christian religion."[26]

In Boyce's discussion of the personal relations in the Trinity, he posited the biblical truth that these relations result "necessarily from the nature of God."[27] At the close of his discussion of the person of Christ as it relates to atonement, Boyce concluded, "The doctrine of the Trinity lies, therefore, at the basis of that of the atonement, and hence the denial of the latter by all those who reject the former."[28] John L. Dagg concurred when he stated, "In the work of salvation, the divine persons co-operate

---

[23] Benjamin Keach, *The Everlasting Covenant: A Sweet Cordial for a Drooping Soul* (London: printed for H. Barnard, 1693), 24.

[24] John Gill, *Body of Divinity*, Baptist Faith Series (Iron Oaks, AR: Baptist Standard Bearer, nd), 138.

[25] John Gill, *The Doctrine of the Trinity Stated and Vindicated* (London: G. Keith, 1752), 150–58.

[26] John Gill, "A Dissertation Concerning the Eternal Sonship of Christ," in *A Collection of Sermons and Tracts,* 2 vols. (London: George Keith, 1773), 2:564.

[27] Boyce, *Systematic Theology*, 138.

[28] Ibid., 325.

in different offices; and these are so clearly revealed, as to render the personal distinction in the Godhead more manifest, than it is in any other of God's works."

In the theology of each of these self-confessed Calvinists, one sees a consistent trinitarian orthodoxy organically related to their entire system of thought.[29] The Second London Confession stated as a conclusion to its article on the Trinity that the "doctrine of the Trinity is the foundation of all our Communion with God, and comfortable dependence on him."[30]

Calvinists believe that their perception of salvation has an intrinsic dependence on the Trinity that is manifest in no other theological system. They believe the doctrines of grace are themselves a manifestation of the necessary coequality of the persons in the Trinity. That which is intrinsic to the glory of one person of the Trinity necessarily involves the glory of the other persons. Each person undertakes to accomplish in the great works of God that which is most appropriate as an expression of the eternal relations within the Trinity. So it is true of creation, providence, and redemption in all its multifaceted excellence. What the Father knows, the Son knows, and the Spirit knows. What the Father decrees, the Son decrees, and the Spirit decrees. That which the Father desires to effect, the Son desires to effect, and the Spirit desires to effect. The scheme of redemption in particular manifests the equality of the three persons of the Trinity in each of these ideas but at the same time shows the eternal distinctions of person. The Father elected, the Son in obedience to the will of the Father procured, and the Spirit, honoring the will of the Father and the obedience of the Son, effects in the personal experience of the elect person. As Dagg reasoned on the basis of the scriptural data:

> The Father alone is not presented as acting in a subordinate office; but appears as sustaining the full authority of the Godhead, sending the Son, and sending the Holy Spirit. . . . In this order of operation, inferiority of nature is not implied, in the subordination of office to which the Son and the Spirit voluntarily consent. The fullness of the Godhead dwells in each of the divine persons, and renders the fulfillment of the covenant infallibly sure, in all its stipulations.[31]

Because every aspect of salvation requires one of infinite power and glory to bring it about, Calvinism rests its soteriology on the doctrine of the Trinity. Another system that does not require the same transactions,

---

[29] Dagg, *Manual of Theology*, 254.

[30] Lumpkin, 253.

[31] Dagg, *Manual of Theology*, 255.

such as an atoning work by a sacrifice equal to the glory of the broken law and the offended deity, or a resurrection from death to life of spiritually incapacitated sinners, does not require the same degrees of power and honor for each respective aspect of salvation and thus is more susceptible to heretical amendment of the doctrines of Christ and the Holy Spirit. Omnipotent power, omniscient wisdom, and eternal glory are necessary at each stage of the development of God's salvation for sinners. In light of this reality, John Dagg discussed the doctrine of the Trinity in his "Book Seven, Doctrine Concerning Divine Grace."

3. The Baptist Calvinist historically has been a consistent advocate of substitutionary atonement. Central to the gospel is the atoning work of Christ. Scripture makes abundantly clear that Christ in His death has taken on Himself the penalty of our sins. "He Himself bore our sins in His own body on the tree," Peter said (1 Pet 2:24 HCSB). Christ "gave Himself for our sins," Paul wrote, "to rescue us from this present evil age" (Gal 1:4 HCSB). "He made the One who did not know sin to be sin for us," he wrote to the Corinthians (2 Cor 5:21 HCSB), and he reminded Titus that Jesus Christ "gave himself for us, that he might redeem us from all iniquity" (Titus 2:14 KJV). The church at Ephesus was admonished to "walk in love, as Christ also has loved us and given Himself for us, an offering and a sacrifice to God" (Eph 5:2 NKJV). The writer of Hebrews argued for Christ's substitutionary atonement throughout. Christ has "put away sin by the sacrifice of himself," being "once offered to bear the sins of many" (Heb 9:26,28 KJV).

Calvinists have with only rare exceptions (e.g., the New Divinity men of the late eighteenth to early nineteenth-centuries) maintained this truth inviolate. John Gill wrote, "Christ interposed, and offered himself in the covenant, to be a Mediator of reconciliation, or to make satisfaction for sin; and so mercy and truth have met together and righteousness and peace have kissed each other."[32] Oliver Hart, in speaking of the way in which Christ as mediator has made intercession for transgressors, argued, "This he did not by laboring to extenuate their crimes, but by offering himself as their sponsor, to stand in their room and stead; bear their sins; make an atonement for their guilt, restore to the law its honors, and answer the demands of justice."[33]

Though Andrew Fuller has sometimes been represented as not accepting substitutionary atonement, there is no convincing and sustained evidence for such a proposal. As he surveyed the blessings that come to the Christian, he preached, "All those threatenings which belonged to him heretofore no longer stand against him, but are reckoned, by the judge

---

[32] Gill, *Body of Divinity*, 232.
[33] Oliver Hart, "Christ, The Mediator," *Philadelphia Association Minutes,* 186.

of all, as having been executed on Jesus his substitute, who was 'made a curse for us.'" In a funeral sermon preached in 1790 entitled "Christ Our Substitute in Death and Judgment," Fuller described Christ's work in the context of Isaiah 53. His expository comment after quoting several phrases is pointed: "He bore the wrath due to our sins. The shaft of vengeance spent itself in his heart!"[34]

James P. Boyce also gave several pages to his discussions of the substitutionary aspect of Christ's suffering and demonstrated how effective substitution depends on orthodox Christology. Boyce wrote, "It was, therefore, not the human nature of Christ that was substituted for us, but Christ himself; yet it was not Christ in his divine nature that suffered, but value was given to the suffering from its being the suffering of one who also essentially possessed the divine nature."[35]

It is no surprise that each of these also argued that the atonement was either by design or by nature effectual only for the elect. But this particularity renders the atonement necessarily substitutionary. *Substitutionary*, in fact, seems to imply effectuality and particularity. If the death of Jesus genuinely removed the judicial verdict against sin, then who among those for whom Christ has died will also suffer for his own sins? For this reason many that do not hold to a definite effectual atonement remain open to other options concerning Christ's death. Though each of these has a degree of applicatory truth in their formulation, their true power is borrowed from the central motif of substitution. The victory theory of Lutherans, the moral influence theory of liberals, and the moral government theory of Arminian Grotians have been propounded to bypass the supposedly offensive implications of a truly substitutionary and propitiatory atonement. The Calvinist has the greatest stake in maintaining the biblical view of Christ's suffering in such a way as to redeem, reconcile, and forgive sinners. "If we died with Him, we shall also live with Him" (2 Tim 2:11 NKJV). A Calvinist pastor will always proclaim a substitutionary atonement.

4. The Baptist Calvinist historically has been a consistent advocate of religious liberty. In his massive *A History of News England with Particular Reference to the Baptists,* Isaac Backus defended and explained Baptist life as orthodox, growing, Calvinistic, and thoroughly committed to religious liberty. He included narratives of how Obadiah Holmes and John Clarke suffered for the faith of Baptists, and he also included their confessions of faith so that the world might be aware of their Calvinistic orthodoxy. Clarke wrote:

---

[34] Andrew Fuller, *The Works of Andrew Fuller*, 3 vols. (Philadelphia: American Baptist Publication Society, 1845), 1:280, 476.

[35] Boyce, *Systematic Theology*, 325.

> All things with their causes, effects, and circumstances
> and manner of being, are decreed by God. . . . The spe-
> cial decree of God concerning angels and men is called
> predestination. . . . Election is the decree of God, of
> his free love, grace, and mercy, choosing some men
> to faith, holiness and eternal life, for the praise of his
> glorious mercy. . . . The cause which moved the Lord
> to elect them who are chosen, was none other but his
> mere good will and pleasure.[36]

The confession of Obadiah Holmes includes that (1) God's providence extends "to the least creature and action," including the reality that "no man can come to the Son but they that are drawn by the Father to the Son"; (2) "God hath laid the iniquity of all his elect and called ones, upon him"; and (3) "none have the power to choose salvation, or to believe in Christ for life; it is only the gift of God."[37] Clarke and Holmes suffered, Holmes being mercilessly whipped, for their witness as Baptists. By the blood of their suffering they argued for liberty of conscience and separation of church and state. Clarke's work, *Ill News from New England,* described the context in which their suffering in Massachusetts came about, and he included an extended defense of liberty of conscience based on the lordship of Christ and the sovereignty of God.

Backus described the continued struggle for religious liberty in Massachusetts after the Revolutionary War. The irony of the situation was that the Baptists maintained more purely the original theological position of the Puritan churches on this doctrine than the Massachusetts churches. As Backus noted, "In general, their faith and practice come the nearest to that of the first planters of New England of any churches now in the land, excepting in the single article of sprinkling infants." Backus then gave fourteen articles of faith divided between soteriological articles and the implications of those truths for the formation of the church.

After affirming the fall of humanity in the sin of Adam, Backus represented the Baptists as believing "that in infinite mercy the eternal Father gave a certain number of the children of men to his beloved Son, before the world was, to redeem and save; and that he, by his obedience and sufferings, has procured eternal redemption for them." The next article stated that "by the influence of the Holy Spirit, these persons individually, as they come into existence, are effectually called in time, and savingly renewed in the spirit of their minds." He went on to affirm justification

---

[36] Isaac Backus, *A History of New England with Particular Reference to the Denomination of Christians called Baptists,* 3 vols. (Newton Mass.: Backus Historical Society, 1871), 1: 206. This was reprinted in one volume by Arno Press in New York, 1969.
[37] Ibid., 207–8.

by faith based on the imputation of the righteousness of Christ, perseverance of the saints, and regenerate church membership as well as several other articles related to the church and the preaching ministry. Baptists, therefore, held to the original intent of the "planters" of New England in producing a church composed of visible confessing saints called by sovereign grace, which governed its own affairs, disciplined its own membership, and selected its own ministers. Baptists held to all those and believed the only way to maintain such an ideal in perpetuity was through the New Testament ordinance of believer's baptism.[38]

John Leland joined in the Baptist struggle for religious liberty both in Virginia and Massachusetts. Leland believed that "Christ did, before the foundation of the world, predestinate a certain number of the human family for his bride" and that, therefore, "Jesus died for his elect sheep only" and would call them effectually and would keep them by His power to "bring them safe to glory."[39] Because of this Leland also believed that "every man must give an account of himself to God, and therefore every man ought to be at liberty to serve God in that way that he can best reconcile it to his conscience."[40]

The rationale for this position, beyond the fact that the exposition of the text combined with the regulative principle of biblical authority yielded this viewpoint, was clearly Calvinistic. Because of the fall, the human will is in bondage; only the effectual call of God can open the heart to believe. God has determined that all His elect shall come and no power of hell can keep Him from saving His elect and thus building His church. In order, therefore, to build a church of living stones with a principle of holiness as their driving motivation, one must eliminate all factors of external coercion. God builds His church through the preaching of His called and sent ministers and not through government sponsorship or carnal intervention.

5. The Baptist Calvinist historically has been a consistent advocate of missions and evangelism. John L. Dagg was one of the most respected men in Baptist life until his death in 1884 when he was over 90 years old. His books of theology, apologetics, and ethics gained wide distribution among Southern Baptists. His theology text was the first used to teach Southern Baptist ministerial students at the Southern Baptist Theological Seminary in Greenville, South Carolina. Broadus remarked that his theology was "remarkable for clear statement of the profoundest truths, and for devotional sweetness." He also wrote gratefully on the

---

[38] Ibid., 3:232.

[39] John Leland, *Writings of John Leland*, ed. L. E. Greene (New York: Arno Press, 1969), 625.

[40] John Leland, "Rights of Conscience," in Baker, *A Baptist Sourcebook*, 40.

"pleasing impulse it gave to theological inquiry and reflection" in his own life.[41]

Dagg gave expression to a warm, evangelical Calvinism throughout his *Manual of Theology*. He believed in the covenant of grace established before the foundation of the world in the eternal consultations within the triune God. Such an intra-Trinitarian agreement extends "to all the works of God: 'Who worketh all things after the counsel of his will.'" The covenant in particular treats the salvation of people as the result of the operation of all three persons of the Trinity. In this Trinitarian context of the covenant of Grace, Dagg described election: "All who will finally be saved, were chosen to salvation by God the Father, before the foundation of the world, and given to Jesus Christ in the Covenant of Grace."[42]

For the Son's part in the Covenant, Dagg stated, "The Son of God gave his life to redeem those who were given to him by the Father in the Covenant of Grace."[43] He reasoned through the entire issue and determined that the most scriptural and most reasonable view of Christ's work is that He has borne the wrath of God for His people in accordance with the principles of distributive justice.[44] The outward external call apart from regeneration always fails. But "the Holy Spirit effectually calls all the elect to repent and believe."[45] This divine work Dagg described as omnipotent and, just as God's purpose in initial creation proceeded unresisted, "equally unresisted is the power by which he new-creates the heart."[46] Dagg identified the internal operation that produces this effectual, unresisted calling as regeneration.

In another context, Dagg discussed the work regeneration in its broadest sense of sanctification proceeds with faith as its foundation. He is quick to add, however, even in that context, that regeneration in the sense of the new birth, the new creation, or being raised from death to life precedes faith and is the efficient producer of it.[47] God's love toward His people operates as an efficient cause before it operates as a motive, and "faith is produced by its efficient power."[48]

Within the context of these expositions, Dagg turned aside those objections that assumed the doctrines of grace render evangelism useless. He argued instead that God's character requires evangelism, and His prom-

---

[41] John A. Broadus, *Memoir of James Petigru Boyce* (New York: A. C. Armstrong & Son, 1893), 112f.
[42] Dagg, *Manual*, 309.
[43] Ibid., 324.
[44] Ibid., 327–31.
[45] Ibid., 331.
[46] Ibid., 333.
[47] Ibid., 279–82.
[48] Ibid., 281.

ise renders its success certain.[49] Then in a positive way in his *Manual of Church Order*, Dagg wrote, "Every Christian is bound to do what he can for the conversion of others, and for spreading the knowledge of truth," but this responsibility falls especially on the gospel minister who has been especially prepared and called, a call that includes a "sincere desire to glorify God, and save souls."[50] In a section on the "Duty of Baptists" Dagg asserted, "It is our duty to labor faithfully and perseveringly to bring all men to the knowledge of the truth." He affirmed that the Great Commission "requires us to preach the gospel to every creature; and we ought to be foremost in obeying it." He pointed to the far-reaching consequences of the obedience of William Carey and the English Baptists as well as the providential conversion of Judson and Rice to be regarded as "a special call of God on American Baptists to labor for the spread of the gospel throughout the earth."[51]

This duty was not merely theoretical to Dagg. During his pastorate at Fifth Baptist in Philadelphia, he remarked that "souls were given me in reward for my labor, not in large crowds, but in sufficient number to keep me encouraged." He, along with friends in the Philadelphia Association, discussed, "Can nothing be done to build the walls of Jerusalem in these troublous times?" Together they drew up a constitution for the Pennsylvania Missionary Association that eventually became the Pennsylvania Convention. When the Association had made some progress in collecting funds, Dagg received a visitor one day asking if there were any in the city "who cared for the souls that were perishing in the interior, where he had for some time been laboring as a missionary, self-sustained."[52] That man, Eugene Kincaid, became the first agent of the Missionary Association, and under his labor the Baptist cause in Pennsylvania enlarged.

Under the leadership of Oliver Hart, the Charleston Association raised funds to "support a missionary to itinerate" in places of South Carolina destitute of the gospel. They managed to procure the services of John Gano, who devoted himself to the work, "and his ministrations were crowned with remarkable success. Many embraced and professed the gospel."[53]

None preached the truths of the doctrines of grace with greater fervor than Spurgeon. But without any fear of its being a contradiction, he would say, "Anybody who calls off the thoughts of the church from soul-

---

[49] Ibid., 315–17, *et al.*

[50] John L. Dagg, *Manual of Church Order* (Charleston: Southern Baptist Publication Society, 1858), 243, 245.

[51] Ibid., 302, 303.

[52] Dagg, *Autobiography*, 30.

[53] Benedict, 2:135.

saving is a mischief-maker."[54] He also proposed, "If any minister can be satisfied without conversion, he shall have no conversions. God will not force usefulness on any man. It is only when our heart breaks to see men saved, that we shall be likely to see sinners' hearts broken."[55]

Calvinists are no less committed to the evangelistic preaching of the gospel than they are to the necessity of the incarnation. Christ's fervency for the glory of His Father in descending to earth is the model for our fervency in preaching this good news. The Son of God came down from heaven because appropriate means, consistent with the glory of God, are necessarily entailed in the decree of salvation (Heb 2:10). He commanded that repentance and forgiveness of sins be preached in the world for the same reason (Luke 24:45–47). Without atonement there is no forgiveness; without preaching there is no repentance and faith. When one objected that election precludes evangelism, Dagg responded, "The objection to election applies equally to every part of the divine purpose, and proceeds on the supposition that God has predetermined the end without reference to the means by which it is to be accomplished."[56]

Obadiah Holmes, mentioned above, included in his confession an article on God's ordained means of calling his elect: "I believe," he wrote, "although God can bring men to Christ, and cause them to believe in him for life, yet he hath appointed an ordinary way to effect that great work of faith, which is by means of sending a ministry into the world, to publish repentance to the sinner, and salvation, and that by Jesus Christ."[57]

6. The Baptist Calvinist historically has been a consistent advocate of Christ-centered preaching. Baptist Calvinists have been clear and consistent in their Christ-centered emphasis. Every Christian knows the glory of Christ and sees in Scripture and feels in his soul the preeminence of Christ as the avenue to salvation and the glory of God.

Richard Fuller, a strong Calvinist who served churches in South Carolina and Maryland, had a homiletic compass that always gravitated toward Christ. In a sermon entitled "The Gospel not a Philosophy, but a Revelation," Fuller consistently led his hearers to see the glory of Christ as constituting the sum of all the revelation that God has given and the answer to all the apparent impossibilities that human reason could never overcome. The revelation meets every longing of the human soul and intellect and "carries along with it self-authenticating credentials; but its

---

[54] Charles Spurgeon, "Travailing for Souls," *Spurgeon's Sermons*, 20 vols. (New York: Funk and Wagnalls, nd), 9:29.

[55] Ibid., 17.

[56] Dagg, *Manual of Theology*, 315.

[57] Backus, *History*, 208.

communications entirely transcend the discoveries which our senses or our reason ever could have made."[58]

Christ is the *wisdom* of God in that His incarnation and death solved the insoluble dilemma of how guilty and unholy creatures could be righteous. Christ is the *power* of God in that that which pure omnipotence could not do as a matter of arbitrary force was done through the incarnation and passion of Christ. "God has but to will," Fuller preached, "and on earth, in heaven, in hell, over the entire universe, all things are controlled by an impulse as direct and irresistible as that communicated by my will to the nerves by which I open and shut my hand." Forgiveness is not a matter of unmitigated omnipotence but a matter of a necessary moral transaction. Because of the Man Christ Jesus, "The Lord of life and glory expiring upon a cross," a guilty unholy one "appears before the inspection of Omniscience clothed in a perfect righteousness."[59]

The gospel also is a revelation of the love of God that comes in the form of "mercy to sinners." No one knows or exhibits love like the one that gave His only Son as a propitiation for sin. Such love is "not a weakness, a blind effeminate attachment overlooking the guilt of its object; but love, holy, righteous, uncompromising in its abhorrence of sin; and yet rescuing the lost and ruined by an interposition before which reason is staggered, imagination recoils, and faith can only wonder, admire, weep, rejoice, adore."[60]

The revelation of this gospel concerns things prepared from eternity. Nothing has taken God by surprise or defeated His purpose of glorifying Himself by preparing a people for a prepared place. It all resides in Christ. "By the redemption which is in Jesus, even the existence of moral evil—that dark mystery—is overruled, so as to reflect amazing splendor upon all the divine perfections and at the same time to exalt those who are saved from among men to an immortality of surpassing blessedness and glory." All are called, but only those that love will come, for the preaching of the gospel is foolishness to those that are perishing but the power of God to those being saved. Faith is "something more than the conviction of the intellect; . . . until love opens our eyes, the things of the Gospel are hidden from us; . . . it is love which comprehends, feels, rejoices in the unsearchable riches of Christ."[61]

Like Fuller, Boyce saw these truths of grace as finding their coherence in the person and work of Christ. Boyce's great sermon on "Christ

---

[58] Richard Fuller, *Sermons by Richard Fuller*, 3 vols. (Baltimore: John F. Weishampel, 1877), 1:19.
[59] Ibid., 26.
[60] Ibid., 29.
[61] Ibid., 29, 33.

Receiving and Eating with Sinners" has a Christ-centered focus that should be the goal of every gospel preacher to emulate. Christ waits on sinners, Christ seeks sinners, and Christ rejoices in the coming of sinners and invites them with all earnestness to come to Him. He "shouts out his triumph throughout the realms of heaven, and the angelic hosts rejoice at the salvation of a single man."[62]

Spurgeon opened the Metropolitan Tabernacle with the unmistakable affirmation of the centrality of Christ.

> I would propose that the subject of the ministry of this house, as long as this platform shall stand, and as long as this house shall be frequented by worshippers, shall be the person of Jesus Christ. I am never ashamed to avow myself a Calvinist; . . . I do not hesitate to take the name of Baptist. . . . But if I am asked to say what is my creed, I think I must reply—"It is Jesus Christ." My venerable predecessor, Dr. Gill has left a body of divinity admirable and excellent in its way; but the body of divinity to which I would pin and bind myself for ever, God helping me, is not his system of divinity or any other human treatise, but Christ Jesus, who is the sum and substance of the gospel; who is in himself all theology, the incarnation of every precious truth, the all glorious personal embodiment of the way, the truth, and the life.[63]

As he developed his thought more, he focused on what, indeed, it meant to preach Christ. In one section pertinent to our intent here, we hear him remind us that if one preaches Christ he must of necessity preach doctrine.

> If I preach Christ I must preach him as the covenant head of his people, and how far am I then from the doctrine of election? If I preach Christ I must preach the efficacy of his blood, and how far am I removed then from the great doctrine of an effectual atonement? If I preach Christ I must preach the love of his heart, and how can I deny the final perseverance of the saints? If I preach the Lord Jesus as the great Head and King, how far am I removed from divine sovereignty?

---

[62] J. P. Boyce, *Selected Writings* (Nashville: Broadman Press, 1989), 81.

[63] Charles Spurgeon, *Metropolitan Tabernacle Pulpit* (Pasadena, TX: Pilgrim Publications, 1961), 1861: 169.

> Must I not, if I preach Christ personally, preach his
> doctrines?[64]

Baptist Calvinists affirm a Christocentric revelation and gospel because that is the emphasis of Scripture. If the Calvinist properly understands Paul's affirmation that our calling is in accord with His own purpose and grace given us in Christ Jesus before the world began (2 Tim 1:9) and that He has given us all spiritual blessings in heavenly places in Christ Jesus, the proper response is to drive every message toward Christ. The Father's purpose of glorifying Himself is Christ-centered, and the Spirit's work of drawing sinners to salvation is the same as drawing them to Christ. If any would see God glorified and sinners saved, then the preacher's exposition must lead to Christ, the one in whom the fullness of the Godhead dwells in bodily form. Election cannot save apart from Christ; irresistible grace cannot save without establishing union with Christ; Christ's death was fully effectual because of who He was. The Calvinist believes that God operates by means that are consistent with His character, and the only one in whom salvation resides in a way consistent with the character of God is Christ.[65]

7. The Baptist Calvinist historically has been a consistent advocate of holiness of life. When John A. Broadus wrote in his *Catechism of Bible Teaching*, "The only sure proof of being a true believer is growing in holiness and usefulness even to the end," he merely stated in shortened form what Calvinistic Baptist theologians and preachers had been saying since the seventeenth century. Benjamin Keach argued strongly for the necessity of holiness as naturally concomitant to justification: "Where justification is, there is also sanctification; a man is not sanctified that is not justified, nor are any actually justified that are not sanctified; though

---

[64] Ibid., 174.

[65] B. B. Warfield, a non-Baptist Calvinist, sets forth the Christ-centeredness of Scripture as a striking evidence of its inspiration. "Another point in which the unity of the bible is strikingly apparent needs our attention next: amid all the diversity of its subject-matter, it may yet be said that almost the whole book is taken up with the *portraiture of one person*. On its first page he comes for a moment before our astonished eyes; on the last he lingers still before their adoring gaze. And from that first word in Genesis which describes him as the 'seed of the woman' and at the same time her deliverer—with occasional moments of absence, just as the principal character of a play is not always on the stage, and yet with constant development of character—to the end, where he is discovered sitting on the great white throne and judging the nations, the one consistent but gradually developed portraiture grows before our eyes. Not a false stroke is made. Every touch of the pencil is placed just where it ought to stand as part of the whole. There is nowhere the slightest trace of wavering or hesitancy of hand. The draughtsman is certainly a consummate artist. And, as the result of it all, the world is possessed of the strongest, most consistent, most noble literary portraiture to be found in all her literature." Warfield, *Works,* 1:438.

it is true, 'God justified the ungodly . . .' yet God doth not leave them unsanctified by the Spirit."[66] The Christian, therefore, is "not to work for Life, but from Life." If one is justified, then assuredly faith has been wrought in his heart by the Holy Spirit, a "Principle of Life wrought in the Soul" which causes one to "live a Holy Life and renounce all Sin and Iniquity from a Principle of Faith." The Christian sees sin as "so hateful unto God, and so abominable in his Sight" that out of love to Christ he desires to "do all things whatsoever he commandeth him."[67]

John Gill, sometimes falsely reputed as an antinomian and thus an enemy to holiness, showed the true tendency of the Calvinist view of redemption by contending,

> Redemption is a deliverance from sin, from all sin, original and actual; and that not only from the guilt of sin, and the punishment due unto it; but in consequence of redeeming grace, the redeemed ones are delivered from the dominion and governing power of sin, and at last from the being of it. Christ saves his people from their sins; he does not indulge them in them.[68]

True effectual grace produces true love for, pursuit of, and increasing attainment of true holiness.

Abraham Booth (1734–1806), the English Particular Baptist preacher noted for his book *Reign of Grace*, wrote in his personal confession of faith, "I believe the absolute necessity of regeneration in order to eternal life; and am fully persuaded, that *without holiness,* that is, a real love of God producing cheerful obedience to his commands, *no man*, whatever his religious pretensions or professions may be, shall see the Lord." In a sermon on Gal 5:22–23, Booth outlined every manifestation of the fruit of the Spirit as arising from the dual sources of revealed truth and the Spirit's efficacious work. "Every holy disposition," he contended, "so far as it is really holy in its exercise, is under the influence of divine authority, and is produced by divine agency, through the instrumentality of truth." After his full exposition of the text, Booth closed with this: "Such, my brethren, is the morality of the New Testament. So perfectly fitted are the genius of the gospel, and the doctrines of grace, to produce in the heart, and to manifest in the life, those tempers 'against which there is no law.'"[69]

---

[66] Benjamin Keach, *Exposition of the Parables* (Grand Rapids: Kregel, 1974), 547, 548.

[67] B. Keach, *Display of Glorious Grace* (London: S. Bridge, 1698), 60.

[68] John Gill, *Collection*, 1:10.

[69] Abraham Booth, *The Works of Abraham Booth*, ed. Michael Haykin (Springfield, MO: Particular Baptist Press, 2006), 29,41, 49. This is volume one of a projected three-volume set.

For the Calvinist, the divine purpose in election, atonement, and effectual calling is the gathering of a people zealous of good works. Because regeneration is an immediate and sovereign operation of God, it alters the affections and necessarily gives rise to hatred of sin and remorse for it. The new heart embraces Christ and His righteousness and then seeks to practice righteousness because Christ is righteous (1 John 3:7). The Calvinistic Baptist in a way consistent with his system expects holiness in increasing measure in all the people of God.

8. The Baptist Calvinist historically has been a consistent advocate of regenerate church membership. The *Summary of Church Discipline* of the Charleston Association said that "a particular gospel church consists of a company of saints incorporated by a special covenant into one distinct body." It is not to be built "with dead, but living materials. None have a right to church membership, but such as Christ will own as his sincere followers at the last decisive day." If a man is not born again, he may not enter the kingdom of God "or in to a gospel church." In a later chapter they emphasize again that a church's members "must be truly gracious persons. None are fit materials of a gospel church, without having first experienced an entire change of nature. . . . None but such have a right to ordinances." P. H. Mell, the outspoken Calvinist from Georgia, began his book of *Corrective Church Discipline* with the statement, "It is the Saviour's will of precept that the constituents of His churches shall be regenerated persons. He authorizes none to receive the ordinance of Baptism, and to have a lot among His visible people, but those who believe with the heart that He is the Son of God."[70]

An article that appeared in the *Baptist Record* in 1882 and was reprinted in the *Christian Index* examined the anxious-bench method of evangelism and found it as a whole "pernicious." The abuse connected with this system has "resulted in grievous injury to our churches by filling them with an unconverted membership; and this last is one great reason . . . why our efficiency as a denomination is not commensurate with our numerical strength."[71]

One need never fear that Baptists who are Calvinists will go lightly on this Baptist distinctive of regenerate church membership. Historically their commitment to the new covenant in which God writes His law on the heart has made them zealous for receiving only those that can articulate an experience of grace. The gradual compromise of the ideal of regenerate church membership as indicated by our misleading numbers has coincided with the loss of two practices essential for maintaining

---

[70] Mark Dever, *Polity* (Washington, D.C.: Center for Church Reform, 2001), 118, 122, 422.

[71] *Christian Index*, November 9, 1882, 1.

this distinctive. One is care in receiving members, and the other is care in maintaining spiritual health in the entire congregation through close attention to both formative and corrective discipline.

Concluding Remark: Issues that mark Southern Baptists so strongly found vocal and articulate advocates from Calvinistic ranks. In contemporary Southern Baptist life, among their strongest defenders will be Calvinists. What an anomalous, even tragic, irony if those that birthed the Convention and fostered its foundational strengths with such a firmly grounded theology should now be seen as enemies of its mission and its effectiveness in the world. Any policy, any determination, any resolution that seeks the repression, or elimination, of Calvinism from the ranks of Southern Baptists would be a theological tragedy and historical suicide. In fact, one could argue along with P. H. Mell that exactly the opposite should be the case:

> In conclusion, it becomes a serious and practical question—whether we should not make these doctrines the basis of all our pulpit ministrations. If this be, indeed, the gospel system, sustained by such arguments, and attested by such effects, every minister should be imbued with its spirit, and furnished with its panoply; it is not necessary, indeed, that we should present its truth, always in the form of dogmatic or polemic theology—though even these should not be entirely neglected, if our people are not, as yet, thoroughly indoctrinated—but our hearers should never be left in doubt as to the fundamental truths, that sinners are totally depraved, and utterly helpless; that men must be regenerated by God's Spirit, and justified by the righteousness of Christ imputed to them, before they can obtain God's favor; that God's people are created by him, in Christ Jesus, unto good works, which he had before ordained that they should walk in them, and that they are kept by God's power through faith, unto salvation; that God is the sovereign ruler of the universe, and the author of everything, morally good, in the creatures. In short, that the sinner has destroyed himself, but in God is his help. And, surely it will not impair the efficiency of the minister, for him to remember that his sufficiency is of God.[72]

---

[72] P. H. Mell, *Calvinism: An Essay Read before the Georgia Baptist Ministers' Institute* (Atlanta: Geo. C. Conner, 1868; reprint Cape Coral: Christian Gospel Foundation, 1988), 19, 20.

At the same time, for a Baptist Calvinist to deny that true work is done for the glory of Christ by non-Calvinists would be to close one's eyes to the evidence and often to our own experience. I was reared in a First Baptist Church of a county seat town in Mississippi. I was baptized at 11 (before I was converted) as were most of my youthful peers (many of whom it became clear were also unconverted). We had many more members than we had active participants in the church, and I never saw a case of discipline in my 18 years of close participation in the church's activities. The only message I ever heard on election amounted to an Arminian dismissal of it. In spite of that, I had a pastor that loved the Bible and defended its full truthfulness and inspiration. He defended the deity of Christ, His resurrection, His glory, and the necessity of knowing His atoning work for the forgiveness of sins. He was infectiously joyful about the life of a Christian, loved his people, and loved me in particular. Though I was not converted under his ministry, his influence in preaching and in personal piety kept me in or near the fold even when I was not a Christian. Many things about the church could have been purer: evangelism could have been more careful without diminishing its zealous execution, and doctrinal instruction could have been more historically confessional and robust. No church or pastor, however, could have been more conscientious in attempts to nurture and encourage a young man toward Christian devotion.

We urge brethren to a massive doctrinal recovery that will result in grace-centered, truth-centered, Christ-centered preaching and a conscientious regard for removing the corrupting factors from church evangelism. At the same time, along with lamentable corruptions, we must not underestimate the true good that has been done throughout the theological spectrum of evangelical Baptists through their earnest love for the Bible and for the salvation of people. We still have much room to find a glorious unity in the person and work of Christ and a charitable judgment of sincerity toward one another. None of us stands as master of Christ's servants, but to his own master each of us stands or falls.

A Southern Baptist Dialogue

Calvinism
General Evaluation

Calvinism: Cause for Rejoicing, Cause for Concern

Malcolm B. Yarnell III
Director, Center for Theological Research
Southwestern Baptist Theological Seminary
Fort Worth, Texas

Behold, how good and how pleasant it is
    For brothers to dwell together in unity!
It is like precious oil upon the head,
    Coming down upon the beard,
    Even Aaron's beard,
    Coming down upon the edge of his robes.
It is like the dew of Hermon
    Coming down upon the mountains of Zion;
    For there the LORD commanded the blessing—
    life forever.

            —Psalm 133 NASB

How Texans Build Biblical Bridges

OUT OF A DESIRE FOR CLARITY AND FOCUS, we will consider Southern Baptists in general and Texas Baptists in particular. Alongside our fierce defense of local church independence, Southern Baptists west of the Mississippi River are interested in Christian unity. For instance, the first association of Texas Baptist churches, which began in 1840, was self-consciously entitled, "The Union Baptist Association." And earlier this month the Southern Baptists of Texas Convention (SBTC) resolved to pursue unity. But in direct contradiction to much ecumenism, the convention declared that unity is to be pursued only on the basis of "sound doctrine."[1] Recently, I reviewed the minutes of that first

---

[1] Southern Baptists of Texas Convention, "The Importance of Sound Doctrine for True Unity," adopted 13 November 2007; Internet, http://www.sbtexas.com/missions/07resolutions.htm, downloaded 22 November 2007.

association and pondered the beginnings of the Baptist witness in Texas, as well as the foundational beliefs of B. H. Carroll and Southwestern Baptist Theological Seminary.

The Union Baptists first attempted to gather in June 1840 in Independence, Texas. Two of the four ministers, Abner Smith and Ariel Dancer, were not only soteriologically Calvinistic but also pragmatically antimissionary. Indeed, the first Baptist churches in Texas were personally led and long inspired by Daniel Parker.[2] He was fanatically active in Baptist life, spreading his "two seeds" doctrine as far and wide as possible. He proclaimed and wrote that it was foolish to present the Word to the non-elect and that the elect would be won without missionaries.[3]

When the missionary Baptists realized they could never work with antimissionary Calvinists and remain true to the Great Commission, no matter how hard they might try, they formed the Union Association on their own. Thus, the remaining two ministers from that fateful June 1840 meeting gathered a group of missionary Baptists in October of the same year in Travis, Texas. T. W. Cox was elected the moderator, but R. E. B. Baylor, ordained Baptist preacher, state judge, and founder of Baylor University, was the theological giant in the Union Baptist Association. The first part of Baylor's personal motto, *Pro Ecclesia-Pro Texana*,[4] is clearly manifested in the "Bill of Inalienable Rights" adopted by the association:

> Each Church is forever free and independent, of any and every ecclesiastical power formed by men on earth, each being the free house-hold of Christ. Therefore every ordination and power granted by the Churches emanating as they do directly from the Church, those who are thus ordained or upon whom such powers are conferred, must be to her forever obedient.[5]

As you can see, Texas Baptists, who brought their pristine Baptist theology with them from many states both north and east, were committed churchmen before Landmarkers J. R. Graves and J. M. Pendleton ever

---

[2] These Calvinistic churches later formed "do nothing" associations, considering it a point of pride to do exactly that with regard to organizing Christian efforts for evangelism and mission. Harry Leon McBeth, *Texas Baptists: A Sesquicentennial History* (Dallas: Baptistway Press, 1998), 22–23.

[3] Walter B. Shurden, *Not a Silent People: Controversies That Have Shaped Southern Baptists*, 2nd ed. (Macon: Smyth & Helwys, 1995), 26–27.

[4] Guy B. Harrison Jr., "Baylor, Robert Emmett Bledsoe," *Encyclopedia of Southern Baptists*, 4 vols. (Nashville: Broadman, 1958–1982), 1:150.

[5] *Minutes of the First Session of the Union Baptist Association* (Houston: Telegraph Press, 1840), 9–10.

came to their ecclesiastical doctrines.[6] Leaving the hyper-Calvinists to kill their witness ever so slowly, the missionary Christians in the Union Baptist Association in the Texas of yesterday pursued a healthier path of biblical orthodoxy and missionary ecclesiology. Leaving the ecumenists to pursue their agenda, the missionary Baptists of today are pursuing the "unifying and healthy" path of biblical theology, soteriology, and ecclesiology, for we believe "true biblical unity is based upon certain unalterable doctrinal confessions as revealed in God's inerrant Scripture."[7] If I can translate the Texas resolution into postmodern missional language, it might sound like this: traditional missionary Baptists will build bridges with others all day long, but only on the basis of scriptural doctrine, only by the means of scriptural proclamation, and only for the purposes commanded by our Triune God in Scripture, for Scripture alone reveals what is truly relevant.

Defining Calvinism

Before proceeding, it may be helpful to develop a taxonomy for understanding Calvinism in the Southern Baptist context. In recent debates over Calvinism in the Southern Baptist Convention (SBC), many have noted a lack of clarity over what both proponents and opponents mean by the word *Calvinism*. Delineating the differences between classical Calvinism, Baptist Calvinism, and hyper-Calvinism may help us progress toward unity around what Southern Baptists consider essential doctrines.[8]

Classical Calvinism

Classical Calvinism is that Calvinism which began with the work of leading magisterial Reformers such as Ulrich Zwingli, Martin Bucer, and most notably, John Calvin. The philosophical basis of classical Calvinism was subsequently propounded in the work of Scholastic theologians such

---

[6] E.g., John Piper *et al.*, "Baptism and Church Membership at Bethlehem Baptist Church" (9 August 2005); Internet, http://www.desiringgod.org/media/pdf/baptism_and_membership.pdf, downloaded 26 November 2007; Timothy George *et al.*, "That They May Have Life: A Statement of Evangelicals and Catholics Together," *First Things* (October 2006): 18–26.

[7] "The Importance of Sound Doctrine for True Unity."

[8] Liberal Calvinism, neoorthodox Calvinism, and postmodern Calvinism are subjects worthy of consideration in their own right but tangential to the current context. Also not considered here is the debate over the relationship between Calvin and Calvinism. See R. T. Kendall, *Calvin and English Calvinism to 1649* (New York: Oxford University Press, 1978); Paul Helm, *Calvin and the Calvinists* (Carlisle, PA: Banner of Truth, 1982); Kevin Dixon Kennedy, *Union with Christ and the Extent of the Atonement in Calvin*, Studies in Biblical Literature 48 (New York: Peter Lang, 2002).

as Theodore Beza, William Perkins, and the Heidelberg Theologians. Various groups and synods made numerous attempts to codify competing visions of the Calvinist system in canons and confessions, such as the two Helvetic confessions,[9] the Belgic Confession,[10] the Remonstrance,[11] the Synod of Dort,[12] and the Westminster Assembly.[13] After the Synod of Dort, Arminians, among whom the leading theologians are Jacobus Arminius and John Wesley, broke completely with Calvinists, who bind themselves to the historical doctrines codified at Dort and Westminster.[14]

The five heads of the Synod of Dort provide classical Calvinists with their acronym of TULIP (originally, ULTIP): unconditional predestination, limited or particular atonement, total human corruption, irresistible grace, and final preservation. Fisher Humphreys correctly noted, "Anyone who accepts unconditional predestination should have no trouble accepting the other four ideas [that] follow naturally from unconditional predestination."[15] By unconditional predestination, classical Calvinism understands not only positive election, which Scripture definitely affirms, but also negative reprobation, which is their mere logical supposition.[16] After the line is crossed into philosophical theology with speculation regarding the divine decrees, little holds the Christian theologian back from embracing the soteriological doctrines of classical Calvinism in their entirety.

Moreover, the philosophico-theological system of classical Calvinism may not be reduced to soteriological matters alone. As a premier classical Calvinist scholar, Richard Muller remarked, "It would be a major

---

[9] *Reformed Confessions of the Sixteenth Century*, ed. Arthur C. Cochrane (2d ed.; Louisville: Westminster John Knox, 2003), 97–111, 220–301.

[10] Ibid., 185–219.

[11] *Articuli Arminiani sive Remonstratia* (1610), in *The Creeds of Christendom: With a History and Critical Notes*, 6th ed., 3 vols., ed. Philip Schaff (1931; reprint, Grand Rapids: Baker, 1993), 3: 545–49.

[12] *Canones Synodi Dordrechtanae* (1618–1619), in *The Creeds of Christendom*, 550–80 (ET, 581–97).

[13] *Confessio Fidei Westmonasteriensis* (1647), in *The Creeds of Christendom*, 600–73.

[14] For an invaluable theological introduction, consider Karl Barth, *The Theology of the Reformed Confessions,* trans. Darrell L. Guder and Judith J. Guder (Louisville: Westminster John Knox, 2002). For a historical perspective of Westminster, the most important English Calvinist assembly, consider Robert S. Paul, *The Assembly of the Lord: Politics and Religion in the Westminster Assembly and the 'Grand Debate'* (Edinburgh: T&T Clark, 1985); and Nicholas Tyacke, *Anti-Calvinists: The Rise of English Arminianism c.1590–1640* (New York: Oxford University Press, 1987).

[15] Fisher Humphreys, "Traditional Baptists and Calvinism," *BHH* 39.2 (2004): 57.

[16] "God once established by his eternal and unchangeable plan those whom he long before determined once for all to receive unto salvation, and those whom, on the other hand, he would devote to destruction." John Calvin, *Institutes of the Christian Religion*, 3.21.7, ed. John T. McNeill, LCC, 20–21, trans. Ford Lewis Battles, 2 vols. (Philadelphia: Westminster Press, 1960), 2:921.

error—both historically and doctrinally—if the five points of Calvinism were understood either as the sole or even as the absolutely primary basis for identifying someone as holding the Calvinistic or Reformed faith."[17] The Synod of Dort was merely a negative reaction to the Reformed aberration of Arminianism. For a complete understanding of classical Calvinism, one must turn to the confessions of Zurich, Bern, Basel, Geneva, Lausanne, Heidelberg, and Westminster, among others. Muller correctly noted that what we are referring to here as classical Calvinism "makes very little sense" unless one also adopts other doctrines such as "the baptism of infants," "the identification of sacraments as means of grace, the so-called amillennial view of the end of the world."[18] Conversely, classical Calvinism denies concurrent emphases on "adult baptism, being 'born again,' and 'accepting Christ,'" and is uncomfortable with evangelical language advocating a "personal relationship with Jesus Christ."[19]

In other words, from a traditional Baptist perspective, genuine classical Calvinism is, to say the least, unacceptable and, perhaps more correctly, utterly reprehensible. Although we could spend much time here deconstructing the unbiblical nature of classical Calvinism, consider the example of the murder of Michael Servetus by the Genevan Calvinists. While admittedly a heretic, Servetus was still a precious human being created in the divine image, and for Calvin to advocate his murder is inexcusable. As Thomas Grantham, a General Baptist who was writing systematic theology before John Gill began his inventive career, wisely asked, "O *Calvin*, why didst thou (like *Cain*) thy pious Brother slay, Because he could not walk with thee, in thy self-chosen Way?"[20] Calvin only weakly apologized regarding the condemned Baptist, "I had never entertained any personal rancor against him."[21] Servetus was burned at the stake by the Reformed not only for his anti-Trinitarianism, for which he was wrong, but also for his antipaedobaptism, for which he was right.[22]

Baptist Calvinism[23]

To understand Baptist Calvinism, it may be helpful to distinguish three major theories of Baptist origins: Historical Succession, Protestant

---

[17] Richard A. Muller, "How Many Points?" *CTJ* 28 (1993): 426.

[18] Ibid., 428

[19] Ibid., 430–31.

[20] Thomas Grantham, *A Dialogue between the Baptist and the Presbyterian* (London, 1691; reprint, Fort Worth: Center for Theological Research, forthcoming 2007), 21–22.

[21] Roland H. Bainton, *Hunted Heretic: The Life and Death of Michael Servetus, 1511–1553* (Boston: Beacon, 1953), 209.

[22] Ibid., 207–8.

[23] "Reformed Baptists" is not used, as that term has been applied to particular Baptist churches unaffiliated with the Southern Baptist Convention.

Branch, and New Testament Pattern. The Historical Succession theory seeks to trace in history a succession of baptizing churches stretching back through history to the first church of Jerusalem.[24] The Protestant Branch theory finds the origin of modern Baptist churches in either the continental Reformation with the Anabaptists or the English Reformation with the Separatists.[25] The New Testament Pattern theory is less concerned with a traceable historical succession or with a Protestant origin than with the marked tendency that Christians who take New Testament theology seriously often become Baptist.[26]

Whichever of the above theories one holds, the Particular Baptists are without doubt two to three decades behind the General Baptists in their development. The first English Baptists, which all historians agree are the forefathers of today's Baptists, were not classical Calvinists, although they developed *out* of the Calvinist context. The first English Baptists, under the leadership of Thomas Helwys, explicitly rejected predestinarian Calvinism as unbiblical.[27] Moreover, Stephen Wright recently argued that the Particular Baptists did not at first develop a separate denomination but had long intimate relations with the General Baptists.[28] The split between General and Particular Baptists came only with the hardening of predestinarian theology amidst the political posturing of the Particular Baptists in adopting the Second London Confession. Yet even then these early Calvinistic Baptists were careful to distinguish themselves over against both Calvinistic Presbyterians and Calvinistic Independents or Congregationalists by presenting a distinct ecclesiology, even as they adopted the Westminster Confession and the Savoy Declaration as models for their own confession.[29]

Whether one prefers Zurich in 1525, or Amsterdam in 1609, or London in 1633 or 1638 as the favored origin of modern Baptists, the point is that in every historical instance, the Baptists explicitly rejected, or at the least significantly modified, the theological method and numerous

---

[24] J. M. Carroll, *The Trail of Blood* (Lexington, KY: Ashland Avenue Baptist Church, 1931). J. M. Carroll was the brother of the founder of Southwestern Seminary and an original trustee.

[25] B. R. White, *The English Separatist Tradition: From the Marian Martyrs to the Pilgrim Fathers* (New York: Oxford University Press, 1971), ch. 6; James R. Coggins, *John Smyth's Congregation: English Separatism, Mennonite Influence, and the Elect Nation*, Studies in Anabaptist and Mennonite History 32 (Scottdale, PA: Herald Press, 1991).

[26] Robert A. Baker, *The Baptist March in History* (Nashville: Convention Press, 1958), 3.

[27] Thomas Helwys, *A Short and Plaine proofe by the Word, and workes off God, that Gods decree is not the cause off anye Mans sinne or Condemnation. And That all Men are redeemed by Christ. As also That no Infants are Condemned* (London, 1611).

[28] Stephen Wright, *The Early English Baptists, 1603–1649* (Rochester, NY: Boydell & Brewer, 2006).

[29] Lumpkin, 235–40.

dogmatic conclusions of the Reformed. Baptists, in all three instances, moved *away from* or developed *out of* the Calvinist context. They implicitly retained certain beliefs and explicitly rejected other beliefs of the classical Calvinists. The problem is that not all modern Baptists agree on exactly how much should be retained and how much rejected. The relevant theological lessons we can learn today from the origins of Baptist Calvinists for our current subject are threefold: first, Baptists came to their beliefs in the Reformed context; second, Baptists came to their beliefs and were compelled to separate from the Reformed churches due to biblical convictions; and third, Baptists have therefore always had both an appreciation for and a healthy distrust of Calvinism.

This appreciation and distrust is not due so much to historical factors but to the fact that Reformed theology intentionally seeks to reflect on biblical truth. Although it does so with great theological creativity, Calvinism takes the biblical text seriously. Baptists, too, take the biblical text seriously but more so. This confluence between Baptist and Calvinist explains why Baptist Calvinism is a long-standing phenomenon. It also explains why Baptist confessions sometimes appear to have a Calvinistic tone to them, even as they reject classical Calvinism's extrabiblical inventions. For instance, the Union Baptist Association explicitly affirmed both divine sovereignty and human freedom in the third of its eleven articles of faith, thus setting itself to address the premier Augustinian-Calvinist question, though not in Calvinistic terms.[30]

Thus, even as Texas Baptists at their foundation reacted against antimissionism, Campbellism, and Calvinism, they simultaneously responded to the Calvinist question.[31] Anecdotally, Texas Baptists have always alternated between both defense of their Baptist Calvinist brethren in Louisville and warnings to those same brethren. On the one hand, Texas Baptists distanced themselves from George M. Fortune and J. M. Fort, the latter opining that "the Baptist Theological Seminary at Louisville was the greatest curse upon the denomination and Christianity ever tolerated."[32] On the other hand, Texas Baptists fully supported B. H. Carroll as he led the attack against W. H. Whitsitt, the president of Southern Seminary, because they worried the seminary was undermining Baptist ecclesiology through historical revisionism.[33]

The New Hampshire Confession of 1833, which is the basis of the Baptist Faith and Message of 1925, subsequently revised in 1963 and

---

[30] *Minutes of the First Session of the Union Baptist Association*, 8.

[31] McBeth, *Texas Baptists*, 33–35.

[32] Ibid., 115.

[33] Alan J. Lefever, *Fighting the Good Fight: The Life and Work of Benajah Harvey Carroll* (Austin: Eakin, 1994), 84–94.

2000, actually represents a turning away from the Second London Confession.[34] Dortian Calvinism, as James Leo Garrett Jr. terms that synod's soteriological doctrines,[35] is well represented in the London Baptists' second confession. Unconditional predestination is affirmed, both from the standpoint of positive election (10.1–3) and, arguably, from negative reprobation (10.4). The Second London Confession also affirms limited atonement (11.3–4), total corruption (6.2), irresistible grace (9.4, 10.2), and final preservation (17.1–2).[36]

The New Hampshire Confession was the culmination of a significant undermining of the Calvinism of the Regular Baptists, who championed the Second London Confession at Philadelphia and Charleston. On the one hand, the work of Benjamin Randall in the New Hampshire area modified the Calvinistic tenor of the surrounding churches, preparing for the development of the New Hampshire Confession.[37] On the other hand, the Separate Baptists, an especially fruitful branch of the family arising during the Great Awakening, were either adamantly opposed to confessions of any kind, or if willing to accept the Philadelphia Confession, were careful to deny it specific authority.[38]

In 1787, when the Separate and Regular Baptists, who joined under the name of United Baptists in several states, formed their union in Virginia, they agreed that the Philadelphia Confession should have no "tyrannical power." They were willing to affirm the essentials of orthodox soteriology, but the essentials were severely limited to the statement "that the doctrine of salvation by Christ, and free and unmerited grace alone, ought to be believed."[39]

---

[34] Timothy George strongly asserts that the New Hampshire Confession "follows the Reformed orientation of the Philadelphia Confession" but only mildly admits "its treatment of the doctrines of grace is briefer, less specific, and more susceptible to theological ambiguity." George, "Introduction," in *Baptist Confessions, Covenants, and Catechisms*, ed. Timothy and Denise George (Nashville: Broadman & Holman, 1996), 12.

[35] James Leo Garrett Jr., *Baptists and Calvinism: An Informational Examination* (Birmingham: The Alabama Baptist, 2007).

[36] *Confession of Faith Put Forth by the Elders and Brethren of Many Congregations of Christians* (London, 1677), in Lumpkin, 241–95.

[37] Lumpkin, 360–61.

[38] In 1792, the South Association of Separate Baptists in Kentucky answered some queries: "1. What was the Separate Baptists first constituted upon, in Kentucky? *Ans.* The Bible. . . . 3. Did those terms [of union with the Regular Baptists] oblige us to receive any part of the Philadelphia Confession of Faith? *Ans.* No." John T. Christian, *A History of the Baptists*, 2.3.1; Internet, www.pbministries.org/History/John%20T.%20Christian/vol2/history2_part3_01.htm, downloaded 20 November 2007.

[39] David Benedict, *A General History of the Baptist Denomination in America* (Boston: Manning & Loring, 1813), 60–62; cited in H. Leon McBeth, *A Sourcebook for Baptist Heritage* (Nashville: Broadman, 1990), 165–66. See W. Wiley Richards, "Southern Baptist Identity: Moving Away from Calvinism," *BHH* 31.4 (1996): 28–29.

It should cause little wonder then that, soon after, when the New Hampshire Confession was published in the manuals of Brown, Pendleton, and Hiscox, it quickly supplanted the strict Calvinism of the Second London/Philadelphia/Charleston Confessions as the favored symbol of most Baptist churches. The New Hampshire Confession's long-standing local popularity has caused not a few of the new Calvinists in the SBC heartfelt concern. Indeed, one admitted that after discovering his church's confession was "less than Calvinist," he decided to use that standard for church membership but dusted off a different standard, the Second London Confession, for the church's leadership.[40]

The New Hampshire Confession downplays most of the doctrines that the Synod of Dort and the Second London Confession emphasized. There is no hint whatsoever of unconditional predestination, for the questions of particularity and reprobation are never addressed. Rather, New Hampshire immediately affirms that election is "perfectly consistent with the free agency of man," then proceeds to teach the benefits of a biblical doctrine of election: it effectively elevates divine wisdom, promotes humility among men, encourages Christian proclamation, and provides assurance (9). The debate between general and particular atonement is left unaddressed: Christ simply "made atonement for our sins by his death" (4). There is a doctrine of corruption, but the Augustinian doctrine of original sin is muted: all are "now sinners, not by constraint but choice" (3). As for irresistible grace, it is replaced with a strong statement regarding the freeness of salvation: "Nothing prevents the salvation of the greatest sinner on earth except his own voluntary refusal to submit to the Lord" (6). Ultimately, the only soteriological distinctive of the Synod of Dort to be clearly confessed in the New Hampshire Confession, and in its Southern Baptist descendants, is final preservation (11).[41]

Hyper-Calvinism[42]

The full history of "High Calvinism," if the particular historian appreciates the movement, or "hyper-Calvinism," if the historian does not, is better rehearsed elsewhere. However, from a traditional Southern Baptist perspective, this third type of Calvinism is as acceptable as classical Calvinism. Having led several groups of faculty and students to tour the Northamptonshire Association churches that turned the British

---

[40] Mark Dever, "Which Confession?" *FJ* 61 (2005): 4–9.

[41] *The New Hampshire Confession* (1833), in Lumpkin, 361–67.

[42] Hyper-Calvinism is treated after Baptist Calvinism because it flourishes best in the Baptist context. Hyper-Calvinism is less likely to occur in a classical Calvinist context due to the latter's temporal sacramentalism and emphasis on covenantal community. Muller, "How Many Points?," 428–29.

tide against the hyper-Calvinism of John Brine and John Skepp, I can personally attest that not only are Texas Baptists consistently offended by hyper-Calvinism, but so are Baptists in South Carolina, Tennessee, Alabama, Georgia, Florida, Mississippi, Louisiana, and Missouri. The missionary theology of Andrew Fuller and the passionate evangelism of William Carey are inspiring precisely because these men forsook the rigid Calvinism of their forefathers and launched the modern missions movement as a result of their departure from strict Reformed theology. Fuller's passionate advocacy of faith as a duty for all people consistently trumps the hyper-Calvinistic argument that faith is only available to those possessing a warrant to believe.[43] To argue, like the hyper-Calvinists, that sinners should not be freely offered the gospel or invited to respond with faith and repentance, is anathema to missionary Baptists.

For instance, Texas Union Baptists adopted articles of faith that have been interpreted as Arminian: "We believe that Christ died for sinners, and that the sacrifice which he has made, has so honored the divine law that a way of salvation is consistently opened up to every sinner to whom the Gospel is sent, and that nothing but their voluntary rejection of the Gospel prevents their salvation."[44] While the claim that such a statement is necessarily Arminian is doubtful, it is definitely not a Calvinist sentiment. The sixth article of the New Hampshire Confession is similarly non-Calvinist:

> That the blessings of salvation are made free to all by the Gospel; that it is the immediate duty of all to accept them by a cordial, and obedient faith; and that nothing prevents the salvation of the greatest sinner on earth except his own voluntary refusal to submit to the Lord Jesus Christ, which refusal will subject him to an aggravated condemnation.[45]

Although B. H. Carroll referred to the Philadelphia Confession, he preferred the New Hampshire Confession.[46] Indeed, the founding confession adopted by the board of trustees, and subscribed to by the faculty of Southwestern Seminary was the New Hampshire Confession. The New Hampshire Confession, with one significant correction—the word "visible" was replaced by the word "particular" in the article on the

---

[43] Andrew Fuller, *The Gospel Worthy of All Acceptation: Or the Obligations of Men Fully to Credit, and Cordially to Approve, Whatever God Makes Known* (London, 1785).

[44] Robert A. Baker, *Tell the Generations Following: A History of Southwestern Baptist Theological Seminary, 1908–1983* (Nashville: Broadman, 1983), 32; *Minutes of the First Session of the Union Baptist Association*, 8.

[45] Lumpkin, 363.

[46] Lefever, *Fighting the Good Fight*, 67, 73.

church, removing even an implicit affirmation of the fictitious invisible church promoted by classical Calvinism—was declared the "permanent" articles of faith of the seminary.[47] When the faculty elected to speak out against the accusations of J. Frank Norris in 1921, they again affirmed their allegiance to the revised New Hampshire Confession. Moreover, they outlined "the fundamentals of Christianity," which could be identified as uniquely Calvinist only by a fertile imagination: "The inspiration of the Bible, the sovereignty of God, the deity of Christ, the personality of the Spirit, the fallen condition of all mankind, Christ's death and resurrection as man's only hope and the regenerating and sanctifying work of the Holy Spirit as the only power that can lift man out of his fallen condition."[48]

The first occupant of the first chair of evangelism in any seminary and the second president of Southwestern Seminary, L. R. Scarborough, was a member of the committee led by E. Y. Mullins that presented the Baptist Faith and Message for adoption in 1925. Mullins was wise to look not to the Abstract of Principles of Southern Seminary, a slim version of the Charleston Confession, for a consensus document for Southern Baptists. Perhaps detecting a theological bulwark against a resurgent Baptist Calvinism, Southwestern was so pleased with the new confession that it was the first Southern Baptist institution to adopt it. And in an extraordinary resolution, the SBC explicitly commended Southwestern for its action, requesting "all its institutions and Boards, and their missionary representatives, to give like assurance to the Convention and the Baptist Brotherhood in general, of a hearty and individual acceptance."[49] Following the Elliott controversy and the promulgation of the 1963 Baptist Faith and Message, Southwestern again affirmed this non-Calvinist statement as its own.[50]

In an excellent article surveying the changing views of Southern Baptists on the doctrine of predestination, Paul Basden has shown how Southern Baptist theologians transitioned away from Calvinism toward non-Calvinism, even outright Arminianism. In the nineteenth century, Southern Baptist writing theologians, as exemplified by Patrick Hues

---

[47] *Minutes of the Board of Trustees of Southwestern Baptist Theological Seminary*, November 1908 (Fort Worth: Archives of the Roberts Library), 21–22; Baker, *Tell the Generations Following*, 142–43. Earlier Baptist Calvinists were also uncomfortable with the concept of an invisible church. The First London Confession does not use the word *invisible* in reference to the church, and the Second London Confession carefully qualifies the Westminster Confession's use of the term by adding, "(with respect to internal work of the Spirit, and truth of grace) may be called invisible." Lumpkin, 165, 285.

[48] Baker, *Tell the Generations Following*, 224–25.

[49] Ibid., 262.

[50] Ibid., 395. This controversy involved *The Message of Genesis*, by Midwestern Seminary professor (at that time) Ralph H. Elliot, published in 1961 by Broadman Press.

Mell, John Leadley Dagg, and James Petigru Boyce, borrowed heavily from classical Calvinists in order to affirm either double predestination or preterition.[51] In the early twentieth century Southern Baptist writing theologians, all of them in or from Texas, moderated the Calvinism of earlier theologians. "While they still affirmed God's election of persons to salvation in Christ, they denied God's rejection of any to eternal damnation." And methodologically, "The revealed will of God in Christ replaced abstract speculation."[52] Finally, after the mid-century, led by theologians affiliated with Southern Seminary and New Orleans Seminary, Southern Baptists even moved toward Arminian positions. Herschel Hobbs, the chairman of the 1963 revision committee, rejected speculation regarding the divine decrees and defined election as an eternal redemptive plan for those who are "in Christ."[53] Hobbs, however, held the line against Dale Moody's Arminianism by protecting the one clear Dortian affirmation in the Baptist Faith and Message, that of final preservation.[54]

With such a history behind Southern Baptists, the SBC in general clearly may be willing to tolerate Baptist Calvinism, but classical Calvinism and hyper-Calvinism are singularly unwelcome. In spite of the efforts of some to promote Calvinism, Basden argued that the "Arminian approach to predestination" would continue for at least three reasons:

> (1) Southern Baptists are committed to foreign missions. . . . They fear that belief in a God who predetermines the eternal fate of every person will eventually undermine missionary zeal. (2) In their own nation, cities, and hometowns, Southern Baptists have greatly emphasized evangelism and church growth. This emphasis, pragmatic though it may be, generally stands on the theological conviction that 'whosoever will may come.' . . . (3) A dispensational view of eschatology, which enjoys popularity across the Southern Baptist Convention, is generally not compatible with Calvinistic theology.[55]

---

[51] Paul Basden, "Predestination," in *Has Our Theology Changed? Southern Baptist Thought Since 1845*, ed. P. Basden (Nashville: Broadman & Holman, 1994), 41–50. The view of preterition involved leaving the non-elect to perish in their sins.

[52] Ibid., 58–59.

[53] Ibid., 62.

[54] M. Yarnell, "The Person and Work of the Holy Spirit," in *A Theology for the Church*, ed. Daniel L. Akin (Nashville: B&H, 2007), 672–73.

[55] Ibid., 71. Regarding the third reason, however, Basden's supporting point that dispensationalism teaches "two seemingly irreconcilable views of salvation" is mistaken. See John S. Feinberg, "Systems of Continuity," in *Continuity and Discontinuity*, ed. J. S. Feinberg (Westchester, IL: Crossway, 1988), 70–71; David L. Turner, "'Dubious

Yet other reasons could be listed as to why Calvinism will find it difficult to triumph, as will become apparent in our evaluative comments.

Causes for Rejoicing and Concern

With this threefold taxonomy in place and a long-standing non-Calvinist Baptist tradition, particularly in Texas, historically established, let us tremble toward a theological and ethical evaluation of Calvinism. I will suggest five causes for rejoicing about Baptist Calvinism and five causes for concern, especially when Baptist Calvinists exhibit tendencies toward classical Calvinism and hyper-Calvinism. These causes rotate around essential Baptist beliefs regarding Jesus Christ, the Bible, the gospel, the Church, and the Christian Life.

1. Jesus Christ

Calvinism is a cause for rejoicing because it takes the Christological definitions of the early church seriously. One cannot pick up a book by a Calvinist such as John Gill and not be impressed with the basic Christian orthodoxy expounded there.[56] The Christological orthodoxy of all three Calvinisms is generally superb. With Calvin all Baptists can heartily agree that the Christology promoted at the Council of Chalcedon is a "pure and genuine exposition of Scripture." With Calvin we also agree that the focus of our Christology should be on the benefits of Christ, an experiential dimension sadly not always reflected in later Calvinism.[57]

One thing that characterizes Baptist belief at the folk level and among our best theologians is the centrality of faith in the Savior and submission to Him as Lord. We may joke at how our children offer the answer, "Jesus," to almost any question put to them, but the phenomenon indicates a deep-rooted Christocentrism. We Baptists love our children, and rather than finding false security in the misleading practice of paedobaptism, we instruct our children about who Jesus Christ is and what He has done for us. This Christocentrism is seen also in the theology of that former hyper-Calvinist, Andrew Fuller. Whereas classical Calvinists such as Herman Bavinck and High Calvinists such as John Gill founded their theology upon philosophical determinism, Fuller preferred personal faith in Jesus Christ and His cross as the foundation for theology.[58]

Evangelicalism'? A Response to John Gerstner's Critique of Dispensationalism" *GTJ* 12 (1991): 263–78.

[56] John Gill, *A Body of Doctrinal Divinity*, 1.30, 2.11.

[57] Bruce L. McCormack, "For Us and Our Salvation: Incarnation and Atonement in the Reformed Tradition," *GOTR* 43 (1998): 284–88, 292–94.

[58] Malcolm B. Yarnell III, *The Formation of Christian Doctrine* (Nashville: B&H, 2007), 154–55.

The cause for concern with regard to Jesus Christ is that the key Reformation doctrine of faith in Christ and the key believers' Church doctrine of discipleship to Christ have been sidelined for speculative reasons by many Calvinists. Classical Calvinists consider even the use of the terminology of Christocentrism to be "imprudent."[59] As I have shown elsewhere, classical Calvinism demotes faith in Christ in order to elevate philosophical speculation regarding the divine decrees and common grace. Fortunately, Baptist Calvinists like John Dagg recognized that speculation should not replace experiential, practical faith in Jesus Christ as Lord and Savior.[60] Non-Calvinist Jerry Falwell went further when he said John 3:16 requires a central focus upon faith in Jesus Christ.[61]

Unfortunately, Baptists enamored with Reformed theology may be tempted to downplay faith in Christ in the rush toward rationalistic doctrines of predestination. Such speculations, especially with regard to eternal justification, are key to the theological development of hyper-Calvinism.[62] Moreover, the debate over lordship salvation (whether saving faith includes faith in Christ as Lord as well as Savior) and antinomian salvation is primarily an intra-Calvinist controversy.[63] Resort to the pastoral legacy of Jonathan Edwards and Andrew Fuller may be helpful here for Baptist Calvinists who are tempted to pursue the rationalist paths of scholasticism. Consider again the psalm that began this presentation. Unless unity is based on the One who is anointed prophet, priest, and king, there is no brotherhood or eternal life. Non-Calvinist Baptists call their Baptist Calvinist brethren to reject clearly and permanently speculative doctrines insofar as they detract from experiential faith in and consistent submission to Jesus Christ as Lord.

2. The Bible

Like Baptists, Calvinists have a high appreciation for the Bible. Conservative theologians in both groups affirm the Bible's inspiration by the Holy Spirit, the inerrancy of the original autographs, the infallibility of the copies, and the unique authority of the Scriptures (*sola scriptura*) for our faith and for our worship (the regulative principle). We agree with one another about much. For this, non-Calvinist Baptists truly rejoice in the stands taken by our taxonomy of Calvinists. This is

---

[59] Richard A. Muller, "A Note on 'Christocentrism' and the Imprudent Use of Such Terminology," *WTJ* 68.2 (2006): 253–60.

[60] Yarnell, *The Formation of Christian Doctrine*, 57–59, 67–70.

[61] Jerry Falwell Jr., "Introduction to Jerry Falwell, 'Becoming Champions for Christ,'" *Live from Liberty*, Television Broadcast (19 October 2007).

[62] See John Brine, *A Defence of the Doctrine of Eternal Justification* (London, 1732).

[63] For the debate between John MacArthur and Zane Hodges, see Millard J. Erickson, "Lordship Theology: The Current Controversy," *SwJT* 33.2 (1991): 5–15.

why non-Calvinists are glad to work alongside Calvinists in the conservative resurgence of the SBC, and in such non-ecclesiastical venues as the Evangelical Theological Society (although there is some warrant to charges that this organization is in danger of detaching itself from its biblical and theological moorings).

Non-Calvinist Baptists, however, detect causes for concern in the way some Calvinists use the Bible. These arise particularly in the theological systematization of classical Calvinism. W. G. T. Shedd, the erudite nineteenth-century defender of the Westminster Confession, described the problem, although he meant it as a panegyric: Calvinism is "that intellectual and powerful system of theology which had its origin in the Biblical studies and personal experience of the two most comprehensive and scientific theologians of Christendom, Aurelius Augustine and John Calvin."[64]

The shift of emphasis is subtle but significant. Calvinism is not just interested in the Bible but in a system that issues forth from ruminations upon the Bible by the fifth-century bishop of Hippo and the sixteenth-century reformer of Geneva. Richard Muller's well-regarded book, *The Unaccommodated Calvin*, illustrates the problem. In this work, as in his Reformed corpus generally, Muller is most particularly interested in presenting Calvin's theology as Calvin understood it.[65] Although Muller's historical method is laudable, his theology is not. As a Biblicist, I am more concerned to present the unaccommodated Christ from the Bible than I am to present the reflections of "the Unaccommodated Calvin" on the Bible.

The rationalist approach to Scripture is found in the Calvinist tendency to rightly divide the Word of truth but then continue dividing it *ad infinitum*. I once entered a dialogue with an accomplished scholar who had read an article of mine on Calvinism[66] and sent me a contrary article of his own. I asked him for the exegetical clue to distinguish between the hidden and revealed wills of God with regard to particular redemption. I have not yet received an answer. Likewise, many important theological distinctions used by Calvinist theologians lack a sufficient biblical basis for the theological load they are asked to bear. These include, among others, the logical ordering of the divine decrees, the covenants of works

---

[64] W. G. T. Shedd, *Calvinism: Pure and Mixed* (1893; reprint, Carlisle, PA: Banner of Truth, 1986), xi.

[65] Richard A. Muller, *The Unaccommodated Calvin: Studies in the Foundation of a Theological Tradition* (New York: Oxford University Press). See Matthew C. Heckel, "Review Essay," *Presb* 31.2 (2005): 101–6.

[66] Yarnell, "The TULIP of Calvinism: In Light of History and the Baptist Faith and Message," *SBC Life* (April 2006).

and grace, and the equation of circumcision with baptism.[67] As Charles Haddon Spurgeon complained about some Calvinists, "They bring a system of divinity to the Bible to interpret it, instead of making every system, be its merits what they may, yield, and give place to the pure and unadulterated Word of God."[68]

Similarly, in the Texas free churches, there is a long-standing distrust of extrabiblical systems. The second article of faith for the Union Baptist Association reads, "We believe the Scriptures of the Old and New Testament are revealed from God, and that they contain the only true system of faith and practice."[69] Considering that the Bible is, by all accounts, not organized as a scientific system, that is quite a statement. Baptists are not as interested in a rationalist system as they are in following the Word of God precisely in their faith and practice. B. H. Carroll was personally led away from God by human philosophies. As a result, after conversion he explicitly rejected any attempt to construct belief upon them: "Whoever in his hour of real need, makes abstract philosophy his pillow, makes cold, hard granite his pillow. Whoever looks trustingly into any of its false faces looks into the face of a Medusa, and is turned to stone. They are all wells without water, and clouds without rain."[70] Non-Calvinist Baptists would call our Baptist Calvinist brethren to reject clearly and permanently speculative doctrines, extra-biblical distinctions, and theological methodologies insofar as they detract from the revelation of the Word of God illumined by the Holy Spirit to the gathered churches. Some forms of Calvinism are simply not biblical enough.

3. The Gospel

Spurgeon's comment, "Calvinism is the Gospel, and nothing else," receives much attention, while his comments regarding hyper-Calvinism's problems are often ignored. Spurgeon understood the gospel and proclaimed it regularly, but his statement here is challengeable not only on the basis of the Bible but also from his sermon. First, Spurgeon's *A Defence of Calvinism* does not explicitly affirm all five points as expressed at the Synod of Dort. He definitely affirms final preservation and probably irresistible grace, and he moderates the doctrine of limited atonement with the sufficient-efficient distinction. But his doctrine of depravity lacks the Augustinian belief in the transmission of guilt, and

---

[67] For a fuller though undeveloped list, see Yarnell, *The Formation of Christian Doctrine*, 155n.

[68] Iain Murray, *The Forgotten Spurgeon,* 2d ed. (Carlisle, PA: Banner of Truth, 1973), 46.

[69] *Minutes of the First Session of the Union Baptist Association*, 8.

[70] Baker, *Tell the Generations Following*, 60–61.

his presentation of the doctrine of unconditional predestination is notably missing the classical Calvinist doctrine of reprobation.[71]

Moreover, from a biblical perspective, Spurgeon's sermon slights the central figure of the gospel, Jesus Christ. The Lord appears but primarily as a means to argue the extent of His atoning work. The prince of preachers laid aside his crown of evangelism on the day he produced this piece, for he was more interested in limiting the recipients of Christ's atoning work than in exalting Jesus Christ. In light of recent worries that Southern Baptists may be losing the gospel, such misdirected attempts surely must raise concerns.[72] Lost priorities are not only evident in this presentation by Spurgeon but also in the evangelistic presentations of John Piper.

Piper's Desiring God Ministries placed three evangelism tracts on the Web for distribution. The first tract is noticeable for its elevation of Piper's "Christian hedonism." Although Piper must be lauded for injecting divine glory into a gospel presentation, it caters to rather than challenges our narcissistic culture: "God gets the praise and we get the pleasure." Piper, busily promoting peculiarities, never discusses the person of Jesus Christ. And when asking what the believer must do, he points them to a church but neglects to exhort them to follow Christ in baptism, as the Great Commission teaches.[73] In the second tract Piper correctly discusses Jesus Christ at length, alongside his passion for glory, but passes quickly over sin and never issues a call for the sinner to believe in Jesus Christ.[74] In the third tract Piper issues a call for faith in Christ, but the tract is written for the struggling believer rather than the lost person.[75]

The Calvinist concern for the gospel is a cause for rejoicing, but the demonstrated confusion of Calvinism with regard to the gospel is a cause for concern. A related cause for concern is the Calvinist doctrine of conversion. The classical Calvinist understanding of faith and repentance, which together define conversion, is troubling. Bavinck demonstrated that the Lutheran recovery of faith was pushed back in the speculative Calvinist *ordo salutis* to a second-order issue, while repentance was

---

[71] Charles Haddon Spurgeon, *A Defence of the Gospel*; Internet, www.spurgeon.org/calvinis.htm, downloaded 25 November 2007.

[72] Tom Ascol, "Have We Lost the Gospel?" Internet, www.founders.org/blog/2007/02/have-we-lost-gospel.html, downloaded 25 November 2007.

[73] Thanks to Cky Carrigan for his helpful analysis of this tract. John Piper, "Quest for Joy," Internet, www.desiringgod.org/ResourceLibrary/Articles/ByDate/1995/1546_Quest_for_Joy/, downloaded 25 November 2007.

[74] John Piper, "Don't Waste Your Life Tract," Internet, www.desiringgod.org/ResourceLibrary/Articles/ByDate/2004/1547_Dont_Waste_Your_Life_Tract/, downloaded 25 November 2007.

[75] John Piper, "The Gospel in 6 Minutes," Internet, www.desiringgod.org/ResourceLibrary/Articles/ByDate/2007/2389_The_Gospel_in_6_Minutes/, downloaded 25 November 2007.

pushed even further back into discussions of the Christian life. While admitting Calvinism is confused about the exact time of regeneration in relation to baptism, Bavinck believed Baptists overemphasized the new birth.[76] Classical Calvinism's emphases seem contradictory to Scripture, especially with regard to the first-order invitation of Christ and the apostles for sinners to repent and believe.[77]

Although classical Calvinists may deny that the Reformed system limits the offer of the gospel to the elect alone, when nineteenth-century Presbyterians sought to revise the Westminster Confession, they complained that it allowed for "no declaration of the love of God towards all men,"[78] a complaint reiterated by traditional Baptists.[79] Shedd's denial of a restricted love depends on an extrabiblical distinction lost on most lay Christians. The elite theologians of Calvinism distinguish between "common grace in the common call" and "special grace in the effectual call." The folk theologians among Baptists recognize no such distinction, for they cannot find it in the Bible.

Non-Calvinist Baptists would call our Baptist Calvinist brethren to reject clearly and permanently speculative doctrines insofar as they detract from a clear presentation of the gospel of Jesus Christ. We must plainly declare the gospel to all people that they are sinners who will die and spend an eternity in hell unless they are born again. We must proclaim that the second Person of the eternal Trinity became flesh in order to reveal Himself to us, died on a cross in order to atone for the sins of the whole world, and rose again from the dead so that those who hear, believe, and confess may have eternal life. As the Word is proclaimed, faith in God and repentance from sin are brought near to the hearts and mouths of men, women, and children by the regenerating work of the Holy Spirit. If you will but believe in Jesus Christ and confess that God has raised Him from the dead, you will be saved. Such salvation results in disciples who publicly profess Jesus as Lord through baptism in a local church, who regularly celebrate the Lord's Supper there, who personally submit to its teaching and redemptive discipline, and who preach the gospel to all nations. This is a gospel on which both non-Calvinist and Calvinist Baptists should be able to agree.

4. The Churches

The Calvinist treatment of the doctrine of the church should be a field for rejoicing and concern. The greatest service of modern Southern

---

[76] Yarnell, *The Formation of Christian Doctrine*, 55–59.

[77] Mark 1:14–15; Acts 2:37–39.

[78] Shedd, *Calvinism: Pure and Mixed*, 23.

[79] Humphreys, "Traditional Baptists and Calvinism," 58–60.

Baptist Calvinists to the SBC has been a renewed focus on ecclesiology. Although not alone in this regard, they have been at the forefront, most notably Mark Dever of Capitol Hill Baptist Church in Washington, D.C. He has emphasized regenerate church membership, especially with regard to church discipline, but has not ignored believers-only baptism and the Lord's Supper. Dever has also been instrumental in publishing and republishing a number of Baptist works on the doctrine of the church.[80]

The Calvinist treatment of ecclesiology is also a cause for concern. Although there is room for disagreement over multiple-elder versus single-elder churches, there is no room for the loss of congregationalism among Baptists. Suppression of democracy in the local church is not just against the Baptist Faith and Message; it is more importantly misinterpreting Scripture. Baptists have never been an elitist people who exalt a clerical hierarchy, Roman or Genevan. Rather, we have emphasized the priesthood of all believers at the same time that we have followed our pastors.[81] It is feared that some manifestations of Calvinism are moving churches away from Baptist identity in a rush to ecumenical relevance encouraged by the fictitious doctrine of the invisible church.

The Calvinist treatment of the history of Baptist churches should also be a field for rejoicing and concern. A number of primary sources and secondary sources might not be widely available today were it not for the efforts of such prominent Baptist historians as Tom Nettles, Timothy George, and Michael Haykin. All of these Baptist Calvinists deserve lauds for publishing works by and about Hercules Collins, John Gill, John Dagg, and James Petigru Boyce, among others. Baptist Calvinist historiography is a cause for rejoicing. But alas, it is also a cause for concern. The original edition of *Baptist Theologians*, edited by Timothy George and David Dockery, emphasized Baptist Calvinists at the expense of Baptist non-Calvinists.[82] In the revision, *Theologians of the Baptist Tradition*, the problem intensified.[83] After reading these otherwise fine collections, one could conclude that Calvinists were the only historically important Baptists. Among the confessions, covenants, and catechisms collected by Timothy George, the only General Baptist confession is the Orthodox Creed, and the covenants and catechisms are similarly skewed

---

[80] Mark Dever, "The Doctrine of the Church," in Akin, *A Theology for the Church*, 766–856.

[81] Yarnell, "Democratic Congregationalism: A Seventh Baptist Distinctive in Peril" (two parts), Internet, sbctoday.com, downloaded 25 November 2007.

[82] *Baptist Theologians*, ed. Timothy George and David S. Dockery (Nashville: Broadman, 1990).

[83] *Theologians of the Baptist Tradition*, ed. Timothy George and David S. Dockery (Nashville: Broadman & Holman, 2001).

toward Calvinism.[84] Again, consider a recent collection of devotional texts introduced by Michael Haykin. While Hercules Collins wrote nearly a quarter of his books to defend passionately believers-only baptism, from the perspective of pious obedience, Haykin saw fit to include excerpts from none of those works.[85] If one did not know him personally, he might wrongly conclude that the seminal Baptist doctrine of baptism was unimportant. Baptist historians would do well neither to privilege nor ignore either Calvinists or non-Calvinists.

Perhaps it would be appropriate to learn a lesson from a British historian. In his highly influential theological biography of Spurgeon, Iain Murray focused on three major doctrinal movements that the prince of preachers opposed: Arminianism, baptismal regeneration, and the downgrade.[86] Of the three, Murray admitted he was most concerned to refute Arminianism. While Arminianism was and is certainly a problem, the wise Calvinist should realize it is not the only problem. What Murray failed to do for British Baptists in 1966 was to rehearse the battle that the last of the Puritans fought with hyper-Calvinism. Three decades after Murray helped lead a Calvinist revival in England, he belatedly addressed the opposing problem. He lamented, "While not accepting the tenets of hyper-Calvinism it may well be that we have not been sufficiently alert to the danger of allowing a supposed consistency in doctrine to override the biblical priority of zeal for Christ and the souls of men."[87] In 1966 Murray, the historical theologian, led a fight against Arminian laxity; in 1995 he regretted he had not forewarned against hyper-Calvinism.

Non-Calvinist Baptists would call our Baptist Calvinist brethren to reject clearly and permanently speculative doctrines insofar as they detract from a strictly biblical understanding of the local churches. Non-Calvinists will also continue to challenge Baptist Calvinists not to forget that New Testament church membership is impossible apart from believers-only baptism, and this truth is what makes us Baptists rather than Presbyterians.[88] But non-Calvinist Baptists must also appreciate the

---

[84] Fortunately, the New Hampshire Confession and the Baptist Faith and Message are included in George and George, *Baptist Confessions, Covenants, and Catechisms.*

[85] *Devoted to the Service of the Temple: Piety, Persecution, and Ministry in the Writings of Hercules Collins,* ed. Michael A. G. Haykin and Steve Weaver, Profiles in Reformed Spirituality (Grand Rapids: Reformation Heritage Books, 2007).

[86] Iain Murray, *The Forgotten Spurgeon* (Carlisle, PA: Banner of Truth, 1966).

[87] Iain Murray, *Spurgeon v. Hyper-Calvinism: The Battle for Gospel Preaching* (Carlisle, PA: Banner of Truth Trust, 1995), xiv. Murray also chides Nettles for his defense of John Gill. Ibid., 130–31n.

[88] See Tom Schreiner and S. Wright, eds., *Believer's Baptism,* NACSBT (Nashville: B&H, 2006). Tom Ascol's proposed 2007 resolution on regenerate church membership entirely neglects baptism; a 2007 resolution by the Southern Baptists of Texas Convention provides baptism its proper place. Jerry Pierce, "Regenerate Church Membership

contributions our Baptist Calvinist brethren have made and will make with regard to maintaining the local church as regenerate. We must unite around the biblical doctrine of the church even as we disagree over minor issues, keeping one another honest about the major issues, and warning one another not to turn a minor issue into a sign of elitism or test of inner fellowship.

5. Christian Life

It is here that I have had the sharpest appreciations for and disagreements with aggressive Calvinism in the SBC. First, I rejoice over the emphasis on speaking the gospel clearly, as many Calvinists teach. Any gospel presentation relying on human manipulation, rather than the Holy Spirit, should be rejected by all Baptists. However, I am concerned that protests against the invitation or altar call have been too negative, proposing no real alternatives. The invitation is certainly not the public profession of faith; that is the role of baptism. But there is biblical support for intense dialogue between preacher and sinner at the end of a sermon (Acts 2:36–40). It should also be remembered that the anti-invitation, anti-application attitude is a sign of hyper-Calvinism.

As a professor, I have vivid memories of dealings with several Calvinist students who displayed interesting attitudes. Most Calvinist students have no difficulty with this non-Calvinist theologian whatsoever, for I make life equally difficult for all my students, Calvinist or not. When we debate the difficult soteriological doctrines, I always assign the partisans to defend publicly the positions of their opponents. But there was a time when some Calvinist students felt distinctly unwelcome at Southwestern Seminary. Recognizing their sincere Christian and Baptist beliefs, I stepped out to provide them with fellowship. Mistaking kindness for total agreement, however, one assumed I was a Calvinist, too, and excitedly asked when I had "converted to the doctrines of grace." Friend, Christians convert to Christ His person, not to Calvin his doctrine.

Then there was the student who, after regretfully fulfilling an assignment to evangelize and then to pen a theological reflection, confessed that she was actually a hyper-Calvinist. Thankfully, she repented and took up personal evangelism, even though it meant she was at first angry with this professor. Next was the student who chided me for disrespecting Reformed doctrine in class. He turned away sheepishly when I reminded him that in the same session, before reprimanding Reformed theology

Resolution Refused," Southern Baptist Texan (19 June 2007), Internet, www.texanonline.net, downloaded 22 June 2007; Southern Baptists of Texas Convention, "Reaffirming Regenerate Church Membership," adopted 13 November 2007, Internet, www.sbtexas.com/missions/07resolutions.htm, downloaded 26 November 2007.

for its rationalism, I read Calvin's *Institutes*, praising his description of the transformative nature of growth in the knowledge of God and man. Finally, there was the student who moved so far into Reformed thought that, in spite of the efforts of both Dr. Garrett and myself, we could not keep him from compromising his Baptist convictions.

The First Texas Bridge Builder

Texas Baptists respect the founder of Southwestern Seminary. Benajah Harvey Carroll was a giant of a man, a compelling preacher of the gospel, a skillful defender of New Testament churches, and a respected organizer of Baptist energies. At the populist level, some argue Carroll was a Calvinist. But Carroll's doctrine of election was corporately in Christ, and reprobation was absent. He embraced neither limited atonement nor a classical doctrine of depravity. He did believe in irresistible grace, but qualified it with contrition. He personally affirmed final preservation, but his second wife happily disagreed. His most recent theological biographer concluded, "Carroll was a Calvinist in line with the moderate tone of the New Hampshire Confession."[89]

To the Dortian Calvinist, Carroll's soteriology may seem inconsistent, but the father of Southwestern Seminary was concerned more with biblical consistency than synodal consistency. Because Carroll believed in the living Word of God first and foremost, he faithfully lived out of the Bible. He possessed "a biblical-pastoral theology of practical value which called the church to evangelism and ethical responsibility." On that biblical and experiential basis J. B. Gambrell commented that the common thread in Carroll's career was that "he championed Christian truth and Baptist unity, faith, and practice."[90]

In the boots of Carroll, the Texas Baptist tradition—as exemplified by the current president of Southwestern Seminary, Paige Patterson, and the founding executive director of the Southern Baptists of Texas Convention, Jim Richards, and prominent pastors such as Jack Graham—indicates that Texas Baptists maintain an appreciative place for Baptist Calvinism, for it is a wide and tolerant Baptist fellowship.[91] However, the Texas

---

[89] James Spivey, "Benajah Harvey Carroll," in *Theologians of the Baptist Tradition*, ed. George and Dockery, 173–74, 177–78; B. H. Carroll, *Colossians, Ephesians, and Hebrews*, ed. J. B. Cranfill (Chicago: Fleming Revell, 1917), Eph. 1.

[90] Spivey, "Carroll," 177–79.

[91] Tony Cartledge, "Seminary Presidents Debate Calvinism," Associated Baptist Press (13 June 2006), Internet, www.abpnews.com/1086.article, downloaded 23 November 2007; Jim Richards, "Distinguishing between Fellowship and Leadership," *Southern Baptist Texan* (23 October 2006), Internet, www.texanonline.net/default. asp?action=article&aid=4838, downloaded 23 November 2007.

tradition also indicates that classical Calvinism and hyper-Calvinism should feel distinctly unwelcome, for it expects personal faith and repentance from preaching.[92]

Perhaps I may be bold enough to speak a word of exhortation on behalf of Texas Baptists, Louisiana Baptists, and many other average Southern Baptists: We non-Calvinists treasure Calvinist Baptists. Like the Union Baptist Association, we believe it decorous to grant one another "the appellation of brother,"[93] and not only in the created sense, or ending with the redeemed sense, but also in the ecclesiastical sense. However, it would be helpful for non-Calvinist Baptists if all Baptist Calvinists would intentionally and publicly refute the errors of classical Calvinism and hyper-Calvinism.

There is also the issue of denominational integrity. Shedd was concerned that in the rush to identify Presbyterianism with modernity, his people were losing their integrity. When the pure beliefs of a people are mixed with others, it weakens them in the long run. "By this method, Calvinism, or Arminianism, or Socinianism, or any creed whatever, becomes mixed instead of pure; a combination of dissimilar materials, instead of a simple uncompounded unity. . . . The purest and most unmixed . . . Lutheranism, or Calvinism, is the strongest in the long run," Shedd wrote.[94] Similarly, it pains me that in the rush to adopt a rationalist creed, some Baptist Calvinists have discovered they no longer wish to be Baptists. When Baptists replace their Biblicism[95] with Reformed rationalism, they risk losing their New Testament identity.

Finally, let me exhort both non-Calvinist Baptists and Calvinist Baptists from the Word of God. For the Calvinist Baptists let me remind you that Paul, the inspired apostle of Jesus Christ, wrote that you must "work out your own salvation with fear and trembling" (Phil 2:12, NKJV). For the non-Calvinist Baptists let me remind you that Paul then went on to say that "it is God who works in you both to will and to do for His good pleasure" (Phil 2:13 NKJV).

---

[92] Jack Graham, "The Truth about Grace," Sermon at Prestonwood Baptist Church (July 2005), Internet, resources.christianity.com/details/pbc/19000101/9290F735-33AF-45FC-83A3-2386D0699096.aspx, downloaded 23 November 2007.

[93] *Minutes of the First Session of the Union Baptist Association*, 13.

[94] Shedd, *Calvinism: Pure and Mixed*, ix.

[95] I do not define Biblicism in the same sense as Gerhard Ebeling, but as a simple commitment to live out of Scripture as God's never-changing dynamic Word. Gerhard Ebeling, *The Nature of Faith*, trans. R. G. Smith (Philadelphia: Fortress Press, 1961), 38.

The Rise of Calvinism in the Southern Baptist Convention: Reason for Rejoicing

Jeff Noblit
Senior Pastor, First Baptist Church
Muscle Shoals, Alabama

REFORMING OUR CHURCHES to become biblically healthy is the most important task on earth. Why do I make such a statement? Because everything is about the glory of God! The church is meant to be the blazing epicenter of His glory. The church is the sole support of truth in the earth. It is the primary source of God's glory both for time and for eternity. As God builds His church the angels stare in amazement. The substance of this essay will be an explanation of seven reasons I believe the rise of Calvinism could be used of God to bring the revival and reformation our churches need to bring Him the glory He deserves.

Overcoming Inerrancy Idolatry and Reclaiming the Sufficiency of Scripture

Some have said that Southern Baptists won the battle for inerrancy but lost the battle for sufficiency. I think that is a good way to say it. I propose that holding to the inerrancy of Scripture without at least an equal passion and commitment to the sufficiency of Scripture (for all faith and practice) is sheer idolatry. It is but a love for a position on the nature of the Bible without a genuine love for the God of the Bible. Jesus said, "If you love Me, you will keep My commandments" (John 14:15).[1] One way to view the inerrancy controversy that was fought and won in our denomination is that we changed the convention's mind but did not change the heart.

The seminaries, which might be viewed as the denomination's mind, have been wonderfully reformed to the inerrancy of Scripture and sound doctrine. For that we are all thankful and praise God. That was the

---

[1] Unless otherwise indicated, Scripture quotations are from the NASB.

providential hand of God. But changing the denomination's mind is not all we need. We need a change of heart, and the heart of the denomination is the local church. Our churches have not been revived, changed, or transformed. Our churches for the most part seem to be far too comfortable in the lukewarm waters of Laodicea (Rev 3:16). I'm convinced the average Southern Baptist church has little concept of a genuine, humble allegiance to the Scriptures for all faith and practice. The notion of the Bible's being sufficient for all faith and practice may get a verbal "Amen," but the substance of that allegiance is about as weighty as the dust on the old statement of faith that lies untouched in the back of the filing cabinet in the church office.

Today's view seems to be that all we really need to know about God, the gospel, and Christ, we learned by the fifth grade. And what we really need are "smart men" to make Christ and the gospel attractive to this sophisticated age. Why do we need a sufficient Bible pressing us toward unflinching obedience when we have so many clever men who can teach us how to grow the church? These men supposedly understand the unique challenges of this modern age. Their methods suggest that God's old gospel and the Holy Spirit are weak when it comes to converting twenty-first-century man. The average Southern Baptist church not only neglects the sufficiency of Scripture in practice but actively rejects it. They have accumulated for themselves sufficient men to show them the way. Man-centered pragmatism in doctrine and practice is the order of the day. And it seems that not one in a thousand has the spiritual discernment to know the difference between man-centered pragmatic messages that merely use the Scriptures and Spirit-filled preachers who faithfully preach the Word (2 Tim 4:2). The true difference between these two in the church is the difference between life and death.

We may have trained our minds to shout inerrancy, but the testimonies from our churches shout that the Scriptures simply are not sufficient. For example, instead of looking to them alone for counseling in our churches, we seem to look to Freud and Skinner and then use the Scriptures to back them up. We function as if Scripture is no match for Freud when God's children are hurting. Another area where we question the sufficiency of Scripture is with our children. We put them in groups of their peers and often place over them a young man not much older than they are as a youth director. So we actually have an older child leading a group of children. The Bible says, "Foolishness is bound up in the heart of a child" (Prov 22:15). So you have the companionship of fools!

God's Word teaches us that God has given children youth directors, and they are called Mom and Dad. It was a glorious day in our church when simply by the grace and providence of God the majority of our men seriously began to assume the responsibility to train their own children in the discipline and instruction of the Lord. We've come to the conclusion that whether our children know and love Christ does not depend on a youth program or a children's program. Those ministries should only complement and be an extension of godly parents. The Scriptures clearly teach this, and they are sufficient.

We've had quite a journey at my church in recommitting ourselves to the sufficiency of Scripture. A few years ago we adopted an unreached people group in Peru, which required a mountainous seven-mile hike to reach them. Fortunately, their dialect was close enough to Spanish that we could take a Spanish translator. We had been talking as a staff about how we did not want to take to the mission field the "hoop-jump, easy-believism" type of evangelism that we had come out of. Most of these people are polytheists. If you give them a 20-minute message on Jesus, they will raise their hand and add Jesus to their list of gods, and that's simply not conversion.

One of my young men asked me, "Pastor, if we're not going to just lead them in a sinner's prayer and then tell them they are saved, then what do we do?" I asked, "What does the Bible say? When Paul and Silas were in jail in Philippi, God miraculously brought the earthquake, the jail doors opened, and the jailor, fearing for his life, asked, 'Sirs, what must I do to be saved?' Paul and Silas responded, 'Believe in the Lord Jesus'" (Acts 16:25–31). Then I asked this staff member, "What's wrong with the Bible? Let's just do what the Bible says; it is sufficient!" The work of praying a "sinner's prayer" is not salvation. It can become a silly superstition and nothing more than a sacrament in Baptist clothes.

Our missionaries marched back into the mountains of Peru, and they preached the gospel. They preached the wickedness and offensiveness of man before a holy God, the lostness of man, and the wrath of God. Then they preached the love of God in Jesus Christ and that Christ came and died for sin, shedding His precious blood. They preached that the Spirit of God must move on a person and that men must repent and believe in Christ. By outward accounts, it didn't work. And they went again and again, and it didn't work. And they went again and preached some more, and it didn't work. And they went again and preached some more, and it didn't work.

I don't know how many times they went back in there with their tents and their backpacks and preached and preached. Then one day an older woman walked up to them in the evening and said, "My heart has changed. Now I know Christ. I see the weight of my sin and the depth of my sin, and I've come to embrace Christ." A teenage boy came later. Then others came. And today there is a thriving little church back in the Andes Mountains of Peru where people love, worship, and rejoice in

Jesus Christ. We needed none of the common, modern methods of evangelism—just passionate, doctrine-filled, Spirit-empowered preaching of the gospel of Jesus Christ. Why? Because the Scriptures are sufficient! They don't need our help. The church really doesn't need another "smart guy." We just need some passionate, obedient, God-honoring preachers who will preach the gospel until God changes lives.

The missionary representative for Peru contacted us sometime ago and said, "We just heard from the International Mission Board that as far as we know the church that was planted among the Jaqaru people by your church members is the only church planted among an unreached people group by a local Southern Baptist church in America without the aid of a career missionary." I was shocked. I thought, "You've got to be kidding." But that's what they said. Now somewhere in Baptist history they're going to have to record that a Calvinistic church did that.

The Calvinist brothers I know have a passion for the sufficiency of Scripture and a passion that it must be lived out in the methodologies of the church. I think the rise of Calvinism will help us overcome the idolatry of inerrancy and help us regain or reclaim the sufficiency of Scripture.

Better Church Splits

We Southern Baptists are good at splitting churches, but not all church splits are bad. The greatest divider of all time was Jesus Christ, who said, "Do not think that I came to bring peace on the earth; I did not come to bring peace, but a sword" (Matt 10:34). Then He added that "a man's enemies will be the members of his household" (v. 36). The blazing light of truth is incompatible with the darkness of error.

According to 2 Cor 6:17, Paul had that same spirit: "'Therefore, come out from their midst and be separate,' says the Lord. 'And do not touch what is unclean; And I will welcome you.'" He tells Christians that they must separate—*split*, if you will—from false professors of the faith. In 1 Cor 5:9–11, he explained, "I wrote you in my letter not to associate with immoral people; I [did] not at all [mean] with the immoral people of this world, or with the covetous and swindlers, or with idolaters, for then you would have to go out of the world. But actually, I wrote to you not to associate with any *so-called brother* if he is an immoral person, or covetous, or an idolater, . . . not even to eat with such a one." Our Lord also split the veil in two when He died. Then He entered death, hell, and the grave, and He split them apart. He's a great splitter.

What I understand today from counseling pastors and hearing of church splits is that most church splits are not good splits. They are usually over power or worldly desires, far too often involving one power-hungry group fighting with another.

Here is an example of what I think is a good split. A young man that I have been mentoring for years—who is a precious, kindhearted, compassionate brother—took a church in a southern state. He was excited to find out that their confession of faith was the New Hampshire Confession.[2] He began to teach that church the New Hampshire Confession of Faith, paragraph by paragraph, line by line. He came to the section on repentance, teaching it just like it was in their own confession. At the end of that message, an older lady in the church approached him and said, "Pastor, I don't agree with that. I didn't experience that, and I'm a Christian. I have asked Jesus to save me."

Compassionately and lovingly he explained to her that the evidence of repentance toward God plus faith in Christ is essential to know if you're truly converted. She became angry and stopped attending church, but she started working the telephone. Because of her persistence, a good percentage of the members wanted the pastor to leave. Finally, they called in a mediator from the state convention. Although this dear pastor is a door-to-door soul winner and a missions-minded church planter, the mediator brought out that he was a Calvinist and that he was incompatible with the church. The whole issue that started the controversy, namely, the doctrine of repentance, was lost. This brother stood on truth and was voted out of his church. A number of members stood with the pastor and left the church. Some may disagree, but that, I think, is a good reason for a church to split—over truth.

When essential doctrine is at stake, the pastor must stand. Peace at all costs is the banner of the coward. The pastor must be long-suffering. Those of us who believe in grace ought to have some; humility should mark us—not the absence of boldness or conviction but true Christian humility (Phil 2:5–8). Nevertheless, many of our professing churches are so doctrinally deficient and spiritually dark that they cannot stand the light of truth. The result of the collision of a Bible-preaching pastor and a spiritually and doctrinally weak church will be either God-sent revival and unity or God-sent division, which may also lead to revival. Splitting over essential doctrine is not only inevitable; it's commanded, and it's commendable.

Paul instructed in Titus 1:9–11 that an "overseer" of the church must hold fast

> the faithful word which is in accordance with the
> teaching, so that he will be able both to exhort in sound

---

[2] The New Hampshire Confession of Faith is a fundamental confession from which our own Baptist Faith and Message was written.

doctrine and to refute those who contradict. For there are many rebellious men, empty talkers and deceivers, especially those of the circumcision, who must be silenced because they are upsetting whole families, teaching things they should not [teach] for the sake of sordid gain.

I agree with Dr. Al Mohler, who wrote in a book endorsement, "We are reaping the harvest of doctrinal neglect. The urgency of this task cannot be ignored. Baptists will either recover our denominational heritage and rebuild our doctrinal foundations or in the next generation there will be no authentic Baptist witness."

I am not calling for a litmus test of the five points of Calvinism. I seldom emphasize a theological system in my ministry. I think too many Calvinists love the system and use God rather than loving God and using the theological systems. I've been guilty of that myself, and we must repent when a theological system rises up as an idol in our own hearts. I am calling for a commitment to sound doctrine that the great majority of us can agree on—basic Bible doctrine that defines and explains the gospel, evangelism, repentance, biblical faith, the marks of regeneration, and what constitutes true assurance of salvation. For example, assurance of salvation should not be that you drove a tomato stake behind the barn and told Satan, "Look there. I asked Jesus to save me, and that tomato stake is a witness." A commitment to sound doctrine requires that the brethren be taught that the Holy Spirit will bear witness with your spirit that you are a child of God (Rom 8:16). We want the omnipotent Holy Spirit, not a tomato stake in our theology and methodology concerning assurance. Why do we clamor for "human" instruments in our religion when God has given us vastly superior spiritual instruments? From my experience, the rise in Calvinism will produce better church splits. And by that I mean that it's healthy for humble, compassionate men to stand on truth even if it divides a congregation.

Exposing and Removing Covert Liberalism

Our churches, for the most part, are more liberal than ever before. Any denomination that holds to the inerrancy of Scripture without an equal commitment to the sufficiency of Scripture will soon find itself right back in the cesspool of liberalism. But it will be worse. It will be covert liberalism—having the label of conservative, Bible-believing evangelicalism on the outside but practicing much of the same old liberalism we fought against so long, only now in new clothing.

I see covert liberalism in much of what I understand about the "pur-pose-driven" or "seeker-friendly" model, the "emerging-church" model, and what I call the "psycho-church" model from pastor Joel Osteen in Houston, Texas. I'm not an authority on any of these models or move-ments, but I don't think you need to be to see the error. A casual glance at an elephant is all one needs to understand he would not be a good family pet. If you are not practicing in the church your conservative theology that you claim to hold, then do not talk about being conservative. You are known by your fruit. There is a hollowness and emptiness in some of the conservatism of the Southern Baptist Convention.

The apostles did not have to study in the seminaries of Jerusalem to discern the error of the Pharisees. And when I read about the seeker church or the emergent church or the Joel Osteen type of church, it's glaringly obvious to me that much of this is not an ingenious new way to present Christ. It's an old, false way of doing church that actually denies the biblical Christ and the biblical gospel, and does not build a biblical church. For example, any preacher who tries to dumb down the doctrine of sin, the depravity of man, and the necessity of repentance is not preaching the true gospel. This approach is not new or clever but wicked—dooming men's souls and leading millions to false assurance. Today the pulpit of the evangelical church to the discerning ear sounds more like Robert Schuller or Oprah Winfrey than Spurgeon or Criswell

A few years ago I decided I would visit some churches that don't see things as I do. So I visited a large, seeker-friendly, Southern Baptist church. The pastor preached on the woman at the well in John 4, and I was careful to listen to everything he said. His message was in effect that the world had done this woman wrong and that she was beaten down and needed Jesus. Although that is true, it is not the primary exegetical meaning of the text. Jesus confronted her about her sin of adultery. The pastor never brought that out. Sin was not mentioned. The evil of sexual immorality was not mentioned. The pastor elaborated on how the world had done this woman wrong. Her life was broken down because of it, and she needed Jesus. His invitation at the end was, "Has the world done you wrong and you need Jesus? Then stand up." About 1,500 people stood up.

Is that the new conservative, evangelical church? This type of preach-ing is nothing but old liberalism, not the gospel of Jesus Christ. From observing the Calvinistic brothers I know, I have become convinced that the rise of Calvinism will help us expose this covert liberalism and call these brothers back to sound doctrine.

Recently a Calvinistic pastor from a Southern Baptist association in the West called me. The director of missions of that particular association had taken it upon himself to stomp out anything that to him looked like Calvinism. So the director of missions began seeking to get this pastor's deacons to fire him. The pastor was brokenhearted. He said, "Brother Jeff, I'm witnessing door to door. We emphasize missions, but they put this label on me because I embrace the doctrines of grace as so many of our Baptist forefathers have." He said, "Of all things, you know what our director of missions is pushing us to do? He's pushing us to read *Blue Like Jazz* by an emerging-church author." When the pastor told me this, I thought, "Isn't it amazing that in some quarters the one identifying with Spurgeon gets rejected, while the one that looks more like Joel Osteen or Oprah Winfrey is embraced?" Far too much in these movements is contrary to the historic doctrines of our forefathers and, more importantly, the doctrines of Scripture.

Unfortunately, many of our churches were in bad shape before these modern methods appeared. People have joined my church from churches that have been torn apart by some of these new models. I say to them, "You'll not be happy here unless you admit that before the new model came in, your church was already doctrinally weak and spiritually anemic. The church would have never embraced the new model had they been grounded and mature." Such churches are trading one form of man-centered shallowness and weakness for another. I do not see churches that focus on the glory of God, that honor Christ, that are saturated with Bible doctrine, embracing a liberal, new model and becoming weak.

We need to remember that our God is a purpose-driven God. Three times in Ephesians 1, the apostle Paul tells us that the gospel and the ministry of Christ is "to the praise of the glory of His grace" (1:6) or "to the praise of His glory" (1:12,14). That's His purpose—His glory. The ultimate purpose has not been and will never be the eternal souls of men being saved. While evangelism is a continual passion and emphasis in my church, it is not the ultimate purpose. God is absolutely powerful enough to redeem every soul that has ever lived, had He wanted to do so. *The ultimate purpose is the glory of God.* Sinners will glorify God either in hell, vindicating His justice which should come against sinners, or in heaven praising His grace that saves us. But we *will* glorify God. Salvation and the church exist to the praise of the glory of His grace because God is absolutely thrilled about being God. He wants the whole universe to see the glories of who He is. For all the universe to see the glories of His love, grace, and mercy, He needed deeply offensive, ungodly rebels and sinners who ought to go to hell to be redeemed and made righteous as His Son is righteous. We all qualify. Today's purpose-driven, emerging, and other modern models seem to me to be too much about the cleverness of man and too little about the glory of God.

A surge in the preaching of the old doctrines of grace is a key to stemming the tide of this covert liberalism. We need preaching that exalts God and declares the sinful depravity of man, that man is God's enemy, that nothing in man is desirable to God, and that we are abhorrent and ungodly in His sight. God loves us because of His greatness, not because we are lovable. We need to preach that we are helpless; that Christ, in love, was the substitutionary sacrifice for sin; and that the power of the Spirit is essential to produce a regenerate heart that is attended by repentance toward God and faith in our Lord Jesus Christ. True Calvinistic preaching in the power of the Spirit—not dry, cold intellectual dissertations, but preaching like that of John Knox, George Whitefield, and Charles Spurgeon—will expose this covert liberalism for the counterfeit and fraud that it is, and will produce true converts that have not just the form of godliness but also its power.

We are called to be prophets. We do not go to man to see what man wants from God; we go to God to see what God has to say to man. The rise of Calvinism will help expose this covert liberalism that has crept in among us.

Restoring True Evangelism

The rise in the doctrines of grace or Calvinism will help us restore true evangelism. I am not suggesting at all that those who come under this broad banner of Calvinism have all the answers and are the perfect models. In fact, I have more kindred fellowship with some semi-Arminian brothers than with some Calvinists. Perhaps to say that Calvinism will help restore true evangelism is shocking to some. Many have declared that the rise in Calvinism will kill evangelism and missions. But they are actually talking about hyper-Calvinism, and I do not know one hyper-Calvinist Southern Baptist. I haven't met one. If there are some, let's put our arms around them, look them in the eye, and say, "Repent. You don't understand biblical theology, and your methodology is out of balance."

Spurgeon was a five-point Calvinist and quite an evangelist. In *A Defense of Calvinism*, he declared that "Calvinism is the gospel, and nothing else." Adoniram Judson and William Carey were great missionaries and were Calvinists or at least Calvinistic. Baptist leaders who are about 35 years of age and older are without excuse and without warrant to believe that Calvinism kills evangelism. Why? Because probably the most used and copied soul-winning training course ever embraced by Southern Baptists was Evangelism Explosion, written by D. James Kennedy, a Presbyterian and a five-point Calvinist.

I have heard that from 7,000 to 12,000 Southern Baptist churches baptize no one in a year. I suspect that if you called those churches and said, "Are you a Calvinist church?" they would reject that categorically. They could be labeled anti-evangelistic, anti-missionary Arminians. You cannot lay the deadness and lack of evangelism of roughly 10,000 Southern Baptist churches at the feet of Calvinism. Those churches were dead already.

In my own church last Sunday, we baptized eight people who shared from the baptistry testimonies of their brokenness, their repentance, and their realization of how deeply offensive and wretched they were before a holy God. Then they testified to the unbelievable love and grace of God that worked on their heart and brought them to see the depth of their sin and to an attitude of repentance to heartily embrace Jesus as their only Prophet, their only Priest, and their only King. We need meaningful testimonies of true conversion in our baptistries. First Baptist Church of Muscle Shoals, Alabama, is possibly the only church or one of very few in the Southern Baptist Convention that has six people on staff in its world missions ministry.

If we were to examine the prominent evangelistic methods of the past 100 years, we would see some troubling results. We have 16.4 million Southern Baptists, and we do well to have seven million in church each Sunday. Dr. Paige Patterson, a man I appreciate and respect greatly, once said he would estimate that 40 percent of the Sunday morning congregation in a typical Southern Baptist church are not truly converted. I think that could be optimistic. If these estimates are valid, then out of 16.4 million Southern Baptists, we may have only three to four million true believers in church on an average Sunday.

A high percentage of our high school graduates have been reported to stop attending church, at least for a while. Some have given the number as high as 88 percent or as low as 70 percent. If we are losing 70 percent of our children, we're failing. Barna reported in one of his recent studies that the divorce rate is greater among Baptists in the South than it is among the unchurched culture. I understand this statistic may be skewed somewhat, but do we feel better if we have *almost* as many? If you look at these statistics and at the millions and millions of non-attending members on our rolls, I think you have to conclude that although these people walked to the front of someone's church building and repeated somebody's prayer, the fruit of their lives does not evidence biblical conversion. When approximately 70 percent of our members give little or no biblical evidence of genuine conversion, we need to reexamine our evangelistic methods!

My mom told me that when she was a girl her family and many other families in the community would load up their wagons and go to the Methodist brush arbor meetings. When the Spirit worked on somebody's heart, that person would often go and pray at the front, or some would just go out in the fields and pray. The old-timers and the pastors discouraged anyone from bothering them. They would say, "Let them pray it through." We need to get back to some of that. Too often when the Spirit of God illumines and awakens people, we rush them into a sinner's prayer and through the baptistry before they ever get to repentance and faith.

What caused me to get deadly honest about returning to true evangelism was practicing church discipline. We had to discipline so many of our converts that we knew something had to be wrong. It's as if God screamed at me and said, "Yes, it is wrong. You don't know what conversion is. You only know how to get results." For 10 years we had averaged almost 200 baptisms a year and led the state in baptisms. Then we did something scary. We went back and did some research on these converts. We found that a significant majority of those we baptized could not be found after a year. God deeply convicted me about this. A change had to take place even though I knew it might reduce our baptismal numbers and the accolades of the denominational offices. But I knew I had to face God concerning those souls, and they didn't look like converts. We had to change the way we were evangelizing, yet remain diligent about going after lost souls. By God's grace we did this and our passion for souls has increased. Now for almost 20 years First Baptist Church of Muscle Shoals has averaged 25–35 percent of our Sunday School attendance at outreach visitation every week. As of this writing, I cannot remember a week when at least one person was not genuinely saved, giving evidence of repentance toward God and faith in our Lord Jesus. What a radical difference in the testimonies of those we are baptizing today in contrast to those we baptized in the past! That's the kind of Calvinism we need.

Dr. Patterson recently declared in a chapel service at Southern Seminary, "Southern Baptists have become the worst of infant baptizers," referring to how many we're baptizing under the age of five. You'll stop that if you do church discipline. You'll find that by the ninth grade you'll have to discipline many of them. Then you will learn to wait until they can give good, biblically defined evidence of the new birth before you baptize them.

I was reading some old records of church business meetings recently, and I was amazed at the way they presented members for baptism. I'm sure it wasn't the same in every association or every church, but the minutes often read something like, "Here's Joe. Joe comes to join the church today by *experience.*" What they meant was that after having spent time with Joe, they concluded he had "experienced" the new birth, evidenced by repentance toward God and faith in our Lord Jesus Christ.

The New Hampshire Confession of Faith says this about repentance and faith: "We believe that repentance and faith are sacred duties, and also inseparable graces, wrought in our souls by the regenerating Spirit of God . . . deeply convinced of our guilt, danger, and helplessness, and of the way of salvation by Christ." Such conviction is what we need to look for before we baptize someone. I don't see a lot of that in the so-called conversions in many of our evangelistic campaigns. Most people come to Jesus today not to flee the wrath of God, but to put another layer of frosting on their lives. The Confession further explains that "we turn to God with unfeigned contrition, confession, and supplication for mercy; at the same time heartily receiving the Lord Jesus Christ as our Prophet, Priest, and King, and relying on Him alone as the only and all-sufficient Savior."

In counseling baptismal candidates, we explain to them the meaning of repentance and faith. If they cannot say with confidence, "Yes, Pastor, that's what's happened to me, and that's what I believe," then we don't baptize them. Thorough biblical counseling is a component of true evangelism. I was greatly helped by Dr. Pendleton's discussion of repentance and faith in his 1833 *Church Manual*, which is a great guide for counseling baptismal candidates. Also of great help was the work of Puritan Thomas Boston on the evidences of spiritual life and Jonathan Edwards's writings on the difference between awakening, conviction, and true conversion. In my church we have reclaimed the view of Pendleton, Boston, and Edwards. As a result I'm convinced we have a truer, biblical view of evangelism.

Rather than our churches becoming more biblically healthy in evangelism, I believe we are becoming more bizarre. I just read in a Baptist state paper that a church was applauded for having "dog evangelism." They had trained dogs to share the gospel, and they may share the gospel better than some preachers. In my own association we had "horse evangelism." A man came through who was a horse whisperer (I'm unclear whether the horse whispers to him or he whispers to the horse), and somehow it involved sharing the gospel. We have "music evangelism" and "drama evangelism" and "muscleman" evangelism. Whatever happened to "the foolishness of preaching" (1 Cor 1:21 KJV)? We need men who know the gospel, whose hearts are aflame with the truth of the great doctrines of the gospel and who will say, "God, I'll preach it, and I'll preach it, and I'll preach it until You bring revival, until You save souls, until You break hearts, until men and women and boys and girls really repent and run to Christ."

Furthermore, where are the results these methods promise? With no accountability or discipline in our churches, we can't find 10 or 12 million of our members, and the ones we find often don't look like Spirit-born converts, biblically speaking. God didn't call us to get "results" but to make disciples. In the spirit of our Baptist forefathers, we believe in the baptism of *disciples* only. Today we have a dumbed-down "gospel," a dumbed-down view of "conversion," and a dumbed-down version of "revival," which is not genuine revival but something created by man. So we have to have dumbed-down churches to keep these unregenerate people happy and coming back to "church," which has become more like Six Flags Over Jesus than the church of the Lord Jesus Christ.

Even more troubling is that we are exporting our shallow evangelistic practices globally. I was recently in Africa at a reformed Baptist pastors' conference. They had 900 people in attendance, and some drove 2,000 kilometers to come. These brothers represent one of the greatest examples of church growth and church planting I know of in the world. It began 25 years ago with five young African pastors who began to see the great weakness of the church in Africa. They began to embrace the old doctrines of grace. Then they started planting churches. The old guard criticized them, scandalized them, and persecuted them. They said, "They're just young kids. They don't know what they're doing." Well, they are not young anymore, but in their mid 40s. And they've planted churches all over that region of Africa.

One of them came to me, realized where I was from, and mentioned the name of a large church not too far from my church. He said, "Do you know about that church?" I said, "Yes, I do." He then said, "I'm a church planter, and this Southern Baptist church has been doing mission work in my area. They claim they've planted 100 churches in the last few years. But I've been to those congregations, and I've been in their meetings. Those people know little about God, Christ, and the gospel. They go through a quick gospel presentation and press for quick results. They declare them all saved and report it as a church plant." This type of shallow easy-believism is going on everywhere. I believe we need some Aquilas and Priscillas who take these "church planters" aside and explain to them "the way of God more accurately" (Acts 18:26). The rise in Calvinism will be an instrument to help us restore truer evangelism that produces lasting fruit and sound biblical teaching.

The Youth of Calvinism

I have been hearing about the Reformed University Fellowship and all the thousands of college students who are embracing the doctrines of grace. Campus Outreach was founded by a Presbyterian church in Birmingham, Alabama, and it's a growing ministry on college campuses. The number of the young people attending John Piper's conferences is amazing. My church held what we called a True Church Conference in February 2008. The theme was "Church Discipline: The Missing Key to True Church Growth." I thought if 75 people showed up, it would be a miracle. But we had almost 500 from 32 states, and many of those were college students and young adults. They were hungry for weighty doctrine and biblical content.

Paul Washer, an associate of mine, heads up HeartCry Missionary Society. He is reformed in theology and a strong, prophetic preacher of the gospel. He told me the other day that people have been putting his sermons on SermonAudio.com, which I understand is the largest sermon downloading website in the world. His sermons have had over 400,000 downloads. My own website ministry has also grown exponentially. We used to count the number of hits and downloads in dozens or a few hundred. Now we're counting them in the thousands and tens of thousands. Our research revealed that the average age of those downloading these messages is quite young. That is encouraging. I believe this is nothing less than a spiritual awakening. No doubt about it, the rise of Calvinism is a youth movement. These young people want a weighty, doctrinally rich Christianity.

Calvinism's Grasp of the New (But Actually Old) Wine

In my early years of pastoring, our baptisms went up as well as Sunday School and worship attendance. I got a lot of accolades for that. I was reformed in my heart, but my theology was somewhat different from my methodology. We were practicing a pragmatic, "hoop-jump" approach to conversion and church membership. The problem was that my theology was not fully directing my methodology. I was bipolar in my ministry! Being convicted that I was disobedient, I led my church to reform our methodologies to flow out of sound theology. It was a difficult road but today the results are glorious.

During the last five to seven years, pastors are increasingly calling and asking me about the reforms we have made at our church. They ask about how we do evangelism and what constitutes true conversion.

They ask about how we do church discipline or our steps to membership. They are intrigued as to how we developed a meaningful membership in which 90 percent of our members are active in service. They also want to know what it means to preach the Word and how to develop a "truth-driven" missions ministry. They are also very interested in parent-driven youth ministry and parent-driven children's ministry. Then they want to inquire about the doctrines of grace. Most of them are frustrated and heartbroken over the lack of lasting fruit in the people they're baptizing. What we share with them is not new wine. It's old wine. It's the old wine of Benjamin Keach, John Bunyan, and John Gill, of Andrew Fuller, Adoniram Judson, and William Carey. It's the old wine of John Dagg and P. H. Mell, of Basil Manly Sr. and Basil Manly Jr., and of James Pettigrew Boyce, John A. Broadus, and B. H. Carroll. This is not new wine. It's old.

I know there are good pastors and good churches, and there are many who have not bowed the knee to Baal. But I believe they are in the minority if you measure a good church by biblical criteria. Sadly, the majority of Southern Baptist churches are more like old wineskins, and I do not think most of them can contain the new wine of truth. Can a bridge be built to connect all these different groups with all these different views and methods and bring us together as one? I don't know. I think building bridges is a noble task, and I'm thankful for the effort. But we have some concerns. One thing about a bridge, as R. C. Sproul pointed out, is that it carries two-way traffic. I refuse to bring in and embrace some things I see under the broad tent of Southern Baptists.

Furthermore, one must consider what type of soil will be on the other side of that bridge. And there are some bodies of water, like the Atlantic Ocean, that no one has even thought of building a bridge across. The divide is just too great. If we expect the SBC to serve God for even another 10 to 30 years, there must be some significant changes. There's a great divide among us, and we need to be honest about it. Ultimately, the bridge must be of God. Unless He builds the bridge, they labor in vain who build it. Jesus was not interested in patching old systems. The old system of Jewish religion was just incompatible with the new wine of truth contained in Christ (Matt 9:14–17). If I have 20 or 30 years of ministry left, I do not plan to spend that time patching old wineskins because it never works.

Calvinism's Focus on the Glory of God

Ultimately, what must consume us and what must possess us is a passion for the glory of God in His church. God glorified Himself in the first creation, but that is not to be compared with the glory He is unveiling in His second or new creation (2 Cor 3:7–18). Remember from Ephesians 1 that all God did through Christ and through the gospel in securing our redemption is to "the praise of the glory of His grace" (v. 6). Calvinism begins with a focus on the glory of God rather than on the needs of man. The doctrines of grace, inherent in Calvinism, utterly exclude boasting and promote humility.

Conclusion

What is the sole support of truth in the earth? Paul admonished Timothy, and by application all pastors, that the pillar and support of the truth in the earth is *the church*. Paul wrote, "But in case I am delayed, I [write] so that you will know how one ought to conduct himself in the household of God, which is the church of the living God, *the pillar and support of the truth*" (1 Tim 3:15, emphasis mine). The office of administering truth is in the church. God has placed it in her hands. If the church and the pastor are weak, the truth falls to the ground. John Calvin commented on 1 Tim 3:15, "How dreadful is the vengeance that awaits them, if, through their fault, that truth which is the image of the Divine glory, the light of the world, and the salvation of men, shall be allowed to fall! This consideration ought undoubtedly to lead pastors to tremble continually, not to deprive them of all energy, but to excite them to greater vigilance."[3]

What is the primary source of God's glory for time and eternity? Again, the answer is *the church*. It is the epicenter, the blazing center of the manifestation of His glory: "To Him [be] the glory in the church and in Christ Jesus to all generations forever and ever. Amen" (Eph 3:21). No wonder the Bible says we must lay down our lives for the church (1 John 3:16).

What causes the angels to stare in amazement according to the apostle Peter? It is the redeeming of His children and the building of His church. Conversion and the building of His church is a miracle so glorious that even the angels are deeply impressed. The salvation of lost souls and the building of the church, according to 1 Pet 1:12 are "things into which angels long to look."

Almost twenty years ago, God led me to form *Anchored in Truth Ministries*. One of our guiding principles states, "The glory of God is everything. God has ordained that He will most glorify Himself through His church. In order for the church to bring Him the glory He deserves,

---

[3] John Calvin, *Commentary on the Epistles to Timothy, Titus and Philemon*, n.p. Calvin's Commentaries in Accordance 7.4.2.

it needs revival and reformation (and it must take place in that order). This revival and reformation will require suffering on the part of God's shepherds, but the glory of God is worth it." I'm convinced that the rise of Spirit-filled, evangelistic Calvinism is an essential agent to the revival and reformation needed in order to build strong, true churches and bring God the glory He deserves.

A Southern Baptist Dialogue

Calvinism
The Atonement

The Design, Nature, and Extent of the Atonement

David P. Nelson
Senior Vice President, Academic Administration,
Professor of Theology
Southeastern Baptist Theological Seminary
Wake Forest, North Carolina

For God so loved the world, that he gave his only Son, that whoever believes in him should not perish but have eternal life. For God did not send his Son into the world to condemn the world, but in order that the world might be saved through him. Whoever believes in him is not condemned, but whoever does not believe is condemned already, because he has not believed in the name of the only Son of God.

John 3:16–18[1]

All this is from God, who through Christ reconciled us to himself and gave us the ministry of reconciliation; that is, in Christ God was reconciling the world to himself.

2 Cor 5:18–19

But now the righteousness of God has been manifested apart from the law, although the Law and the Prophets bear witness to it—the righteousness of God through faith in Jesus Christ for all who believe. For there is no distinction: for all have sinned and fall short of the glory of God, and are justified by his grace as a gift, through the redemption that is in Christ Jesus, whom God put forward as a propitiation by his blood, to be received by faith. This was to show God's righteousness, because in his divine forbearance he had passed over former sins. It was to show his righteousness at

---

[1] Unless otherwise indicated, Scripture quotations are from the ESV.

the present time, so that he might be just and the justi-
fier of the one who has faith in Jesus.

Romans 3:21–26

Introduction

THE DESIRE TO "BUILD BRIDGES" assumes there is some-
thing to be bridged, some divide to be crossed, some uneven ground to be
traversed. I propose that the gospel situated properly within the *missio Dei*
(mission of God) is not only a means, but the preferred means to bridge
whatever divides may exist. Some divides are natural; they come with the
landscape. Some divides are manmade; they may be the unintentional
results of some other project. Or a divide may be intentional, a barrier
erected to keep another from coming into our space, as a means of distanc-
ing and separating. I want to say at the outset that I hope anyone wishing
to divide over any doctrine will do so for the right reason. In Scripture,
those who hold to false teaching are described as those who bring *hairesis*,
a division, into the body of Christ (2 Pet 2:1). We get our word "heresy"
from this word. A heretic is one who "divides" from the truth of the gospel. A heretic must be corrected and thus end his division from the truth,
or else the church must "divide" itself from the false teacher. That is, the
false teachers must be silenced and rebuked (Titus 1:10–16); if they are
recalcitrant, they are to be put out of the church (Matt 18:17). Of course,
we must be very careful about what we label "heresy."

If any teaching is a heresy, then it should be corrected, and those who
hold to it should repent. Otherwise they have divided themselves from
the church already. If, however, a teaching is only a matter of dispute
or disagreement, and not "heretical," then we should disagree with one
another charitably and together publish the good news of salvation to the
nations. It is my intention, therefore, to lay out what I take to be at the
heart of the doctrine of atonement, and to get at what should be obvious,
to establish whether one's position on the "extent of the atonement" is an
issue that demands we build a barrier, or whether it forms a divide that
can be bridged.

I must say one other thing by way of introduction, as a means of making myself accountable before God and before my brothers and sisters.
I believe that the *content* of our discussion matters very much. We are, I
hope, all seeking the truth, and when we argue, we are together arguing
"toward the truth" as C. S. Lewis has taught us to do.[2] It is equally important to consider the *manner* in which we conduct such a conversation. I

---

[2] I owe this insight to Walter Hooper.

believe the Scriptures are clear about this: the truth is to be spoken in love (Eph 4:15). I want to conduct this conversation consistent with the *more excellent way* of Christian love—the way of charity (1 Cor 12:31b). I have been aided recently by a convicting article published by Roger Nicole, "Polemic Theology, or How to Deal with Those who Differ from Us."[3] Nicole posed three questions we must always ask when we find ourselves in disagreement with another.

1. What do I owe the person who differs from me?
2. What can I learn from the person who differs from me?
3. How can I cope with the person who differs from me?[4]

Nicole noted that we usually move straight to the third question, and that our impulse is to figure how we can bash our opponent over the head. That is exactly what I expect in a disagreement—from my soon-to-be seven year-old son. No, as a matter of fact, I expect more from all my children, including my son—and I certainly expect more from adult Christians. We owe one another love (Rom 13); we can learn from those who differ from us. We can and must determine ways to work together for the sake of the gospel and for the glory of our Lord.

One may wonder why I introduce a presentation on the atonement in such a way. Simply put, I begin this way because of the atonement that I begin this way. In light of Christ's atoning death, the love of God that "controls us" (2 Cor 5:14), and the reality that the life of the redeemed is no longer lived for themselves but rather for the One who died and rose for us, Paul said, "From now on, therefore, we regard no one according to the flesh. Even though we once regarded Christ according to the flesh, we regard him thus no longer" (2 Cor 5:16). If I take seriously the atoning work of Christ, then I must relate to every human in a distinctively Christian manner; and whatever disagreements we may have over the theological system named Calvinism, we must form and maintain our relationships to one another in light of the redemptive work of Christ. To do otherwise is to suggest that we do not take seriously the atonement of Jesus Christ.

The Design of the Atonement[5]

It is typical to begin a discussion about the design of the atonement by answering a question like, Why did Christ die? Bruce Demarest, seeking

---

[3] Roger Nicole, "Polemic Theology, or How to Deal with Those Who Differ from Us," *JBC* 19:1 (Fall 2000): 5–12.

[4] Ibid., 5.

[5] The term "atonement" is an English contribution to the theological lexicon. I have not done extensive study of the history of the term, but *OED* indicates that the term

to consider the purpose and intent of the atonement, asked the question, "For whom did Christ intend to provide atonement through his suffering and death?"[6] These are worthwhile questions to ask, and in answering them we do understand better the design of divine atonement. But I think it is helpful to consider the matter from another vantage point, one that is more broad and expansive. To speak of atonement is to speak of the gospel, and to speak of the gospel is to speak of God's mission, the *missio Dei*.

Missio Dei and Atonement

The Scriptures unfold the grand narrative of God's creation of a world and His intention to form for Himself a people who will be a kingdom of priests, created for His glory. This overarching biblical narrative is sometimes referred to with the rubric "creation—fall—redemption" and sometimes as "creation—fall—redemption—restoration." I prefer to view the narrative in the following manner:

Creation—Fall—Redemption—New Creation

In describing the history of God's world in this way we recognize that God created the heavens and the earth (Gen 1). He created people for Himself, made in His image, who tragically fell in sin (Gen 1–3). The rest of Scripture is the grand story of God's redemptive love for His creation (Gen 3-Rev), God's intention is to form a new creation kingdom, that is, a new heaven and new earth (Isa 65:17; 66:22; 2 Pet 3:13; Rev 21:1) in which His people, a kingdom of priests (Exod 19:6; Rev 1:6; 5:10) dwell with the triune Lord forever and ever, to the praise of His glory (Eph 1:3–14; Rev 21–22).

This sort of divine intention constitutes the design of the atonement, and the gospel is to be understood in this context. The means by which God accomplishes His intention is through the cross of Jesus Christ. This is the gospel: "In Christ God was reconciling the world to himself" (2 Cor 5:19).

We tend to develop theories about everything in theology, and the doctrine of atonement is littered with theory-making. I set any such theorizing within the context of *missio Dei* in order to keep the doctrine in

---

"onement" was employed by Wycliff, and "atonement" was employed by Tyndale. In the sixteenth to seventeenth centuries the term meant simply to "set at one," that is, to bring unity, harmony, or concord. The manner in which that union is achieved is rendered variously depending on the use of the term. The idea of reconciliation is prominent, recognizing that once alienated parties who are now reconciled are "atoned," they are "at one." See *Oxford English Dictionary*, vol. 1, s.v. "atone," "atoned," "atonement."

[6] Bruce Demarest, *The Cross and Salvation: The Doctrine of Salvation* (Wheaton: Crossway, 2006), 189.

perspective. On the one hand, I want to guard against making the doctrine of the atonement some scholastic exercise that resorts too quickly to abstraction, and on the other hand, to guard from making the atonement a teaching that is simply about my own personal religious experience. The gospel is God's atoning work in Christ that includes Christ *pro me* (for me)—the personal intention of God (John 10:9; 1 Tim 1:13–14); Christ *pro nobis* (for us), the corporate intention of God to form a people for himself (Rom 5:8; Eph 5:25–27); and Christ *pro mundo* (for the world), the cosmic intention of God to form a good land in which His people may dwell and experience divine blessing (Gen 12:1–3; Rom 8:20–22; Revelation 21–22).

Understanding the design of the atonement in this fashion provides a foundation from which not only to preach the grace of Christ to unbelievers, but also to build up the church, as well as to account for a distinctively Christian manner of living in the world, including our engagement with the culture in which we dwell. The atoning work of Christ subverts, reconciles, and restores. It *subverts*, overturning our thinking, our actions, and the prevailing spirit of the age. It *reconciles*, enabling us to experience the benefits of God's covenant promises (Eph 2:12–13) and bringing to an end the hostility between us and God, destroying enmity between ethnicities (Eph 2:14–22). It *restores* us to union with God in Christ, and by the Spirit of Christ we have life (Rom 8:11) today and in the age to come. We now anticipate the glory of that coming age along with the groaning creation.

We have now explained the gospel somewhat differently than it is often offered in our pulpits. In this sense the gospel is not simply a rescue from hell (which it is) or some secret to a "better life" or "your best life now" (whatever one may mean by that), but the gospel is God's gracious claim upon the lives of ruined sinners (Eph 2:1–10) set in the context of Christ's bride—His church—with a view toward the cosmic plan of God for the ages. Understood in these terms, set within the context of the *missio Dei*, individual believers must account for life in the context of the church, which exists in a world filled with history that is purposeful, meaningful, and has a properly biblical eschatology that forms both watchfulness and faithfulness in all of life. This is a biblical way of situating the doctrine of the atonement.

I wish to return to the questions I introduced previously: Why did Christ die, and for whom did Christ intend to provide atonement through His suffering and death? God is faithful and true;[7] therefore, He always acts according to His nature. This includes both His love and His

---

[7] I have in mind here the biblical concepts of *ḥesed* and *'emet*, which indicate that God always acts according to his covenant loyalty (sometimes translated "steadfast love" or

righteousness. God loves His creation, and God always does what is just. While Adam was God's special creation, made in God's image, Adam was also a rebellious sinner whose sin had to be punished. I want to rephrase the questions above to reflect a more classic and a more holistic way of asking the question: Why did God become man? This question, famously addressed by Anselm, situates the doctrine of the atonement in the context of the life, death, and resurrection of Jesus Christ. The answer, then, is that *the Father sent the Son because God wills to punish sin and to save, by the atoning work of Christ, all who believe.*[8] This is the divine intention of the atoning work of God in Christ that is heralded in texts introduced at the beginning of this essay (John 3, Rom 3, and 2 Cor 5), and in texts like Gen 15:6 and Isa 52–53 (along with many, many other texts). By means of the cross, the triune God's intention is to save all who are in union with the Father through the Son by the Holy Spirit; there at the cross the Lord triumphs over sin, death, and Satan (Col 2:13–15).

By putting the doctrine this way, I want to affirm the righteousness of God who punishes sin, and also the love of God who shows mercy to sinners.[9] A sinner is condemned because he is sinfully corrupt due to his place in Adam's race (Rom 5) and because he condemns himself by refusing the love of God revealed in Christ who died for lost sinners (John 3:17). The atonement, therefore, is about both the justice and the mercy of God.

While the biblical teaching of atonement is stated in various ways, it is aptly summarized in 2 Cor 5:19 where Paul says that "in Christ God was reconciling the world to himself." In this little phrase we have something of the complete doctrine: What is God doing? Reconciling. How did God reconcile? In Christ. For whom did Christ die? The world. To what end did God do this in Christ? To reconcile the world to Himself.

"mercy"—mercy that endures forever), and He always acts according to His nature. He is truth, so He always "does" truth, He always keeps His Word.

[8] In saying this, I am in agreement with Richard Lightner's statement that "the divine design of the atonement was to provide a basis for salvation for all and to secure it to those who believe" (Robert P. Lightner, *The Death Christ Died: A Biblical Case for Unlimited Atonement*, rev. ed. [Grand Rapids: Kregel, 1998], 96). The notion of "belief" as trust is central to the grand biblical narrative. For example, note how significant is the instruction to trust God in the Pentateuch. Repeatedly God's people are called upon to trust Him (and also obey), and it is such trust that is credited to Abraham as righteousness (Gen 15:16). The significance of faith in the intention of God's atoning work should be seen in such a canonical context.

[9] The themes of divine righteousness and mercy are evident in Leviticus 16, a standard text for the doctrine of the atonement. God demands payment for the sins of the people and the offerings are made at the "mercy seat."

The Nature of the Atonement

In discussions of the nature of the atonement, we typically resort to cherished theories, and among evangelicals it has been the case for some time that the penal substitution view has been the reigning theory. I affirm the significance of the penal substitution view as it accounts for the central atonement themes in Scripture, including the necessity of punishment for sin, Christ's propitiatory offering of Himself to satisfy the wrath of God and secure forgiveness for sinners, and the vicarious nature of the atonement as stated in 2 Cor 5:21: "For our sake he made him to be sin who knew no sin, so that in him we might become the righteousness of God." Such affirmations are central to the gospel, and no message of reconciliation and redemption is truly Christian without them.

Further, though, I must note that in the history of Christianity there have been varied ways of stating truths about the atonement, even if some have focused on certain aspects of the doctrine to the exclusion of others in an unfortunate and sometimes devastating manner.[10] Thomas Oden pointed out four "traditions" or "models" of the atonement that occur from the Patristic period on: the exemplar model, the governor model, the exchange model, and the victor model. Oden stated, "All have legitimacy, and none of itself is complete. They are best viewed as complementary tendencies rather than cohesive schools of thought represented by a single theorist."[11]

Set within the biblical context of the *missio Dei*, these motifs are useful rubrics under which we may arrange the vast biblical material about God's saving action in Christ. We affirm that God did triumph at the cross (victor motif); that Christ, who knew no sin, took upon Himself the sins of the world and gave to sinners His own righteousness (the exchange motif); that God does establish a kingdom order at the cross by which He accomplishes His sovereign purpose as ruler of His world (governor motif); and that the cross of Christ promotes a dutiful and loving response of the redeemed to God (exemplar motif).

More specifically, we affirm the necessity of the incarnation and death of Christ for the propitiation of sins (Heb 2:17; 1 John 4:10) and that Christ bore the punishment due sinners upon Himself (Isa 53:4–6, 11–12; Heb 10:1–10,14), thus averting the wrath of God (Rom 3:25) and exchanging our sin for His righteousness (2 Cor 5:21). Those who trust Christ are justified (Rom 4:25; 5:9,18), reconciled (Rom 5:10–11;

---

[10] E.g., the moral influence or example theories.

[11] Thomas Oden, *The Word of Life: Systematic Theology: Volume Two* (New York: HarperOne, 1992), 403.

2 Cor 5:18–21; Col 1:19–20) and redeemed (Mark 10:45; Eph 1:7; 1 Pet 1:18–19). Such is God's love for the world (John 3:16).

The Extent of the Atonement

I gather that there is considerable agreement up to this point on all sides of the debate. Before I enter into an exposition of my position on the extent of the atonement, let me situate this debate in a proper historical-theological context, especially for those who believe that one's position on the extent of the atonement is a matter of theological orthodoxy, which requires that those who depart from your position are heterodox or heretical. The question of the extent of the atonement has variously been ignored, debated, and sometimes treated as a litmus test for orthodoxy.

I know it is irritating to some to hear it, but to some extent (pun intended), we all believe the atonement is limited. That is, none of us, I take it, are universalists. By "limited" we mean different things, and on some points we believe differently about *what* limits the atonement. By "limited" some mean that Christ died only for the elect and that, therefore, the limitation is caused by God, while others hold that Christ died for all mankind and that any limitation is caused by man. I note that many whose views are labeled as "limited atonement" do not prefer that terminology, employing instead the language of "particular redemption." Again I think everyone will agree that only *particular* people are redeemed, but we will likely express the reasons for this differently. These disagreements are not new, and it may help us to recall some significant historical moments in the doctrine of the atonement.

Historical Considerations

Usually when one hears a dispute about the extent of the atonement, the subject is discussed with reference to the Reformation. I hope it is no surprise to anyone that church history predates the Reformation, and it has actually continued after that historical time period.

While the debate was not strictly about the atonement or the extent of the atonement, it is worth noting the extent to which the doctrines of predestination and election figured in the Pelagian controversy of the late patristic period. Questions about the relationship of divine sovereignty and human agency arose, and the Augustinian position on predestination became prominent. Following Augustine's formulations, Gottschalk of Orbais moved to a highly deterministic view of double predestination that included a logical deduction that the atonement of Christ was for the elect only. This led to a dispute between Gottschalk and Hincmar, Archbishop of Rheims.[12]

The debate was as much about the relationship of predestination and the free will of humans as it was the extent of the atonement, with Hincmar insisting that Gottschalk overemphasized grace and virtually denied human freedom. With respect to redemption[13] Hincmar demonstrated that a logical corollary to Gottschalk's predestinarian views was the denial that Christ had suffered for the salvation of the whole world. Gottschalk and his supporters countered that Hincmar's view led to the conclusion that Christ's blood was wasted. In AD 848 the Council of Mainz condemned Gottschalk's double-predestinarian views as heretical, and in successive councils at Quiercy in the mid-ninth century Hincmar managed to have Gottschalk deposed from the priesthood and imprisoned for life, where he died.[14] Beyond the Hincmar-Gottschalk donnybrook, the doctrine of the extent of the atonement, in the terms of today's debate, was not an especially prominent feature of Patristic and Medieval theology.

The Reformation presents a different picture. One might assume from our use of the term "Calvinism" in this context that Calvin had something to say about the atonement in general, and about the extent of the atonement in particular. Calvin did have something to say about the atonement. He affirmed that on the cross Jesus was a substitutionary sacrifice who on the cross satisfied God's justice and wrath and who redeems and reconciles those who repent and believe. Determining Calvin's position on the extent of the atonement proves to be a bit more difficult, and Calvin scholars themselves have something of a dispute about the matter. Michael Thomas noted the diversity of opinion among scholars: "It is certainly striking that R. T. Kendall can assert without hesitation Calvin's 'belief that Christ died indiscriminately for all men', while J. H. Rainbow can give his one work on this theme the subtitle, 'An historical theological study of John Calvin's doctrine of limited redemption.'"[15] As far as I can tell, this dispute remains among Calvin scholars to this day.

---

[12] A summary of the dispute may be read in Jaroslav Pelikan, *The Great Christian Tradition: A History of the Development of Doctrine, vol. 3: The Growth of Medieval Theology (600–1300)* (Chicago: University of Chicago Press, 1978), 80–95.

[13] The term "atonement," of course, was not a part of this discussion.

[14] See *Catholic Encyclopedia*, http://www.newadvent.org/cathen/06682a.htm, accessed November 15, 2007. I note that the *Catholic Encyclopedia* states that none of Gottschalk's views were actually heretical.

[15] G. Michael Thomas, *The Extent of the Atonement: A Dilemma for Reformed Theology from Calvin to the Consensus (1536–1675)* (Carlisle: Paternoster, 1997).

The Reformers who followed Luther and Calvin present us with a mixed picture on the question.[16] Heinrich Bullinger (1504–1575), who served as a prominent pastor in Zurich in the wake of Zwingli's ministry there, held to predestination in a Calvinist sense, but affirmed a doctrine of general atonement. Jacobus Arminius (1560–1609) and the Remonstrants who followed him likewise held to a general or unlimited atonement, though without such a commitment to a Calvinist doctrine of predestination. On the other hand, theologians like Theodore Beza (1519–1605) held firmly to the Calvinist doctrine of predestination and affirmed the doctrine of limited atonement.

The Synod of Dort presents an interesting study of the extent of the atonement. Convened in 1618–1619 to counter the Remonstrants, the Canons of Dort are well known as a classic expression of Calvinist doctrine. Interestingly, there was considerable dispute at the synod over the extent of the atonement.[17] John Davenant was part of the deputation from Great Britain, and his view of universal atonement is evident in volume 2 of his Colossians commentary, *Dissertation on the Death of Christ*. Martinius of Bremem also held to the universal view, and he pressed the synod considerably on the matter, so much so that Gomarus challenged Martinius to a duel at one point.[18] The Canons clearly lay out Calvinistic doctrines of election and predestination, and on the question of the extent of the atonement affirm that the death of Christ "is of infinite value and worth, more than sufficient to atone for the sins of the whole world."[19] The Canons affirm the inability of man to believe, affirm God's gift of faith given to the elect,[20] and then speak of the "Saving Effectiveness of Christ's Death" in the following manner:

> For it was the entirely free plan and very gracious will
> and intention of God the Father that the enlivening and
> saving effectiveness of his Son's costly death should
> work itself out in all his chosen ones, in order that he
> might grant justifying faith to them only and thereby

---

[16] According to Herman Bavinck, "The Reformed theologians accordingly, with their doctrine of particular satisfaction, stood virtually alone. Add to this that they were not at all unanimous among themselves and gradually diverged even further from one another as well." *Reformed Dogmatics: Sin and Salvation in Christ: Volume Three* (Grand Rapids: Baker, 2006), 460. Bavinck provides a helpful survey of the different views on pp. 460–464.

[17] Referring to the various "deputations" or delegations from various places, Thomas states that "The sufficient-efficient formula is implicit or explicit in most of the submissions." Thomas, *Extent of the Atonement*, 138.

[18] Ibid., 147.

[19] Canons of Dort 2.3.

[20] Ibid., 2.6–7.

> lead them without fail to salvation. In other words, it was God's will that Christ through the blood of the cross (by which he confirmed the new covenant) should effectively redeem from every people, tribe, nation, and language all those and only those who were chosen from eternity to salvation and given to him by the Father; that he should grant them faith (which, like the Holy Spirit's other saving gifts, he acquired for them by his death).[21]

The Canons of Dort, therefore, admit the sufficiency of Christ's death to atone for the sins of the whole world,[22] but confirm that Christ's blood effectively redeems all—in the sense of "without distinction"—who are elected and given to Christ by the Father.

The Saumur theologians John Cameron and Moïse Amyraut introduced further controversy into the Reformed churches with their outright rejection of the doctrine of limited atonement. Cameron, a Scottish theologian, argued that God possessed two wills and that in His antecedent will God demonstrated unconditional love for the world by sending the Son, while in His consequent will Christ dies for the elect. He explains this with the language of sufficiency and efficiency: "Christ died sufficiently for all, but effectually for believers only."[23] Amyraut held to a conditional predestination of all people to salvation and a particular predestination of some to faith.[24] The "particular" aspect for Amyraut is rooted in God's absolute will and is associated with the effectual calling by the Holy Spirit in association with the preaching of the Word.[25] Amyraut saw this view of the atonement as crucial to winning and keeping converts from Catholicism, in as much as Catholics abhorred the Calvinist doctrines of election and predestination. Amyraut affirmed the sacrificial, penal, and substitutionary nature of Christ's death.

Confessional statements in the seventeenth through the nineteenth centuries display varied opinions on the extent of the atonement. The Thirty-nine Articles of the Church of England affirm that Christ's offering was "for all the sins of the whole world, both original and actual."[26]

---

[21] Ibid., 2:8.

[22] That the language of sufficiency is employed even at Dort suggests that we should be careful to clarify what is entailed by the typical "sufficiency—efficiency" language used in discussions of the extent of the atonement.

[23] Thomas, *Extent of the Atonement,* 176.

[24] Brian G. Armstrong, *Calvinism and the Amyraut Heresy: Protestant Scholasticism and Humanism in Seventeenth Century-France* (Madison, WI: University of Wisconsin Press, 1969), 158–221.

[25] Ibid., 216–221.

[26] The Thirty-nine Articles of the Church of England, XXXI. See also XV, XVII.

The Westminster Confession of Faith, on the other hand, explicitly affirms limited atonement when it states that Christ's offering is "for all those whom the Father hath given unto him."[27]

Baptist confessions also present varied viewpoints. The Orthodox Creed (1679) affirms that "Christ died for all men, and there is sufficiency in his death and merits for the sins of the whole world,"[28] while The Second London Confession (1689) follows the wording of the Westminster Confession, confirming a limited atonement.[29] The New Hampshire Confession (1833) describes Christ as "an all-sufficient Savior"[30] and in Article 6 on the "Freeness of Salvation" encourages a free offer of the gospel and a duty for sinners to believe. The Baptist Faith and Message, originally penned in 1925 and updated in 1963 and 2000, has no direct statement about the matter, though it, like The New Hampshire Confession, encourages a free offer of the gospel to all.

Andrew Fuller (1754–1815) is in many respects a model figure for those engaged in contemporary debates about Calvinism in Baptist life. Himself a Calvinist, he confronted the hyper-Calvinism of his day and "argued it was appropriate to extend the offer of salvation to all who would hear, regardless of their spiritual state."[31] This sort of commitment to a free offer of the gospel propelled Fuller to support a young man named William Carey, and Fuller thus took his place in the founding of what is now called the "modern missions movement." Much good would come from a fresh return to the works of Fuller by Southern Baptists.[32]

In the contemporary setting among evangelicals the views are equally varied. Prominent figures like John Piper, John MacArthur, R. C. Sproul, and Wayne Grudem hold to a limited atonement, while others like Norman Geisler, Paige Patterson, and James Leo Garrett Jr. affirm unlimited atonement.

---

[27] Westminster Confession of Faith, 1647 8.5.

[28] See The Orthodox Creed, Article 18.

[29] Second London Confession, 1689, 8.5. See also *The Philadelphia Confession, 1742*, 8.5.

[30] The New Hampshire Confession, Article 4.

[31] Paul Brewster, "Andrew Fuller (1754–1815): Model Baptist Pastor-Theologian," Ph.D. diss., Southeastern Baptist Theological Seminary (2007): 86.

[32] For primary source readings on the atonement, I suggest *Gospel Worthy of All Acceptation*" and *Defense of "Gospel Worthy of All Acceptation," In Reply to Mr. Button and Philanthropos*. In particular, section IV, "On the Death of Christ" in *Reply to Philanthropos* is useful in understanding Fuller's view of the extent of the atonement. In addition to the Brewster dissertation I recommend Peter J. Morden, *Offering Christ to the World: Andrew Fuller (1754–1815) and the Revival of Eighteenth Century Particular Baptist Life*, Studies in Baptist History and Thought, vol. 8 (Waynesboro, GA: Paternoster, 2003).

Exegetical Considerations[33]

The texts I submit for consideration are the standard ones adduced; I am more than happy to avoid novelties, and I presume no originality. Again, I wish to set the doctrine of the atonement in the grand redemptive narrative of Scripture. This includes the trajectory set with the Abrahamic, Davidic, and new covenants, and the continual calls to trust Yahweh that form the basis for justification before a righteous God (Gen 15:6; Hab 2:4). Crucial to the doctrine of the atonement is the biblical teaching of an "offspring," a Promised One who is both a royal figure before whom the peoples will bow down (Gen 49:10; Psalm 2) and the Suffering Servant who will provide salvation for the nations (Isaiah 52–53; Psalm 22), consistent with the biblical doctrine of God that Yahweh is both righteous and merciful.[34]

John 3:16–18

I have already noted the significance of John 3:16–18 in the doctrine of the atonement. The classic dispute over this text involves the identification of *kosmos*, which admittedly has varied referents in the Bible. I take the reading of "world" as "all without exception" to be the clearest meaning of the text given the common manner in which such statements are made about Jesus being the Savior of the world in John's Gospel (John 1:29; 4:42; 12:46). In John 1 and 12 *kosmos* is used in the sense of both the earth and all the inhabitants of the earth,[35] indicating that in the incarnation Jesus came to earth for the sake of saving all who would

---

[33] I have found several sources especially helpful in sorting out the exegetical issues, and these I commend to those who want to investigate the subject further: Louis Berkhof, *Systematic Theology* (new ed.; Grand Rapids: Eerdmans, 1996); Bruce Demarest, *The Cross and Salvation*, Foundations of Evangelical Theology: The Doctrine of Salvation (Wheaton: Crossway, 1997); Norman F. Douty, *Did Christ Die Only for the Elect?: A Treatise on the Extent of Christ's Atonement* (Eugene, OR: Wipf & Stock, 1998 [1972]); Wayne Grudem, *Systematic Theology* (Grand Rapids: Zondervan, 1995); Paul Helm, *Calvin and the Calvinists* (Carlisle, PA: Banner of Truth, 1982); Robert P. Lightner, *The Death Christ Died: A Biblical Case for Unlimited Atonement* (rev. ed.; Grand Rapids: Kregel, 1998); James Morison, *The Extent of the Atonement* (Glasgow: London, Hamilton, Adams & Co., 1882).

[34] Ezekiel 18 is instructive on this count, noting the righteousness of God who will judge the wicked, but also showing that He takes no pleasure in the death of the wicked and desires sinners to repent and live (Ezek 18:23,32).

[35] So John 1:10: "He was in the world, and the world was made through Him, and the world did not know him." I take it that this verse, and the surrounding passage, indicate Christ's incarnation ("He was in the world"), Christ's divine agency in creating the world ("and the world was made through him"), and ignorance of Him on the part of the human inhabitants of the world ("and the world did not know him").

believe in Him. Attempts to make *kosmos* mean something other than "all people" or the "universe" are strained and unnecessary.[36]

Let me make three further points about John 3:16. First, while I believe that this text affirms a general or universal atonement, the necessity of faith is equally clear; the benefits of God's saving work in Christ are appropriated by faith. Second, while the love of God is clearly in view in Christ's saving work, so too is God's righteousness. In v. 18 we learn that failure to believe confirms the condemnation of sinners and the justice of God. Third, while I read John 3:16–18 in this fashion, affirming a general view of the atonement, I also affirm the doctrine of unconditional election taught in various places in Scripture, which I believe is in view in a passage like John 10. I will readily admit certain tensions that accrue with affirming both doctrines (i.e., unconditional election and general atonement); I know of no theological system that is biblical that does not have such tensions. I see no contradiction, however, in affirming that Christ lays down His life for His sheep (John 10) and that He came to save "the world." Since His sheep are part of the world, I take Christ's atoning work to be extensive to the whole world and effective for the salvation of His sheep, and equally effective in ratifying the justice of God in condemning unbelievers.

1 Timothy 2:1–6

Paul was instructing Timothy about the "stewardship from God that is by faith" (1 Tim 1:4), which was Paul's way of speaking of the gospel in this context. Paul instructed Timothy about how the people of God should behave since they constitute "the church of the living God, a pillar and buttress of truth" (1 Tim 3:15). Paul gave specific instructions about how these Christians should order their relationships in a gospel manner[37] for the sake of the propagation of the gospel inside and outside the sphere of the church.

In part, this requires a certain manner of praying. We pray for all people, for kings and all who are in high positions, in order to promote an environment of peace. This is good to the God who brings *shālôm* (peace) to the world in the incarnation of the Word (Isaiah 9:6). This God is our Savior and His desire for all people to be saved and come to the

---

[36] Specifically, to say that world refers to "all the elect" or "all without distinction" (i.e., all kinds, classes, or ethnicities) strains the plain meaning of the text.

[37] These are instructions about relationships to all people (2:1), to those in authority in civic affairs (2:2), to those within the church in general (men, 2:8; women, 2:9ff.), and instructions about leaders in the church in particular (3:1–13). This is a means of making the church and the cultural context in which she resides a "gospel" place to the extent possible (2:2–7). This is the stuff of faithful gospel stewardship (1:4).

knowledge of truth. Only one mediator who can accomplish this, "Christ Jesus, who gave himself as a ransom for all" (2:5–6). This repetition of "all" and "for all" is significant. I am aware of the reading by proponents of a limited atonement that "all" means "all without distinction," not "all without exception." Yet I cannot see how this is the most natural reading of the text, since I doubt we are to pray for all without distinction but not all without exception, or that the instruction is simply to pray for all kinds or classes of people.

That phrase "ransom for all" in this context leads me to believe that the one Mediator's death is for all people, not simply "all kinds" of people. This is confirmed in 1 Tim 4:10, where Paul states, "For to this end we toil and strive, because we have our hope set on the living God, who is the Savior of all people, especially of those who believe." I take Paul's use of *malista* here to be an example of a special class set apart from a general class in which it is included,[38] affirming the particular nature of redemption for those who believe within the context of a general atonement. A number of other texts figure into my view of general atonement, and I will survey a few of them briefly.

2 Corinthians 5

Paul's teaching about reconciliation in 2 Corinthians 5 includes the calling of all believers to be "ministers of reconciliation" and "ambassadors for Christ" (2 Cor 5:18,20). To whom are we ministers and ambassadors? To the world which God was reconciling to Himself in Christ (2 Cor 5:19). I am aware that this is the sort of reading that prompts some to object to notions of "hypothetical universalism." Hypothetically, if every person exhibited faith, then, yes, there would be a universal redemption. Nowhere does Paul admit such a thing, nor do I. Many will not believe, and therefore will not benefit from the reconciling work of Christ who saves.

Hebrews 2:9,14–18

This text indicates that Jesus, who is the Son of God who made purification for sins (Heb 1:1–3), suffered and tasted death "for everyone" (Heb 2:9). Jesus has "become a merciful and faithful high priest in the service of God to make propitiation for the sins of the people" (Heb 2:17). While there are arguments about the identity of "everyone" (v. 2) and "the people" (v. 17) by proponents of the varying views of the extent of the atonement. The author of Hebrews is drawing a parallel between Christ's mediatorial role as high priest and the high priestly ministry

---

[38] See, e.g., Gal 6:10; Phil 4:22; 1 Tim 5:8,17; 2 Tim 4:13; Tit 1:10.

of the tabernacle. This analogy, carried on throughout the letter of the Hebrews, presents an interesting dilemma for those who wish to argue that "everyone" and "the people" refer only to those who are particularly redeemed. That is, the high priest entered the tabernacle once per year to make a sin offering for the people, presumably all the nation of Israel. Yet I wonder if anyone is willing to suggest that all of Israel is made up of people who trust God savingly, given the general trajectory of the biblical narrative about Israel. If such a reading is in fact granted, this seems like at least a teaching analogous to "hypothetical universalism," if not universalism itself. I am not suggesting that anyone takes such a reading, but to be consistent, it seems best to read "everyone" and "the people" in general terms, understanding, again, that only those who believe are saved.

2 Peter 2:1; 3:9

Perhaps no texts are more determinative for many proponents of the general atonement than these two. Second Pet 3:9 is oft quoted as a proof text to object to the tenets of Calvinism, though I hardly think this text alone accomplishes what those who use it in such a manner thinks it does. I take God's desire that none should perish in 2 Pet 3:9 to be a statement similar to Paul's in 1 Tim 2:4 and the truth revealed in Ezek 18:23,32 that God genuinely desires the wicked to repent and live, though none will do so without the grace of God.[39]

Second Pet 2:1 has been a subject of considerable debate with respect to the extent of the atonement since it seems to indicate that the false prophets (2:1) whose condemnation is sure (2:3), about whom Peter warns, are those who "deny the Master who bought them" (v. 1). In this instance a term employed to refer to redemption, *agorazō*,[40] is used with reference to those who will be condemned and destroyed.[41] Furthermore, the description of these false prophets with the term *aselgeia*, a term used elsewhere to refer to the ungodly and unregenerate[42] indicates that this reference is to unbelievers who have been "bought" by the Lord, but who fail to benefit from Christ's atoning work due to their unbelief and rebellion.

---

[39] While I believe these texts prove difficult for the supralapsarian position in particular, I do not see that they prove difficult with respect to doctrines like election, predestination, and effectual calling in general.

[40] See 1 Cor 6:20; 7:23; Rev 5:9; 14:3–4.

[41] The term translated "destroyed" (*apōleia*) may be used generally of destruction or more specifically of destruction in hell. The latter appears to be in view here, especially in light of the use with "condemnation" (*krima*). For similar uses of the term see Matt 7:13; Rom 9:22; Phil 1:28; 3:19; 2 Pet 3:7,16; Rev 17:8,11.

[42] See, e.g., Eph 4:19; 1 Pet 4:3; 2 Pet 2:7,18; Jude 4.

1 John 2:2

This is another text often cited by proponents of a general atonement, I think with good reason. The text reads, "He is the propitiation for our sins, and not for ours only but also for the sins of the whole world." John declared that Jesus is the propitiatory sacrifice for sins, and that these sins are not only ours but are the sins of the whole world. We could make various suggestions about what John meant by "the whole world," but 1 John 5:19 seems to clarify the meaning of the term. In that passage the "whole world" refers to those who are "in the power of the evil one," in contrast to those who have been "born of God" in 1 John 5:18. While we could resort to other, more inventive readings, it appears that in 1 John 2:2 we have another reference, like 1 Tim 4:10, to the truth that the atonement is general in its extent, while its saving effect is limited to those who believe.

Theological Considerations

Now I wish to point out some of the chief theological considerations related to the extent of the atonement. I hope to make some important observations, affirmations, and denials, and follow with some significant questions that attend to the matter.

Predestination and Election

Often, one's view of the atonement of Christ is directly related to one's views on predestination and election. Inasmuch as we expect biblical teachings to be coherent, we attempt to connect one doctrine to another reasonably, and this is methodologically virtuous. The extent to which our view of the atonement is controlled by speculative theology about, for example, the logical ordering of decrees, is another matter. I do not consider this approach to be quite so methodologically virtuous.

Whether during the debates of the late Patristic or Medieval periods, those during the Reformation, or in our day, we must recognize that for various reasons one's understanding of predestination and election figures in one's understanding of the atonement for various reasons. The connections are drawn primarily with respect to one's understanding of the decrees[43] as well as the manner in which one understands saving faith, including how one appropriates any particular *ordo salutis* (order of salvation).

I affirm unconditional election, though I recognize that many who hold to a general view of the atonement do not. I affirm the doctrine

---

[43] That is, whether one is attached to a supralapsarian, infralapsarian, or sublapsarian view.

for exegetical reasons, and guard it because of the implications for the Christian life and eternal security. I reject, however, certain doctrines sometimes (but certainly not always) associated with unconditional election, viz. double predestination, a supralapsarian view of the decrees, and a doctrine of eternal justification.

I am curious to hear whether a proponent of the doctrine of limited atonement holds that doctrine primarily because of one's view of the elective decree. That is, is it primarily a logical rather than an exegetical position? Holding to a doctrine for logical reasons is not, in my view, necessarily bad. We hold various doctrines on such a basis, usually as an inference from more directly biblical teachings. For example, I reject what I call the doctrine of divine forgetfulness, that God forgets our sins when He forgives us, because of serious negative implications for the doctrine of God, particularly certain clear teachings of Scripture that must not be rejected.[44] So, I believe my position on that count to be *biblical*, but my reason for holding it is not primarily *exegetical*. Methodologically, I put aside what appear to be logical necessities where I see exegetical reasons to do so.

Another question I have for my friends who hold to a limited atonement concerns the extent to which the *will* of God is determinative in the doctrine rather than the *love* of God. I want to clarify while asking this question that there is no doctrine of the love of God without the righteousness (therefore, justice and wrath) of God, so I am not suggesting that one base one's view of the atonement on a view of God made in man's image. Put another way, I might ask to what extent the *freedom* of God in relation to God's omnipotence figures as a dominant theme from which certain theological positions are deduced—the logical order of decrees, one's view of election, and the design of the atonement, for example.

Instrumentality of Faith

The nature of biblical faith is a significant point in the discussion of the atonement. Only those who are in union with God in Christ are saved. Faith is the means by which one is found in such union (Eph 2:8–9). The Scriptures, from Genesis through Revelation, call people to faith, to trust the Lord. While I affirm the necessity of the Holy Spirit's aid,[45] I still take faith to be an act of human volition. Any view of the gospel must account

---

[44] The most serious problem is that to hold to divine forgetfulness I must affirm that God, who is truth and who is ever faithful, actually believes a lie, viz., that I, a sinner, have never sinned.

[45] As The Abstract of Principles, Article V states, faith is "wrought in the heart by the Holy Spirit."

for this, though we may employ different philosophical tools to do so. I do not understand faith to be a human merit, but rather the instrument by which a sinner receives the gift of eternal life.

Along these lines that I am troubled by the implications of some views of particular redemption that suggest the sins of the elect were atoned for *and* atonement was *applied* at the time of the crucifixion, which implies that the wrath of God is actually removed from persons at the cross.[46] If this is true, then is it the case that the wrath of God is not upon the elect from the time of conception? And, if that is admitted, then what is the nature of Paul's statement to the church at Ephesus that "you were all dead in the trespasses and sins . . . and were by nature children of wrath, like the rest of mankind" (Eph 2:1, 3)? Paul assumed these believers were under the wrath of God, just like all men, and that it was because of God's great mercy and love (Eph 2:4) that God saved them "by grace . . . through faith" (Eph 2:5,8–9). Faith is, in this case, the instrumental means by which the atoning work of Christ is applied to the sinner.[47] This is so obvious that I must ask why any would hold to a doctrinal formulation that suggests otherwise.

---

[46] I note that Charles Hodge addresses this question directly and states that the elect "remain in this state of exposure [to the wrath of God] until they believe, and should they die (unless in infancy) before they believe they would inevitably perish notwithstanding the satisfaction for their sins. It is the stipulations of the covenant which forbid such a result" (Hodge, 557–558). By "covenant" Hodge refers to the covenant between the Father and the Son to save the elect. I am grateful that Hodge admits the necessity of faith, and am not surprised he does so, since there is so much biblical teaching that affirms it. Yet, it is this very point that leads me to reject certain aspects of the limited atonement view that indicate that the wrath of God is *actually* removed from each elect sinner at the time Jesus died. A reference to the assurance that the elect will surely believe because of the covenant does not answer adequately the question of *how* the atonement is applied to the sinner.

[47] Observe the manner in which A. W. Pink speaks of the relationship of reconciliation, by which the wrath of God is removed, and the remission of sins. Reconciliation includes both the propitiatory sacrifice of Christ and the sinners "voluntary and joyful obedience to [God]." He says, "Until both of these are effected, reconciliation is not effected." Pink explains, then, how remission of sins occurs, including the vicarious work of Christ from the incarnation to the resurrection, and then adds, "But *personally* we are not forgiven until we believe. We need to distinguish sharply between the results secured by Christ's death for God's elect, and their being, individually, *partakers* of those effects. Christ purchased and procured a *right* unto our receiving forgiveness, but we do not enter the *enjoyment* of this blessing until our faith is placed in Him." A. W. Pink, *The Satisfaction of Christ: Studies in the Atonement* (Forest City, NC: Truth for Today, 1955), 168–169, 182. I affirm Pink's insistence that faith is necessary for the appropriation of reconciliation and would urge Calvinists to consider the ramifications of arguing to the contrary, whether explicitly or implicitly.

The "Payment for Unbelief" and the "Double Payment" Objections

Largely due to arguments offered by John Owen in *The Death of Death in the Death of Christ*, these are the objections to the general atonement view I most frequently hear. These questions get right to the heart of one's view of the design of the atonement. The questions are posed in the following fashion:

1. *If Christ died for sins, and unbelief is a sin, then must not all sin be atoned for?* The benefits of Christ's death are not enjoyed by any who fail to believe, since faith is the instrument by which the atonement is rendered effective in one's life. The objection offered in the question seems to assume that the atonement works apart from faith. If so, one must wonder whether the cross is the means of salvation, or if election itself is the means of salvation, in which case the question is moot.[48]

2. *If Christ died for the sins of all people, as the general atonement doctrine holds, then are there not two payments offered for the sins of those in hell, the payment offered by Christ on their behalf, and the payment of each condemned person himself in eternal death?* Christ's death is infinite in its extent, but no one enjoys the saving benefits of the atonement apart from faith. Further, the question fails to account for the way in which the work of Christ manifests the righteousness of God, which explains why, in John 3:18, the unbeliever condemns himself by his rejection of the Son. The idea that Christ wastes his blood on the damned ignores the sense in which the cross demonstrates the righteousness of God and serves not only to propitiate for sin, but also to show the justice of God in judgment.[49] Those who reject Christ are rightly condemned.

Two Further Questions

I have two additional questions that are important for Southern Baptists. First, I am eager to learn the various ways in which those who hold to limited atonement handle the question of the love of God for all people. I am especially interested to hear how Reformed theologians who hold that God does not love all people treat the subject of common

---

[48] Thomas argues that such an objection, suggested by Beza at one point, is itself inconsistent with Canon of Dort 2.6, which reads, "However, that many who have been called through the gospel do not repent or believe in Christ but perish in unbelief is not because the sacrifice of Christ offered on the cross is deficient or insufficient, but because they themselves are at fault."

[49] In light of the "wasted blood" charge, I also wonder to what extent the reality of the continued activity of Satan and his servants suggest that Christ's work on the cross "failed" in light of Col 2:15, which teaches that at the cross Christ "disarmed rulers and authorities and put them to open shame, by triumphing over them in him." I maintain that according to divine design, the triumph of the cross is completely sufficient in this respect, and Christ's triumph will be brought to completion at God's appointed time.

grace. Since common grace is frequently discussed in the context of the cosmic effects of the cross, I wonder to what extent a denial of universal love and an affirmation of a doctrine of common grace indicate some sort of inconsistency.[50] Beyond mere curiosity, I believe that Southern Baptists need a reformation of thinking about faith and culture, and I personally believe that the Reformed tradition offers insights from which we can benefit much, including the doctrine of common grace. If we are to resource this theology, though, I think the corollary of the love of God and the common grace of God deserves attention.

Second, and more obviously recognized as an issue in the current debate about Calvinism, is how those who hold to a limited atonement handle the offer of the gospel. I am not asking whether or not we have public "altar calls," since I cannot find warrant for that practice as some sort of sine qua non of biblical liturgy. I am not opposed to altar calls per se, but there are obviously varied ways in which a free offer of the gospel may be given.[51] I have on several occasions fielded criticisms about those who hold to the doctrine of limited atonement and have attempted to explain how their views do not necessarily militate against such offers, but I have found little acceptance of those explanations by

---

[50] Attempts to answer this question by a simple appeal to a doctrine of creation or providence (e.g., appeals to statements throughout Scripture that affirm God's universal care for His creation) do not actually answer my question. That is, I am not asking *if* God cares for the world, since Scripture clearly teaches that He does. Rather, I am asking *why* He does so. Is it because of divine love or not? And if so, in what way is that love granted universally. I take universal statements like John 3:16, 2 Cor 5:19, and 1 John 2:2 to address this very point. In any event, it seems incongruous to speak of common *grace* while denying universal *love*.

Berkhof notes that Kuyper's argument that common grace is simply a blessing of creation "hardly suffices to answer the question, how it is to be explained that a holy and just God extends grace to, and bestows favor upon, sinners who have forfeited everything, even when they have no share in the righteousness of Christ and prove finally impenitent . . . . Reformed theologians generally hesitate to say that Christ by his atoning blood merited these blessings for the impenitent and reprobate. At the same time they do believe that important natural benefits accrue to the whole human race from the death of Christ, and that in these benefits the unbelieving, the impenitent, and the reprobate also share." Berkhof, *Systematic Theology,* 437–38. R. B. Kuiper comments on this same point: "The design of God in the atoning work of Christ pertained primarily and directly to the redemption of the elect, but indirectly and secondarily it also included the blessings of common grace." R. B. Kuiper, *For Whom Did Christ Die?: A Study of the Divine Design of the Atonement* (Grand Rapids: Eerdmans, 1959), 84.

My point, then, is to seek clarification about the nature of love demonstrated on the cross and the doctrine of common grace so often appealed to in the Reformed tradition. I prefer to affirm both, and understand scriptural statements like "God so loved the world" in this fashion.

[51] At the risk of stating what should be obvious, the offer of the gospel or the "invitation" is not synonymous with an "altar call."

some opponents of Calvinism. Clarification about this point alone could do much for the sake of bridge building in the SBC.

To sum up, I hold that the effects of Christ's death are universally extensive, that they are cosmic in scope. Only that which is in union with God in Christ, however, receives the *redemptive* and *restorative* benefits of Christ's death. All who are "new creations" by means of faith, along with the restored creation itself, benefit from the atonement in this manner.

What Is at Stake Regarding the Doctrine of the Atonement: Two Potential Problems

Regarding the Nature of the Gospel

With respect to the extent of the atonement, I believe there is some room for disagreement; as regards the nature of the atonement, however, we cannot sustain substantial disagreement and remain partners in the gospel. That is to say, we may have disagreements about the extent of the atonement, even sharp disagreements, and yet remain partners in the gospel with a Great Commission passion. Precisely because we agree on the nature of the atonement, that "God so loved the world that he sent his only begotten Son that whosoever believes in him should not perish but have everlasting life" and "that in Christ God was reconciling the world to himself" (2 Cor 5:18–19). My worry is simply this: that the gospel is not regularly preached in the pulpits of our churches. My colleague Nathan Finn has written about this in the past, and I am not sure I can improve on his assessment.[52] I am aware that he was sharply criticized for his claims, but I think he is correct in his critique. This is my single greatest worry for our convention: that we are losing the gospel. To a large extent this is because we have failed to teach the atonement in the richness and fullness of the canonical exposition of the doctrine.

Regarding the Offer of the Gospel

While I have mentioned this as a question for those who hold to a limited atonement, there are potentially troubling implications for the offer of the gospel on both sides of the debate. As previously noted, a limited view of the atonement may minimize or extinguish the free offer of the gospel. On the other hand, the unlimited view of the atonement may

---

[52] See Nathan Finn, "Some Possible Solutions for What Ails the SBC" at http://nathanafinn. wordpress.com/2006/12/05/some-possible-solutions-for-what-ails-the-sbc-part-141/ and http://nathanafinn.wordpress.com/2006/12/09/some-possible-solutions-for-what-ails-the-sbc-part-142/.

promote a cheap offer of the gospel that may undermine the gospel altogether. This may be the result of simple homiletical silliness, or it may be a more considered deduction from general atonement to the belief that we may dispense with the doctrines of election and effectual calling, thus producing "inhumane" presentations of the gospel.[53] By this I mean that our offers of the gospel sometimes seem to imply that God has nothing to do with salvation. By both our methods and our rhetoric, this seems apparent to me. As a result, we fail to treat sinners as the humans they are, sinners for whom Christ died. Our gimmicks and rhetorical tricks are not worthy of the gospel of Christ, and they are not consistent with the more excellent way of love that we should express for people.

I admit that these are *potential* problems. I can't say that either view of the atonement *causes* these aberrations. When Paul confronted antinomianism, for example, he didn't argue that grace *causes* antinomianism; a doctrine of grace that is disordered in one's theology leads to the problem. One's view of the extent of the atonement, improperly situated in relation to other doctrines, may well lead to an excess of some kind.

Conclusion

I have raised some important questions for my Calvinistic friends. I hope I have been clear and charitable. You likely have determined that, while I have my share of questions about the doctrine of limited atonement or particular redemption, I do not believe that our differences deter us from building bridges. Frankly, I am not worried that Calvinists are going to ruin the SBC, and I certainly do not believe that their presence among us signals the eventual death-knell of missions and evangelism in our convention. In fact, the real dangers to the future of the SBC have little to do with Calvinism in my view.[54] To argue that Calvinism necessarily has a deleterious effect on evangelism and missions is inconsistent with both my personal experience and with history (not to mention the

---

[53] I am thankful to my colleague Pete Schemm for suggesting this description of the problem.

[54] Among my concerns, beyond the potential loss of the gospel in our churches, are (1) that we are not more fully engaged in the Great Commission enterprise—though there seems to be a genuine movement of reformation on this count, for which I am grateful to God; (2) the lack of preaching that is truly biblical, i.e., preaching that respects the biblical teaching and textual-canonical form of the Scriptures; (3) the failure to connect doctrine and life (by this I do not mean "practical" preaching that is typically little more than pop-psychology and self-help advice, but rather the formation of a way of reading and interpreting the Scriptures that naturally connects to the formation of a Christian way of life); and (4) that so many of our congregants spend their time listening to purveyors of false doctrine (e.g., John Hagee and Joel Osteen), which they do not readily recognize for what it is.

Scriptures). Some of the most evangelistic people I know are five-point Calvinists, and that includes some missionaries who are among the most faithful Great Commission Christians I know.

If those of *any* theological position, Calvinist or otherwise, who do not take seriously the Great Commission mandate and the free offer of the gospel, then they should repent. My experience is that most people fail to share the gospel not because of considered soteriological positions, but because we are self-centered and care so little for the lost; ultimately we love ourselves more than we love God. This is a problem not limited to Christians of one particular soteriological view. We might refer to it as an unlimited problem among believers.

Dr. Mohler has mentioned "the stewardship of the moment" that is before us. I want to remind us of that stewardship for the entire SBC. There is a lost world with billions of people who need the redeeming gospel of Jesus Christ. The mission of God is clear, and we have been called to carry the gospel to the nations. How tragic it would be if we failed to make the most of the moment offered to us. Yet I am optimistic for our convention, that we will find our way back to the more excellent way of Christ, and that we will, as faithful ministers of reconciliation and ambassadors for Christ, herald the good news "that God was in Christ reconciling the world to Himself."

The Biblical Confirmation of Particular Redemption

Sam Waldron
Academic Dean, Professor of Theology
Midwest Center for Theological Studies
Owensboro, Kentucky

Introduction

MY PURPOSE IS TO SHOW that the doctrine of particular redemption is biblical and makes much more sense of the teaching of the Bible than the doctrine of general redemption or universal atonement. No approach to the question of the extent of the atonement can make any progress until the issue or question at stake is clearly understood. The question which the extent of the atonement is intended to answer is, For whom did Christ die?

Several points of clarification are necessary as to what this question is not. First, the question is not, For whose benefit did Christ die? Let me stipulate several things with regard to this question. Many people who benefit from the death of Christ are not elect. Many benefits of common grace flow out of Christ's death. Many temporal benefits come to the non-elect as a result of Christ's death. I admit, therefore, that many besides the elect benefit from Christ's death.

Second, the question is not, Is the atonement limited? All evangelical Christians who believe that only some will ultimately be saved by Christ's death hold to a limited atonement. They concede, in other words, that in some sense the atonement is limited. Arminians and Amyraldians limit the efficacy of the atonement by affirming that some for whom Christ died will nevertheless be lost. Calvinists limit its extent. The question is not, therefore, whether the atonement is limited but whether it is limited in its extent or its efficacy.

Third, the question is not, Is the atonement precious enough in itself, or did Christ suffer enough, to satisfy the justice of God against every single human being? There is no limit to the value of the precious blood of Christ. The original, historical statement of the five points of Calvinism in the Canons of Dort (second head, Article 3) affirms, "The death of the Son of God is the only and most perfect sacrifice and satisfaction for sin, and is of infinite worth and value, abundantly sufficient to expiate the sins of the whole world."

My understanding of the question contrasts with each of these. The question, For whom did Christ die? properly means, "In whose place did Christ substitute Himself?" This is the specific meaning biblically of the words *for whom*. The preposition *for* in the Bible is correctly taken by evangelicals and Southern Baptists as implying the specific idea of substitution. Hence, when we ask if the Bible teaches that Christ died generally for all men without exception or particularly for the elect, it is the Bible's meaning of *for* which must control our understanding of the question. This is also what the question is normally taken to mean within the Reformed tradition. Furthermore, only with reference to this precise question do I have any interest in defending a particular redemption or a limited extent for Christ's atonement.

I have two points to make about this question. I will deal first with the proofs of particular redemption and then with the problems often raised against it.

The Proofs of Particular Redemption Stated

The Substitutionary Nature of the Atonement

The Argument's Statement. The nature of the atonement as substitutionary curse-bearing demands particular redemption. When we say that Christ died for sinners, we mean that He engaged in the work of substitutionary curse-bearing for sinners. The question that Calvinists have pressed based on this (generally agreed upon) evangelical doctrine is, If Christ actually substituted Himself for me and bore the curse for my sins, how can I ever bear that curse? Since the time of John Owen's great treatise, *The Death of Death in the Death of Christ*,[1] Calvinists have pressed the implications of substitutionary atonement on their opponents. Will a just God punish the same sins twice? It cannot be. Double jeopardy is as unjust in the divine court as it is in human courts. If God propitiated His wrath toward me in a truly substitutionary and penal sacrifice, how can He still be angry at me? Did God in Christ actually redeem, reconcile, and propitiate His anger against us on the cross? Then I cannot and will

---

[1] John Owen, *The Works of John Owen* (Edinburgh: The Banner of Truth Trust, 1967), 10:140–425.

not ever experience that anger. Those for whom Christ died cannot die for their sins.

The Argument's Support. Vast support can be marshaled for the idea that the nature of the atonement requires that all those for whom Christ died be actually and ultimately saved. John Murray argued that within the inclusive concept of obedience, the work of Christ must be understood under four specific categories: sacrifice or expiation, propitiation, reconciliation, and redemption.[2] As these categories define the nature of the atonement, Murray proceeds to argue that they require the doctrine of particular redemption.[3] Each of these categories underlines the nature of the atonement as substitutionary curse-bearing. Only by muffling or receding from the idea of substitutionary curse-bearing or penal substitution can the evangelical defenders of a hypothetically universal atonement maintain their view. The strictly substitutionary nature of the atonement cannot, however, be evaded. Though many passages could be cited in support of particular redemption, I will examine only two here and refer to others subsequently.

> And they sang a new song, saying, "Worthy are You to take the book and to break its seals; for You were slain, and purchased for God with Your blood *men* from every tribe and tongue and people and nation. You have made them *to be* a kingdom and priests to our God; and they will reign upon the earth" (Rev 5:9–10[4]).

In these verses the four living creatures and 24 elders sing. The occasion of their singing is the accession of the Messiah to the throne of God described in the previous verses. This event occurred at the resurrection and ascension of our Lord when He was made both Lord and Christ (Acts 2:36) and sat down on the right hand of God (Heb 1:3). It is crucial that this temporal standpoint be understood because, after worthiness is attributed to the Lamb, three aorist (past) tenses describe the basis for His worthiness. Each of these describes events that preceded His ascension to the throne and His taking of the book. They are followed by a contrasting future tense which further accentuates the significance of the aorists.[5]

---

[2] John Murray, *Redemption Accomplished and Applied* (Grand Rapids: Eerdmans, 1951), 19–24.

[3] Ibid., 62–63.

[4] Unless otherwise indicated, all Scripture quotations are from the NASB.

[5] There are textual variants with regard to the tense of the verb, but the future tense is the best supported reading and the only one which makes good, doctrinal sense.

The point is that the aorists describe events that occurred at the time of and by means of the death of Christ. The first aorist clearly establishes this in its reference to the death of Christ: "For You were slain." The next aorist must also, therefore, refer to an event which occurred at the time of and by the death of Christ. By His death and at the time of His death, He "purchased for God with Your blood *men*." There was, therefore, real penal substitution ("blood") resulting in a real purchase of men. The redemption here so realistically described is not a reference to the time when men are personally converted or justified. It is a reference to a transaction that occurred at the time of the death of Christ, by the blood of Christ, and on the cross of Christ. There is redemption or purchase on the cross, and it is a particular redemption. It is not a redemption of all men in general. It is a redemption of certain men in particular as the language makes clear: "*men* from every tribe and tongue and people and nation."

So realistic is the idea of redemption at the death of Christ and on the cross of Christ that the third aorist describes the blessing it bestows. Those so redeemed are constituted "a kingdom and priests to our God." No longer are those so purchased regarded as the slaves of sin but as a royal priesthood. As individuals are personally brought to Christ, they enjoy the status secured for the Church on the cross of Christ. This redemption is, however, not only particular; it is also effectual. The song ends with a future tense which predicts the glorious, future display of this status conferred by the blood of Christ and on the cross of Christ to the people of God: "They will reign on the earth." In the new age and on the new earth all those purchased at and by the death of Christ will reign with Him as a royal priesthood. Such a description of the redemption affected by the death of Christ requires a clear penal substitutionary view of the atonement and with it a particular redemption.[6]

"For the love of Christ controls us, having concluded this, that one died for all, therefore all died" (2 Cor 5:14). Here is a second text that illustrates the realism with which the New Testament presents the atone-

---

[6] The doctrine of general redemption seems to jeopardize the great Protestant doctrine of the finality or perfection of Christ's redemption. This finality is implied by the aorists of Rev 5:9–10. If Christ "made purification for sins and then sat down on the right hand of God" (Heb 1:3), if He "perfected forever those who are sanctified" (Heb 10:14 HCSB), and if He could say "it is finished" when He gave up His spirit (John 19:30), this certainly seems to ascribe an efficacy and virtue to Christ's atonement that it lacks in the view of general redemption. Nothing is finished or perfected or secured or guaranteed by the cross itself on the premises of a general redemption which only makes salvation possible and which only supplies a provisional salvation. See John Murray's chapter on "The Perfection of the Atonement" in *Redemption Accomplished*, 51–58.

ment as substitutionary curse-bearing.[7] The reference of the pronoun, "all," will, of course, attract attention in a discussion of the extent of the atonement. I regard it as designating all those in Christ who are part of a new creation (v. 18). This, however, is not the most significant thing about this text for the present debate.

The crucial assertion of this text is that there is an inseparable relation between the idea of substitution and the idea of representation. This is affirmed when Paul said that "one died for all, therefore all died." However, the logic behind Paul's assertion is that substitutionary death means representative death. One having died for all means that all died. In itself this assertion is significant enough. It means that if Christ died for someone, that person died on the cross. How then can they die again for their sins in the lake of fire by the second death? Substitution is here viewed in a highly realistic fashion.

> Therefore we have been buried with Him through baptism into death, so that as Christ was raised from the dead through the glory of the Father, so we too might walk in newness of life. For if we have become united with *Him* in the likeness of His death, certainly we shall also be *in the likeness* of His resurrection, knowing this, that our old self was crucified with *Him*, in order that our body of sin might be done away with, so that we would no longer be slaves to sin; for he who has died is freed from sin. Now if we have died with Christ, we believe that we shall also live with Him (Rom 6:4–8, emphasis added).

The implication of Christ's substitutionary death is even more compelling from the standpoint of particular redemption. Paul asserted in Rom 6:4–8 that union with Christ in His death inevitably and inseparably carries with it the idea of union with Christ in His resurrection.

The advocate of general redemption is, therefore, faced with an excruciating admission. Upon his view, every single man without exception both died in Christ and was raised with Christ in His resurrection to walk in newness of life. How can he affirm this and avoid the implication that all those for whom Christ died will be saved?[8]

---

[7] The KJV ("that if one died for all, then were all dead") obscures the meaning of the verse by its translation of the aorist verb *apethanon* as "were dead."

[8] Murray, *Redemption Accomplished*, 69–71, prosecutes this argument much more fully and ably than I have here. In a number of places in Paul's description of union with Christ, there is an intentional ambiguity in which he slips back and forth from union with Christ in His historical work to union with Christ in our personal salvation. Besides Rom 6:1–11, see Rom 5:1–11; Eph 2:1–10; Col 2:10–3:4. This intentional ambiguity is

The Argument's Soundness. Some have thought to answer this argument by saying they agree that Christ died substitutionarily and suffered the penalty of all men's sins. They add that men do not go to hell for sin or at least not for most sins but only because they reject Christ and commit the sin of unbelief. Christ did not, they say, die for the sin of unbelief. They conclude that the issue is not the sin question but the Son question. How is such an argument to be answered?

Three responses are adequate to answer such an argument. First, the Bible teaches that men do go to hell for more reasons than just their unbelief (Matt 16:27; Rom 2:5–16; Rev 20:12; 21:8). Second, this doctrine implies that anyone who has not heard the gospel and, thus, could not have committed the sin of unbelief, is saved. If this is true, then those who have never heard the gospel are saved, and the need for missions is at an end. The Bible, however, teaches that all those without faith in Christ are lost for their failure to obey the work of the law written in their hearts (Rom 2:12a,14–15). Third, if Christ did not die for the sin of unbelief, then no one who has heard the gospel can be saved because every Christian commits the sin of unbelief both before and after he is saved (Matt 17:17,20; 26:69–75).

The Argument's Significance. Before I move on to the other arguments for particular redemption, I want to consider the significance of this argument for the peculiarly Calvinistic view of the atonement. As Warfield asserted, the Reformed faith is simply biblical Christianity come into its own. Calvinism does not, and Calvinists should not, look at themselves as elite Christians holding exotic and superior views utterly unlike those of other Christians.[9] Calvinism is merely the outcome of common evangelical doctrines understood in a strictly and consistently biblical way. Particular redemption is simply the penal substitutionary view of the atonement taken seriously. It is the idea of "Christ alone" strictly understood. We do not invite our opponents to adopt exotic doctrines but only their own doctrines carried out with biblical consistency.

The Restricted Recipients of the Atonement

A number of the specific and explicit statements of the Bible regarding those for whom Christ died demand particular redemption. Those who

---

a manifestation of Paul's conviction that all those for whom Christ died will actually and vitally participate in the blessings He procured for them on the cross.

[9] I have found Warfield summarized in this way in several places but have been unable to track down these exact words. See, however, B. B. Warfield, *The Works of Benjamin B. Warfield* (Grand Rapids: Baker Book House, 1981), 5:355, where Warfield says, "In Calvinism, then, objectively speaking, theism comes to its rights; subjectively speaking, the religious relation attains its purity; soteriologically speaking, evangelical religion finds at length its full expression and secure stability."

hold to universal or general redemption customarily dismiss this line of evidence because they assume that their view is inclusive of the passages that teach that Christ died for the Church or for the elect. If Christ died for all men, they reason, then among these He certainly died for the elect. On general principles this seems to be a fairly superficial response to the evidence particular redemptionists bring forward in this regard. If Christ died equally for all men without exception, it is surprising that the Bible so often specifies a more limited group as the focus of Christ's death.

Several passages assert not merely that Christ died for a specific group of people but that, fairly interpreted, He died only for those people. Some of these passages deserve at least brief comment.

> All that the Father gives Me will come to Me, and the one who comes to Me I will certainly not cast out. For I have come down from heaven, not to do My own will, but the will of Him who sent Me. This is the will of Him who sent Me, that of all that He has given Me I lose nothing, but raise it up on the last day. For this is the will of My Father, that everyone who beholds the Son and believes in Him will have eternal life, and I Myself will raise him up on the last day (John 6:37–40).

John Murray commented on this passage, "Security inheres in Christ's redemptive accomplishment. And this means that, in respect of the persons contemplated, design and accomplishment and final realization have all the same extent."[10]

> I am the good shepherd, and I know My own and My own know Me, even as the Father knows Me and I know the Father; and I lay down My life for the sheep. . . . But you do not believe because you are not of My sheep (John 10:14–15,26).

When Jesus asserts that He lays down His life for the sheep, the term "sheep" is exclusive. Only believers given to Christ by the Father and kept by the Father for Christ are the sheep. Others are goats (see Matt 25:32–33). It is unnatural in the extreme to think that we may say in spite of such language that Christ lays down His life for the goats as well as for His sheep.

> Greater love has no one than this, that one lay down his life for his friends. You are My friends if you do what I command you (John 15:13–14).

---

[10] Murray, *Redemption Accomplished*, 64.

Here Jesus asserts that the focus of His laying down His life is His friends. Immediately upon affirming this, He limits the sphere of His friends to those who do as He commands. Such language cannot be reconciled with the idea that Christ also lays down His life for those who are not His friends.

> I ask on their behalf; I do not ask on behalf of the
> world, but of those whom You have given Me; for they
> are Yours (John 17:9).

The old argument frequently made by Calvinists for particular redemption from this passage still appears unassailable to me. Here Christ limits the sphere of His intercession to those given Him by the Father. This is clearly a reference to the elect. He so limits His intercession upon the eve of His atoning death. This demands the question: If He does not and will not intercede for those not given to Him by the Father, is it conceivable that He will then die for them for whom He will not pray? It is not.

> Husbands, love your wives, just as Christ also loved
> the Church and gave Himself up for her (Eph 5:25).

Christ is presented here as the model of the kind of exclusive love which husbands ought to have for their wives. It may be that in some relationships we are to exhibit a love which is also to be bestowed on others in general. This is emphatically not the kind of love Paul is here designating. Paul used Christ's love and atoning sacrifice for the Church as an illustration of the kind of exclusive love a husband is supposed to have for his wife. It is not possible, given the exclusive kind of love under discussion, to think that Christ sacrificed Himself for those who compose no part of His Church.

The Guaranteed Effects of the Atonement

The guaranteed effects of the atonement directly demand particular redemption. The Bible teaches that the atonement does more than merely make possible, or make provision for, the salvation of those for whom Christ died. It secures and guarantees salvation for them. Several texts are relevant to this truth. Philippians 1:29, for instance, teaches that we are given faith for Christ's sake: "For to you it has been granted [or "given" KJV, HCSB] for Christ's sake, not only to believe in Him, but also to suffer for His sake." Because Christ died for us, we are given the faith to believe in Him.

Romans 8:28–39, especially verse 32, is the classic statement of this truth. Romans 8:32 reads, "He who did not spare His own Son, but delivered Him over for us all, how will He not also with Him freely give us all things?" Paul argued here from the greater to the lesser. If God gave His Son to die for us, He will surely grant to us all lesser gifts connected with our salvation. The context determines what gifts Paul refers to, and the context is permeated with the gifts of God's sovereign grace that flow from God's electing and predestinating mercy. Hence, God will certainly give to all those for whom Christ died the effectual calling into Christ (vv. 28,30) and sovereign preservation in Christ (vv. 34–39). Thus, we have an explicit statement that all those for whom Christ died will be effectually called and preserved in Christ. The death of Christ guarantees the salvation of all those for whom He died. Therefore, His redemption is particular.

The Covenant Context of the Atonement

The context of the atonement demands particular redemption. The covenant is the context of Christ's work. Christ's blood is covenant blood. The covenant in view is explicitly and repeatedly identified as the New Covenant, which is one of the most frequently stated truths of the New Testament (Matt 26:28; Mark 14:24; Luke 22:20; 1 Cor 11:25; Eph 2:12–13; Heb 10:29; 13:20). Jesus' blood redeems and atones only in connection with this new covenant. Only by ratifying the new covenant and, thus, securing its saving benefits does Christ's death save. Hebrews 7:22 asserts, "So much the more also Jesus has become the guarantee of a better covenant." Hebrews 8:6 likewise affirms, "But now He has obtained a more excellent ministry, by as much as He is also the mediator of a better covenant, which has been enacted on better promises."

The Bible makes explicitly clear that all men are not included in this covenant. This covenant is made only with those in whose hearts the law is written, whose sins are remembered no more, and who are brought to know the Lord. Furthermore, the covenant is one which secures the salvation of those in it (Jer 31:31–34). If the entire context of the atonement is covenantal, then its extent must be as wide as, but only as wide as, the covenant. This consideration demands particular redemption.

The Problems with Particular Redemption Discussed

The difficulties raised against particular redemption do not undercut or even address all the clear biblical evidence for particular redemption. As long as that evidence is clear and unassailable, the doctrine stands. At best, then, these arguments are difficulties with particular redemption, rather than true objections to it.

The Universal Terms

The most common objection to particular redemption is derived from that class of passages which speak in universal terms of those for whom Christ died. Arminians and others who argue against particular redemption believe that such universal terms include each and every individual in the human race, but this is not necessarily the case.

First, universal terms are often restricted by their context in the Bible. For example, by the phrase "all the inhabited earth" in Luke 2:1, Luke referred only to the Roman world. When Matthew explained that "all Jerusalem" was troubled with Herod at the visit of the magi, he surely did not mean to include every person in the city (Matt 2:3; 3:5). And when Jesus told His disciples, "You will be hated by all because of My name" (Matt 10:22), He meant "all" kinds of people; otherwise 3,000 would not have been saved when Peter preached on the day of Pentecost (Acts 2:41; also see Matt 3:5; 4:23; 21:10; Mark 1:5; Luke 16:16; John 3:26; Acts 2:5; 1 Cor 15:22; Heb 2:9; 1 John 2:2 with 1 John 5:19).

Second, universal terms are often directed against Jewish exclusivism. The New Testament in its polemic against such exclusivism emphasizes that God's salvation has been extended to every nation and class. When the New Testament says, therefore, that Christ died for all the world, it frequently means Jew and Gentile alike. The terms "all men" and "world" are corporate terms (John 1:29; 6:33,51; Rom 11:11–15; 1 Tim 2:1–6).

Third, the universalism of the New Testament passages in question is not a provisional or potential universalism, as taught by Arminians, but a prophetic universalism. The world, they say, is provisionally redeemed, potentially saved by Christ's death. There is, however, a prophetic universalism in the Bible. The prophets predicted that the world would certainly be saved. This kind of biblical universalism deals in certainties not potentialities (Ps 22:27–29; 72:8–11,17–19; 86:9; Isa 2:2–4; 66:23–24; Jer 3:17; Joel 2:28; Zech 14:9; also John 12:32; Rom 5:18; 2 Cor 5:19; Rev 21:1,24). The New Testament passages that attribute a universal significance to the death of Christ may be (and must be) understood within the trajectory of this prophetic universalism. I may make my point this way. If the Bible says that Christ died for the world, then the world will be saved. A saved world will be the result of Christ's death. This does not require, however, that each and every individual member of the human race be saved. The question, we may say to our congregations, is not whether the world will be saved. Christ's death has secured that. The question is whether you will be part of it.

As an illustration, suppose a plague was sweeping the United States that killed everyone in every city to which it came. Suppose a medical researcher developed a cure just before it reached the city of Owensboro where I live. Swift action was able to distribute this cure to most of Owensboro. As a result only one-third of the city died from the plague. Despite the death of one-third of the inhabitants of Owensboro, would it not be true and proper to say that Owensboro had been saved by this researcher? Owensboro can properly be said to have been saved in spite of the fact that one-third of its people died. Even so the world can be said to be saved despite the death of many members of the human race. Both Owensboro and "the world" (as well as "all men") are corporate terms which do not necessarily connote the each and every type of universalism required by general redemption.

The Free Offer

Another objection raised against particular redemption is derived from the free offer of the gospel. The pressing question here is, How can we invite and call each and every man to be saved if Christ did not die for each and every man? This is a difficult question involving deep mysteries, but enough is clear to remove the immediate difficulty.

The problem is not to be solved by denying the free offer of the gospel to everyone who hears the gospel. The idea has been spread by some that particular redemption makes men deny the free offer. This is false. Most people who believe in particular redemption also believe in the free offer. I emphatically am one of them. God not only commands but also desires the salvation of everyone who hears the gospel, whether they are elect or not. This view is embedded in the Canons of Dort themselves (third and fourth heads, Article 8): "As many as are called by the gospel are unfeignedly called. For God has most earnestly and truly declared in His Word what is acceptable to Him, namely, that those who are called should come unto Him. He also seriously promises rest of soul and eternal life to all who come to Him and believe."

The solution to this difficulty is to be found in realizing that a common manner of preaching the gospel has no biblical warrant. The free offer of the gospel does not require us to tell men that Christ died for them. Yes, it is true that this is the way the gospel is commonly preached. It is so commonly preached in this fashion that it may seem incredible to think that this way of preaching is utterly without biblical precedent. The fact is, however, that the gospel does not present men with a theory about the extent of the atonement. It presents men with Christ Himself in His all-sufficient ability to save. Of course, if the free offer of the gospel meant telling unconverted sinners, "Christ died for you," then particular redemption would be inconsistent with the free offer. But nowhere in the Bible is the gospel proclaimed by telling unconverted sinners that Christ died for them. Never, for instance, do the apostles do this in the book

149

of Acts. The Church is told that Christ died for her but not the unsaved recipients of the gospel offer. The assurance that Christ died for me is never presented as the reason I should take Christ as my Savior. Instead, the assurance that Christ died for me is presented as the triumphant conviction of one who already possesses assurance of his salvation (Gal 2:20).[11]

The Apostasy Passages

The final class of passages which present a difficulty to particular redemption speak of apostasy from the Christian faith. They appear to teach that some for whom Christ died will perish. They present, as such, a puzzling difficulty for those who hold to particular redemption. Four passages are frequently mentioned:

> For if because of food your brother is hurt, you are no longer walking according to love. Do not destroy with your food him for whom Christ died (Rom 14:15).

> Then the weak person, the brother for whom Christ died, is ruined by your knowledge (1 Cor 8:11 HCSB).

> How much severer punishment do you think he will deserve who has trampled under foot the Son of God, and has regarded as unclean the blood of the covenant by which he was sanctified, and has insulted the Spirit of grace? (Heb 10:29).

> But false prophets also arose among the people, just as there will also be false teachers among you, who will secretly introduce destructive heresies, even denying the Master who bought them, bringing swift destruction upon themselves (2 Pet 2:1).

---

[11] Murray (Ibid., 65) responds to the objection that particular redemption undermines the free offer of the gospel by saying, "This is grave misunderstanding and misrepresentation. The truth really is that it is only on the basis of such a doctrine that we can have a full and free offer of Christ to lost men." Murray proceeds to argue that only particular redemption enables us to offer men what is actually offered in the gospel. I agree with Murray but also want to admit that there are mysteries involved in the relation of the free offer and particular redemption which I do not fully understand. The fact that I do not understand these mysteries is, however, no reason for me or anyone else to reject either side of this tension. There are also mysteries in the doctrine of the Trinity, for instance, but no evangelical thinks the doctrine of the Trinity should therefore be rejected.

The present polemic for particular redemption, it must be remembered, is obligated only to provide a plausible interpretation which fits with the clear biblical evidence for particular redemption. Such a plausible interpretation is available. Four general observations alleviate the difficulty presented by these passages.

First, all these passages are speaking exclusively of professing Christians. Whatever they may teach, then, they cannot teach universal redemption. Second, by limiting the death of Christ to professing Christians, these passages actually refute universal atonement. In 1 Cor 8:11, for example, the death of Christ is brought forward as a special motive for dealing kindly with brothers. What sense does this make if Christ died for everybody else too? According to Heb 10:29, the blood of Christ is trampled not by everybody but by one who was a professing Christian. It makes no sense to regard this trampling as an aggravation of a professing Christian's sin if Christ died for absolutely everyone.

Third, many opponents of particular redemption in our day believe in eternal security. For such opponents of particular redemption, these passages prove too much. If we interpret these passages as they do, they disprove not only particular redemption but also the preservation of saints. Hebrews 10:29 is speaking not only of one for whom Christ died but one who was sanctified. Second Peter 2:1 is speaking of one who was bought not only in the sense that Christ died for him, but also in the sense of conversion (2 Pet 2:1,17–22; Jude 4–5).

Fourth, and this is the solution to these difficult passages: those mentioned are described according to their external and visible profession and privileges, not according to inward and spiritual reality (Rom 14:15; 1 Cor 8:11). If these passages imply that a brother can perish, such a one is described only as to his visible profession. For a true brother cannot perish (Rom 14:4). Second Peter 2:1 speaks of one bought by the master bringing swift destruction upon himself. Those who are truly bought or redeemed, however, cannot perish (Rev 5:9; 14:3–4). According to inward reality, on the other hand, these false teachers are dogs or pigs (2 Pet 2:22) and predestined to be damned (2 Pet 2:3; Jude 4). Hebrews 10:29 speaks of one sanctified by the blood of Christ. Those who are truly sanctified, however, have been perfected forever through Christ's death (Heb 10:10,14) and enjoy the blessings of the new covenant (Heb 10:15–18). Those mentioned in Heb 10:29 are only sanctified, therefore, in terms of their external attachment to the covenant people for whom Christ died.

Admittedly, this solution raises questions of its own. Nevertheless, the Bible often uses the language of appearance and profession. Perhaps the clearest illustration of this is the one John Owen pointed out in his exposition of the apostasy passages. Second Chronicles 28:23 reads, "For he sacrificed to the gods of Damascus which had defeated him, and said, 'Because the gods of the kings of Aram helped them, I will sacrifice to them that they may help me.' But they became the downfall of him and all Israel."

It is not Ahaz but the Word of God itself and the human author of 2 Chronicles which refers to "the gods of Damascus which had defeated him." This is clearly a reference not to the truth of the matter but to what appeared to be the case and what Ahaz thought or professed to have been the case. Similarly, the apostasy passages speak in the language of appearance and profession—not the language of reality.

Conclusion

Whatever the reader may think of the explanations I have given in relation to the difficulties often raised concerning the doctrine of particular redemption, I urge him to remember that these difficulties do not form actual objections to the doctrine. They do not overturn or even address the pillars of particular redemption raised in the earlier part of this essay. Objections must be addressed, but just because they are treated last in order, they must not be allowed to obscure in the mind of the reader the solid evidence presented.

I am far from thinking that the opponents intend to minimize the glory of Christ in their teaching about the extent of His atonement. Nevertheless, I must conclude with my own testimony. It appears to me that particular redemption greatly glorifies Christ. That is why I love the doctrine of particular redemption. I love it because it teaches that Christ's death without addition or assistance secures the salvation of His people. I love it because it refuses to withdraw from the implications of a penal substitutionary view of the atonement. I love this doctrine because it means that my assurance of salvation is exclusively this—that Jesus died for me.

Particular redemption, therefore, gives rise to singing: "Dear dying Lamb, thy precious blood shall never lose its power till all the ransomed church of God be saved to sin no more."

A Southern Baptist Dialogue

Calvinism
Theological Stereotypes

Southern Baptist Non-Calvinists—
Who Are We Really?

Chuck Lawless
Dean, Billy Graham School of Missions,
Evangelism, and Church Growth
The Southern Baptist Theological Seminary
Louisville, Kentucky

Introduction

LIFE SEEMED SO LESS COMPLICATED when I was a young Southern Baptist pastor serving in Ohio and a seminary student being trained in Louisville, Kentucky. I knew my basic theology was right: God's inerrant Word, Jesus' virgin birth, substitutionary atonement, and victorious resurrection are essentials to our faith. I knew that we were all called to do the work of the Great Commission (Matt 28:18–20). *Calvinism* was a nasty word associated only with an unloving God and declining evangelism, though, of course, the words *eternal security* were fully acceptable.

Later I met two men—one an evangelist/pastor, the other a missionary—who were both self-identified, five-point Calvinists whose hearts beat with evangelism and whose church growth and missions methodologies were progressive. I would not fully accept the five-point Calvinism of these men, but they showed me an evangelistic Calvinism that challenged my paradigm. They broadened my perspective and gave me an appreciation for Calvinists committed to doing the work of the Great Commission—all of which makes my assigned task to discuss misconceptions about non-Calvinists in the Southern Baptist Convention that much more challenging.

As I work toward accomplishing this task, I begin with three preliminary but foundational remarks. First, defining *non-Calvinist* in Southern Baptist life is difficult indeed. LifeWay Research has shown that 85 percent of pastors interviewed indicated that they are not five-point Calvinists, but does that finding necessarily indicate that these men are not Calvinistic at some level?[1] If Steve Lemke is correct that most Baptists "really are between two- and three-point Calvinists," what exactly does it mean to be a non-Calvinist in our context?[2]

As I write today, I hardly write as a non-Calvinist if *non-Calvinist* means a complete rejection of the TULIP. I write rather as one who affirms without reservation the Abstract of Principles of Southern Seminary without adhering to all five points of Calvinism—a description that includes several of us who have written for this book.[3] Hence, according to the findings of LifeWay's study, I am aligned with, at least at some level, the vast majority of Southern Baptist pastors. I speak simply as one who does not identify himself as a five-point Calvinist and who, at times, has himself been mischaracterized because of this doctrinal position.

Second, I realize that any portrayal of theological stereotyping almost inevitably falls into extremes and caricatures. Just as some of the five-point Calvinists writing in this book argue that they are at times wrongly portrayed as hyper-Calvinists, I contend that some concerns raised about non-Calvinists are based on extreme examples on the other side. The extremes, though, are often loudest and easiest to spot and provide the most available source for good preaching fodder. We often turn to them in making our point and in so doing wrongly paint entire groups of people with the same biased brush. Hence, we develop stereotypes that are not helpful.

Third, I speak primarily as a single voice, though I have spoken with and worked with enough Baptists across the non-Calvinist/Calvinist spectrum that I feel comfortable speaking with the collective "we." I can only assume that there are exceptions to the general conclusions I reach, but such is the nature of all stereotypes.

With these preliminary remarks in mind, we proceed to four stereotypes about non-Calvinists that I believe we find today in Southern Baptist life.

Stereotype 1. Non-Calvinists are more concerned about numbers than theology. In a denomination that evaluates much by numbers (the number of new members in a church, the number of baptisms in a local body, the number of dollars given to the Cooperative Program, the number of churches planted, etc.), it would not take much to make this claim

---

[1] See Libby Lovelace, "10 Percent of SBC Pastors Call Themselves 5 Point Calvinists," www.bpnews.net/printerfriendly.asp?ID=23993.

[2] Steve Lemke, "The Future of Southern Baptists as Evangelicals," www.nobts.edu/Faculty/ItoR/LemkeSW/Personal/SBCfuture.pdf.

[3] The Abstract of Principles is one of the confessional statements of The Southern Baptist Theological Seminary in Louisville, Kentucky. For a copy of the statement, go to www.sbts.edu/About_Us/Beliefs/Abstract_of_Principles.aspx.

about our entire denomination—a denomination that Danny Akin has rightly recognized is still "theologically weak."[4] Couple that reality with the fact that some of the strongest critics of Calvinism have been mega-church pastors, and it is easy to see why this stereotype of numbers over theology might develop.[5]

So it is not surprising that one blogger wrote in critiquing the theology of certain megachurch pastors:

> There is a new hatred like never before for the TRUTH of these doctrines [the doctrines of grace]. I say, let them play their games and count their numbers. . . . Often the only reason these men get the platforms they do is because of the numbers they produce and not necessarily the quality of their biblical understanding and ability to teach sound doctrinal truth.[6]

To be fair, this blogger raises serious concerns that must be heard. In much of Southern Baptist life, the opportunities one has to speak on large platforms seem to be directly proportional to the size of one's church (and we too seldom question whether the majority of that growth has its source in conversions or transfers). In addition, in a denomination of more than 42,000 churches, some men *are* more concerned about numbers than about teaching sound doctrinal truth. The concerns of this blogger are thus duly noted.

That is not to say, however, that this stereotype fits all of us who are not five-point Calvinists. Many of us, led by men like Jerry Vines and the late Adrian Rogers—both who clearly do not fit in the Calvinist camp in the SBC—cast our votes at Southern Baptist Conventions in the late 1970s and the 1980s because we recognized that the core problem in the SBC was then a theological one. Calvinist and non-Calvinist alike understood with Dr. Vines that how the Baptist views his Bible does indeed matter.[7] Many of us remain concerned about theology, recognizing that no victory is secure unless we are ever diligent to guard the ground gained. Indeed, the rise of Calvinism in the SBC has challenged many to return to the Word to determine and solidify their own beliefs—a consequence that can only be viewed as positive.

---

[4] "Interview with Danny Akin," sbcoutpost.blogspot.com/2005/07/interviewwith-danny-akin.html.

[5] Among those who have publicly raised concerns about some component of Calvinism are Jerry Vines, Johnny Hunt, Jack Graham, and the late Adrian Rogers.

[6] Posting at elbourne.org/archives/2005/07/12/ johnny-hunt-on election/, 17 July 2005.

[7] At the 1988 SBC Pastor's Conference, Vines preached the message, "A Baptist and His Bible." This message has been considered by some a pivotal moment in the conservative resurgence of the SBC. See www.jerryvines.com/Detail.bok?no=55.

Intentionally teaching theology is the work of the church, and there the correction must start. That teaching begins with pastors who preach the Word and who pour themselves into the lives of young men who themselves will be leaders of the church. In that setting first, and then in our seminaries, the leaders of today and tomorrow must be warned that a church *can* still grow with a wrong theology, but those numbers gained will not reflect a New Testament church. Though not all of us would agree with John Calvin at every point, he was right that the Word of God is "purely preached and heard" where there is a true church.[8] That purely preached and heard Word is still worth our taking a stand, and it absolutely must be the text to guide church growth.

Many of us, however, are also genuinely concerned about numbers. Because God mandated that we make disciples (Matt 28:18–20), it seems logical at least to ask the question, "Is God *using* us to reach nonbelievers and make disciples?" Numbers are one means to answer this question. The numbers matter *not* because we want to build our kingdom or impress our denomination but because we genuinely long for God to use us in His work. The numbers, when properly understood and used, are but one tool for evaluating our ministry.

Will Metzger, who has strongly called for a God-centered evangelism, has reminded us that even while we must leave the results to God, we should be "building a holy dissatisfaction with non-results. We are not content with fishing yet never catching any fish (Luke 5:4–11) or having empty seats at God's kingdom banquet (Luke 14:15–24)."[9] When the numbers suggest that God is *not* using us to change lives, our asking "why not?" neither questions God's authority nor threatens His sovereignty.

In fact, someone had better ask "why not" in a denomination that is reaching no more nonbelievers today than we did in the 1950s.[10] Perhaps the question's answer will take us to "we are not preaching the Word as we claim," or "pastors are not evangelizing as they should," or any other obstacle to God's blessing our churches. But it is the numerical question that forces us to evaluate more deeply.

The Calvinist Charles Spurgeon perhaps best expresses this view. Even as he warned against the wrong use of numbers, he also said:

> I am not among those who decry statistics, nor do
> I consider that they are productive of all manner of
> evil; for they do much good if they are accurate, and

---

[8] John Calvin, *Calvin's Institutes*, ed. Donald K. Kim (Louisville: Westminster John Knox, 2001), 129 [4.1.9 in the *Institutes*].

[9] Will Metzger, *Tell the Truth: The Whole Gospel to the Whole Person by Whole People* (Downers Grove: IVP, 1984), 25.

[10] See "SBC in 'evangelistic crisis,' but would be worse off without resurgence, study says," www.bpnews.net/bpnews.asp?ID=20723, November 2007.

if men use them lawfully. It is a good thing for people to see the nakedness of the land through statistics of decrease, that they may be driven on their knees before the Lord to seek prosperity; and, on the other hand, it is by no means an evil thing for workers to be encouraged by having some account of results set before them. I should be very sorry if the practice of adding up, and deducting, and giving in the net result were to be abandoned, for it must be right to know our numerical condition. It has been noticed that those who object to the process are often brethren whose unsatisfactory reports should somewhat humiliate them: this is not always so, but it is suspiciously frequent. I heard of the report of a church, the other day, in which the minister, who was well known to have reduced his congregation to nothing, somewhat cleverly wrote, "Our church is looking up." When he was questioned with regard to this statement, he replied, "Everybody knows that the church is on its back, and it cannot do anything else but look up." When churches are looking up in that way, their pastors generally say that statistics are very delusive things, and that you cannot tabulate the work of the Spirit, and calculate the prosperity of a church by figures. The fact is, you *can* reckon very correctly if the figures are honest, and if all circumstances are taken into consideration if there is no increase, you may calculate with considerable accuracy that there is not much being done; and if there is a clear decrease among a growing population, you may reckon that the prayers of the people and the preaching of the minister are not of the most powerful kind.[11]

Are there men and churches in the SBC who ignore the importance of sound theology and allow numbers to drive their ministry? I wish that were not the case, but I am not naïve enough to think otherwise. We are absolutely right to be concerned when churches dilute the gospel message in the name of contemporary outreach. We are little different today than we were 30 years ago if the message we preach is not grounded in Scripture.

On the other hand, are we not right to be concerned that some Southern Baptists *never* ask the numerical questions, who rest on their theology

---

[11] Charles Spurgeon, *The Soul Winner* (Grand Rapids: Eerdmans, 1963), 17–18.

even as their churches reach no one for God's glory? Should we not also be concerned about churches that rejoice in their "growing deep" while ignoring the need to go out, who become more a classroom than a missionary church? I am, of course, implying that many of these churches are strongly Calvinistic churches. My sincere hope and prayer is that I have myself just drawn a caricature that men like those contributing to this book will prove wrong in their writings and in their ministries.

To summarize, please do not assume that all of us who ask numerical questions belong to the camp that emphasizes numbers over theology. Some of us are in fact concerned about both.

Stereotype 2. Non-Calvinists promote pragmatic church growth. The leaders of the Church Growth Movement, beginning with its founder Donald McGavran and his disciple C. Peter Wagner, have not been five-point Calvinists. Read works by church growth writers, and you will understand why so many question the pragmatism of the movement. While qualifying his comments to say that only men of God doing God's work in God's way reap God's blessings, Wagner nevertheless asserts, "Clearly, the chief criterion that determines which strategy we choose is whether it accomplishes the goal. . . . It would be irresponsible to invest time, energy and money in some process that would not achieve your objectives."[12] Wagner likewise quotes McGavran saying, "As to methods, we are fiercely pragmatic."[13] George Hunter, distinguished professor of evangelism and church growth at Asbury Theological Seminary, has even noted that John Wesley was a church growth strategist long before church growth was in vogue; Wesley was, in Hunter's words, "an unapologetic *pragmatist* in the choice and development of strategies, models, and methods."[14]

To be fair to Wagner, he calls his approach "consecrated pragmatism," but it is only a short drive from this position to "do whatever it takes" and "if it works, it must be God blessed." No wonder Calvinist John MacArthur describes a Sunday evening wrestling match between church employees as "not an obscure example" of churches entertaining rather than preaching and worshipping.[15] I am convinced that MacArthur sometimes employs extremes to set up a straw man argument, but you can easily see why he goes where he goes and is then so readily followed by his readers.

---

[12] C. Peter Wagner, *Strategies for Church Growth* (Ventura: Regal, 1989), 28.

[13] Idem, "Pragmatic Strategy for Tomorrow's Mission," in *God, Man and Church Growth*, ed. A. R. Tippett (Grand Rapid: Eerdmans, 1973), 147.

[14] George Hunter, "John Wesley as Church Growth Strategist," wesley.nnu.edu/wesleyan_theology/theojrnl/21–25/21–02.htm.

[15] John MacArthur, *Ashamed of the Gospel* (Wheaton: Crossway, 1993), 71.

My colleague Don Whitney, in telling the story of his own Baptist journey, recalled that he, too, found a disturbing "atheological bent among Baptists" and a "church growth pragmatism" prevalent where he pastored in Chicago.[16] A campus minister in my state likewise sees pragmatism rampant in the SBC, and he registered his concerns in the same blog where he noted an anti-Calvinist stance by a megachurch pastor who played a role in the SBC's conservative resurgence:

> At this point, "whatever works" is all the theology needed. Their theology is whatever builds bigger churches and more baptisms. In other words, they have become the servants of whatever theology justifies their methodologies of evangelism and church growth. To this date, that theology is best described as "Gone with the Wind."[17]

Describing the theology of the conservatives who led the resurgence as "Gone with the Wind" is seriously overstated, but the concern about pragmatism is a helpful reminder that we are *not* to be driven by the winds of culture. Nevertheless, not all non-five-point Calvinists succumb to the temptation of pragmatism. If pragmatism is deemed to be using *any* method necessary in order to increase our numbers—most especially anything that relegates the preaching of the Word to a backseat—we must not go there. I would, though, want to make three points here.

First, asking the question, "Is it working?" with regard to our ministries and the results our ministries produce is not fundamentally a wrong question. At its most basic level, this evaluative question may lead us to what we should have been doing in the first place. I am reminded of a church consultation that Dr. Rainer and I completed several years ago. We listened to the pastor (in a mainline church) express his concern that nothing he tried was working in reaching his community—and then we also heard his preaching. He was a good communicator except that he largely ignored the Bible. Our advice was simple: why not try preaching the Bible? Several months later he called to tell us, "You'll not believe how these people are responding to my preaching now!" Yes, we would, because we knew that he should have been expositing the Word in the first place. His ministry was stronger because he first asked, "Is it working?" (or more specifically, "Why is it not working?").

---

[16] Donald A. Whitney, "Why I Am a Baptist," in *Why I Am a Baptist*, ed. Tom Nettles and Russell D. Moore (Nashville: Broadman and Holman, 2001), 194.

[17] Michael Spencer, "Smelling Calvinism on My Breath: How the SBC Looks from under the Table," accessed at www.boarsheadtavern.com/archives/2005/10/11/20034054.html.

Second, as stated earlier, church growth numbers *are* one means of evaluating whether what we are doing is working. We *can* ask the question, "Is it working?" without ever assuming that we will drop the preaching of the gospel if it appears that preaching is not producing results. Our biblical commitment to preaching the Word must never allow us to drop this method, but it also does not preclude our evaluating methods in other areas.

Where we who study church growth numbers have been off target is in asking *only* the baptismal numbers. Not only is that problematic because our understanding and practice of baptism are often skewed, but it also ignores other numerical questions that should be asked. For example:

- How many believers daily practice the spiritual disciplines of Bible intake and prayer?
- How many Christian fathers are praying with their spouses and discipling their children?
- How many believers are intentionally developing relationships with nonbelievers, loving them and planning to share Christ with them?
- How many Christians are using their gifts through a local church?
- What percentage of our church members have served at least short-term on the mission field?

All these questions are important, and all demand a numerical response. Do not be afraid to ask the numerical questions, beginning with the baptismal numbers when properly understood and evaluated, but ask additional numbers as well. Use the numbers as one tool to evaluate whether we are reaching people and whether those reached are being rightly discipled.

Third, at a more advanced level, the "Is it working?" question sometimes forces us to ask missiological questions. We are sometimes so sensitized to the dangers of pragmatism, as we should be, that we confuse pragmatism with contextualization. Is it pragmatism to sing hymns and choruses in a more upbeat fashion so that we might lead to worship a generation that has seldom heard an organ played live? Is it necessarily pragmatism to use PowerPoint and a projection screen as supporting tools for a sermon outline in order to present the Word to a video-driven culture? Is it pragmatic to use handmade instruments and employ the native rhythmic movement of the Ghanaians in West African worship, knowing that nonbelieving Ghanaians are more likely to attend this service than the service baptized in Western methodologies? Some of these questions give rise to the debate about the regulative principle, but even that principle must be fleshed out in the context of differing cultures. We must begin to think missiologically, and the "Is it working?" question often takes us there.

Without specific regard to the regulation of worship, Charles Spurgeon is again insightful in his discussion regarding cultural adaptation in soul-winning:

> Mr. Hudson Taylor, a dear man of God, who has laboured much in Inland China, finds it helpful to dress as a Chinaman, and wear a pigtail. He always mingles with the people, and as far as possible lives as they do. This seems to me to be a truly wise policy. . . . If we can put ourselves on a level with those whose good we seek, we shall be more likely to effect our purpose than if we remain aliens and foreigners, and then talk of love and unity. To sink myself to save others is the idea of the apostle. . . . Come down to those who cannot come up to you. You cannot pull people out of the water without stooping down and getting hold of them. If you have to deal with bad characters, you must come down to them, not in their sin, but in their roughness and in their style of language, so as to get a hold of them. I pray God that we may learn the sacred art of soul-winning by adaptation.[18]

Is this pragmatism? Perhaps it is for some who believe that to change anything based on the recipient of the message—the audience, if you will—is to move in the wrong direction. For others of us, a concern for relevance and a commitment to contextualization should not be negatively equated with the unhealthy, gospel-diminishing pragmatism that marks some churches today. We long for biblical church growth, including increasing numbers of souls converted and discipled, and will strive toward that end without compromising the gospel message.

Stereotype 3. Non-Calvinists use faulty approaches to evangelism and are unconcerned about regenerate church membership. I heard this characterization from a student in my class who returned to me an uncompleted personal evangelism report form, stating, "I don't believe we're supposed to call people to respond to Christ," and "I can't believe you're actually requiring us to initiate some kind of evangelistic act with somebody." In addition to attitudes like this student's—who, by the way, did not pass that little exercise—I have heard about and often seen poor approaches to evangelism that should concern us all:

---

[18] Spurgeon, *Soul Winner*, 269–70.

- Gospel presentations that omit the necessity of repentance
- Tracts that speak of "receiving Jesus" but say nothing of believing and turning
- The implication that repeating somebody else's prayer is all that is required to become a believer
- The suggestion that "walking an aisle" is what it takes for God to accept you as His child
- Approaches that focus more on what we get in salvation than on the God who has given His Son for us
- The implication that following Christ is a one-time decision that need not affect the rest of your life

My own experience in first hearing the gospel marked the way that I would poorly do evangelism early in my Christian life. I first heard about Christ when God planted in my seventh-grade classroom a crazy, fanatical 12-year-old Pentecostal preacher whose goal that year was to win me to the Lord. His approach was simple: he met me at the classroom door each morning and told me, "Chuck, it's a good thing you lived through the night." He would then continue, "If you hadn't, you'd be in hell right now. *But* you can receive Jesus into your heart right now." His technique was suspect, but somewhere in the midst of that message God drove truth into my heart, and my life has never been the same. I thank God for that young man who did not always get it right in how he evangelized.

We could, I am certain, list other examples. The resurgence of Calvinism in the SBC has, in fact, helped many of us to reemphasize the importance of presenting the "whole gospel to the whole person," in Metzger's terms.[19] Mark Dever has also rightly noted, "The Christian call to evangelism is a call not simply to persuade people to make decisions but rather to proclaim to them the Good News of salvation in Christ, to call them to repentance, and to give God the glory for regeneration and conversion."[20] These reminders are not only helpful, but they are simply necessary in today's SBC.

Non-Calvinists would still want to be heard in at least four areas. First, please do not assume that our approach to evangelism is faulty if we sometimes use a tract in a one-time encounter. Surely the content of some tracts is faulty ("Will You Be a Clown for Jesus?" comes to mind), but poor content in one tract should not automatically rule out the overall methodology. The Graham School at Southern Seminary has produced a tract that keeps the emphasis where it ought to be—on God who is Creator and Redeemer—and calls nonbelievers to do what they ought

---

[19] Metzger, *Tell the Truth.*
[20] Mark Dever, *Nine Marks of a Healthy Church* (Wheaton: Crossway, 2004), 137.

to do—repent and believe. The "Experiencing God's GRACE" tract (GRACE being an acronym for God, Rebellion, Atonement, Conversion, and Eternal Life) calls for repentance and belief, followed by aligning oneself with a local church.[21] Because we know that this tract explains the gospel well and calls for the proper response to the gospel, we are unashamed to use it even in one-time encounters. The Word of God is powerful enough to change hearts the first time that truth is heard.

Second, please allow us to talk about "persuading" others to believe without assuming that we somehow turn anthropocentric and trump God's sovereignty when we work to convince. Clearly, changing the heart is the work of God (John 16:8; Eph 2:4–5), but still we must often work through proper apologetics and passionate reasoning to teach others the truth of the gospel. For me personally, that means working to convince a particular loved one that the Bible is indeed true and that logically there cannot be multiple ways to God when competing religions claim exclusive truth. Day in and day out, we want to be like Paul, persuading men and women to believe (2 Cor 5:11). So strong should be our desire that we do not give up easily, all the while knowing that God gives the increase (1 Cor 3:6). The desperate state of lost humanity demands nothing less.

Third, understand that many of us who still use a public invitation following the preaching of the Word are striving to do so with utmost integrity. We are aware of the dangers of the invitation system, and we do not necessarily disagree with Jim Elliff's assertion that "there is much potential harm, in our inviting them [that is, hearers of the gospel] to the front of the church and then assuring them that their short walk or tearful response proves their conversion."[22] At the same time, we contend that the problem is not in offering an opportunity for a public response to the Word; instead, the problem is (as Elliff recognizes) in assuring people that their public response is a guarantee of their salvation.

Yet is it not possible to welcome a public response while clearly teaching that the physical response is not the means by which one is saved? If the Word of the cross is the power of God unto salvation (1 Cor 1:18) and if following Jesus is ultimately a public endeavor, why not provide an opportunity for someone to respond immediately after hearing the preached Word? Proper understanding of, and teaching about, the invitation rests in the hands of the one who extends it. When done well, the invitation is simply an opportunity to express publicly one's faith in Jesus.

---

[21] For a downloadable copy, go to www.sbts.edu/pdf/GRACE.pdf.

[22] Jim Elliff, "Southern Baptists: An Unregenerate Denomination," www.founders.org/library/elliff1.html.

Fourth, please do not be gravely concerned if we still use the word *decision* and lead a repentant sinner to pray a prayer. We recognize major concerns with "deciding" to follow Christ, such as assuming that we can decide in our own power or that making an intellectual decision is all that is needed for salvation. Both errors, though, can be avoided by a proper presentation of the gospel and a right understanding of the response that the gospel demands.

Here Reformed theologian Wayne Grudem is most helpful to many of us. Not only does he call unredeemed sinners to "decide to depend on Jesus," but he also asserts that true saving faith "comes only when I make a decision of my will to depend on, or put my *trust* in, Christ as *my* savior." Of course, Grudem understands regeneration as producing saving faith, and he is thus unafraid to speak about making a decision for Christ.[23] The decisionism of today's SBC *is* problematic, but many of us remain unconvinced that dropping *decision* from our evangelistic vocabulary is a necessary response—understanding still that the decision is but a first step in one's walk with Christ.

Again Grudem addresses the prayer of repentant sinners in a way that we find beneficial:

> Finally, what shall we say about the common practice of asking people to *pray* to receive Christ as their personal Savior and Lord? Since personal faith in Christ must involve an actual decision of the will, it is often very helpful to *express* that decision in spoken words, and this could very naturally take the form of a prayer to Christ in which we tell him of our sorrow for sin, our commitment to forsake it, and our decision actually to put our trust in him. Such a spoken prayer does not in itself save us, but the attitude of the heart that it represents does constitute true conversion, and the decision to speak that prayer can often be the point at which a person truly comes to faith in Christ.[24]

I am aware that for some my admission of using tracts, giving an invitation, engaging in persuasion, calling for a decision, and asking repentant sinners to pray a prayer automatically places me in the camp of those who do faulty evangelism. In that sense I may have painted myself as the stereotype I am attempting to debunk. I can only trust, though, that the reader understands my commitment to a proper presentation of

---

[23] Wayne Grudem, *Systematic Theology* (Grand Rapids: Zondervan, 1994), 702–4. Italics in original.

[24] Ibid., 717.

the gospel that precedes conversion *and* to a right understanding of the church and its role following conversion—which then brings us to the discussion about regenerate church membership.

In 2006 and 2007, Tom Ascol presented to the Southern Baptist Convention resolutions on integrity in church membership.[25] Both remained with the resolutions committee, and the Convention twice voted down a motion to bring the resolution to the floor. Mark Dever responded to the Convention's vote, calling it a "serious mistake."[26] Denny Burk has noted, "Some people will be tempted simply to dismiss Ascol and Dever as cantankerous Calvinists and to give no real consideration to concerns that are connected to Calvinism."[27] Burk affirms Ascol's resolution and calls the issue a *Baptist* concern rather than a Calvinist one.[28] With that position I and others who would not square with Ascol and Dever on all five points of Calvinism concur.

To the surprise of many perhaps, Donald McGavran, the non-Calvinist founder of the Church Growth Movement, clearly tied together evangelism, disciple-making, and responsible church membership. Listen to these words penned in the late 1970s, and see if they do not speak to the SBC situation today:

> A decision is often the first step. However, we deceive ourselves if we believe that a person who has made a decision for Christ, who has prayed, "I accept Jesus Christ into my life," has truly become a disciple. We must make sure that he or she really follows Christ, really lives as a disciple. The goal is that day by day, hour by hour, minute by minute, one lives yielded to Christ as a responsible part of the Body. This is what it means to be a disciple. A *decision* suggests a brief moment of time; a *disciple* suggests a lifelong task. The word *decision* inadequately describes the lifelong commitment called for in Scripture. We do well to use the more biblical concept of disciple and to evaluate our effectiveness in that context.[29]

---

[25] See Tom Ascol, "2007 Resolution on Integrity in Church Membership," www.founders.org/blog/2007/05/2007-resolution-on-integrity-in-church.html.

[26] See Mark Dever, "Southern Baptist Mistake," blog.togetherforthegospel.org/2006/08/southern_baptis.html.

[27] Denny Burk, "Southern Baptist Mistake," www.dennyburk.com/?m=200608.

[28] Ibid.

[29] Donald A. McGavran and Winfield C. Arn, *Ten Steps for Church Growth* (San Francisco: Harper and Row, 1977), 52–53. Italics in original.

McGavran continued:

> Believers must become part of the church; *otherwise the reality of their belief is in question.* This high view of the church must be maintained. A low view of the church, held by secular relativists, is that belonging to the church is more or less a matter of choice. If you like it, you belong; if you don't, you don't. Church Growth Christians reject any such low view.[30]

Hear then the words of Kent Hunter, popularly known in church growth circles as "The Church Doctor":

> The Church Growth Movement is many things. But above all, it is an ecclesiology. . . . All of this means that church membership means something. It is not a fad. It is not just the fashionable thing to do. . . . Churches that get involved in church growth take on a new or renewed spirit of membership account-ability. Membership is not a theoretical response to the gospel. A disciple is a responsible member of the body of Christ. . . . It should not surprise any-one, therefore, that membership conservation and reclamation are important church growth tasks. If members are important to Christ, how can a church "file" people away in an "inactive file"? Like bodies in drawers at a spiritual morgue, many churches have piled and filed those they unaffectionately call "dead wood." A growing church must recognize that these important people are not dead wood but people for whom Jesus died. Furthermore, an inactive Christian, in the view of Christian discipleship, is an oxymo-ron—a set of words that contradict one another. Unwilling to allow such contradictions, many churches that want to grow begin to seek out those people on their inactive list. . . . They also want to be more accu-rate in their reporting methods. It is not uncommon, therefore, to see on a church report a membership figure much lower than previous years—because of a renewed commitment to seek out and care for each individual.[31]

---

[30] Ibid., 31. Emphasis mine.

[31] Kent Hunter, "Membership Integrity," in *Church Growth: State of the Art*, ed. C. Peter Wagner with Win Arn and Elmer Towns (Wheaton: Tyndale, 1986), 93–94.

I do not pretend that all church growth proponents today have maintained the high view of church membership voiced by early Church Growth Movement leaders. I *can* affirm that, as the dean of the Billy Graham School of Missions, Evangelism and Church Growth, I say a hearty amen to that understanding of church growth. Surely those who are Calvinists and those who are not can build unity across that bridge.

Stereotype 4. Non-Calvinists do not like Calvinists. The origin of this stereotype is not difficult to determine. Just read the blogs, where the keyboards have been churning out passionate arguments on both sides of this issue, and sometimes with less than charitable words. I do not speak here for all non-Calvinists, but I hope I speak for many when I state that it is not Calvinism per se that concerns us, and it is certainly not Calvinists. Our Baptist history would be filled with gaping holes if we removed the likes of James P. Boyce, William Carey, Andrew Fuller, and Charles Spurgeon.

What concerns us, rather, is:

- The strong five-pointer who has determined that we are less than gospel preachers because we do not accept all five points
- The Calvinist who spends more time trying to convince us of his truth than he does sharing Christ with his unbelieving neighbor
- The young student who in his zeal for Calvinistic truth attempts to change his church overnight and then pronounces the church "unregenerate" because the congregation does not follow his poor (that is, dumb) leadership
- The strongly Calvinistic pastor who has determined that he must reform his church before he can ever invite nonbelievers to attend, which means that he will never get around to evangelism
- The young zealot who somehow finds glee in God's condemnation of the wicked.

Are these stereotypes on the other side? Surely so, but as I stated early in this chapter, the extremes are usually the loudest and the easiest to spot. As a matter of fact, the loudest on both sides of this discussion will probably aim their arrows at anyone who attempts to build bridges to the other side. Still, though, we must present ourselves as Christians joining in the same battle to make a dent in the darkness of this world.

Conclusion

Do you remember my opening illustration about the two men, the evangelist-pastor and the missionary, who first showed me an evangelistic Calvinism? I still do not agree with them on all of the five points, but I am OK with that fact.

I have seen these men in action. I have watched the evangelist-pastor get almost out of control when his love for personal evangelism sweeps over him in the pulpit and in personal conversations. I have listened to him tell story after story of his striving to reach his neighbors for Christ. I have been with the missionary on the field when he works night and day to introduce Jesus to an unbelieving world. I have watched him weep over his longing to take the gospel to unreached people groups. I have had the privilege of seeing these brothers in Christ do the work of the Great Commission.

To these kinds of five-point Calvinists I will gladly build a bridge any day.

Southern Baptist Calvinism: Setting the Record Straight

Nathan A. Finn
Instructor of Church History
Southeastern Baptist Theological Seminary
Wake Forest, North Carolina

Introduction

SEVERAL YEARS AGO A COLLEGE SOPHOMORE and interim youth minister read two books wherein the authors argued for a Calvinistic understanding of salvation.[1] Perhaps like many Southern Baptists, what little this collegian knew about Calvinism was mostly incorrect, based on stereotypes rather than reality. In fact, he was so jaded toward Calvinism that he likely would not have purchased the books had he known the authors' convictions. The young man was unnerved when he found these books both compelling and winsome. He spent a few days studying Scripture and investigating Calvinism before finally concluding that he had become a Calvinist.[2]

While almost a decade later I remain a convinced Calvinist and a Southern Baptist, multitudes of Christians continue to be uncomfortable with the doctrines of grace, including some fellow Southern Baptists. While many believers have thoughtfully considered Calvinism and rejected it based on their understanding of Scripture, multitudes have written off Calvinistic theology as a result of misunderstandings of Calvinism or misinformation about Calvinists. This is not to imply that only non-Calvinists are guilty of misrepresentation; Southern Baptists

---

[1] The two books were J. I. Packer, *Knowing God* (Downers Grove, IL: InterVarsity, 1993), and John Piper, *Future Grace* (Eugene, OR: Multnomah, 1995).

[2] For the purposes of this chapter, the word *Calvinism* will be used for those who affirm all five of the classical points of Calvinism. *Non-Calvinist* will be used as a generic term for those who do not affirm all five points. This usage is consistent with the structure of the Building Bridges Conference, where an earlier version of this chapter was first presented. The five points of Calvinism are often referred to as the "doctrines of grace," a term I use several times in this chapter.

on both sides of the Calvinism aisle sometimes spread misinformation. But because non-Calvinists are in the majority in the SBC, their stereotypes are more widespread than those made by Calvinists.[3] Furthermore, because non-Calvinists often have larger platforms within the convention, their opinions—even when incorrect—tend to carry considerable weight. This leads to many Southern Baptists' being at best hesitant regarding the doctrines of grace at a time when Calvinism is becoming an increasingly popular view among younger Southern Baptists.[4]

This chapter assesses some of the most common mischaracterizations of Southern Baptist Calvinists. My goal is to correct some myths about SBC Calvinists and provide a more accurate picture of what Calvinistic Southern Baptists actually believe. With this in mind, a few words about methodology are in order. Because this chapter pertains to Calvinism in the SBC, I cite only Southern Baptist Calvinists. Though SBC Calvinists are in substantial agreement with Calvinists in other traditions concerning the doctrines of grace, I want to allow Calvinists in the convention to speak for themselves.[5] In an effort to be fair to non-Calvinists, this chapter only addresses stereotypes that can be documented. My engaging in hearsay will do nothing to further the conversation and build bridges among Southern Baptists. Because this chapter is devoted to common caricatures, the bulk of my interaction is with popular media, including sermons, denominational periodicals, Weblogs, and short books. As a final word, while numerous stereotypes of SBC Calvinism persist, for the sake of space, this chapter focuses on five pervasive myths that can be easily documented.[6]

---

[3] Libby Lovelace, "Is TULIP Blooming In The SBC? LifeWay Research Publishes Findings On Calvinism," available online at www.lifeway.com/lwc/article_main_page/0%2C1703%2CA%25253D163839%252526M%25253D200903%2C00.html?(accessed November 14, 2007).

[4] Possible reasons for Calvinism's growth among younger Southern Baptists are numerous. For scholarly proposals, see C. Douglas Weaver and Nathan A. Finn, "Youth for Calvin? Reformed Theology and Baptist Collegians," *BHH* (Spring 2004): 40–55, and Anthony Chute, "When We Talk about Calvinism, Let's Be Honest," unpublished paper delivered at the annual meeting of the Evangelical Theological Society (November 2007): 9–13. I have a copy of Chute's paper in my possession. For a recent popular discussion of Calvinism's surge among younger Southern Baptists and other evangelicals, see Collin Hansen, "Young, Restless, and Reformed," *Christianity Today* (September 2006), available online at www.christianitytoday.com/ct/2006/september/42.32.html (accessed November 14, 2007).

[5] While numerous historic Baptist figures were Calvinists, I mostly interact with contemporary Calvinistic Southern Baptists. This is in part because history is limited as an apologetic tool in this matter and in most matters. As Anthony Chute notes, "Southern Baptists have always had a wide variety of concerns and have selected their heroes accordingly." See Chute, "When We Talk About Calvinism, Let's Be Honest," 8.

[6] I am indebted to Timmy Brister, M.Div. student at The Southern Baptist Theological Seminary and proprietor of the Weblog "Provocations and Pantings" for providing me

Myths about Southern Baptist Calvinism

Four key assumptions guide this chapter. I assume that, as a general rule, Southern Baptist Calvinists and non-Calvinists agree on the basics of the gospel. All parties agree that Jesus Christ is the divine Son of God who was incarnate in the virgin Mary, lived a life of perfect obedience to God's law, provided a penal substitutionary atonement for sinners on the cross, and was resurrected after three days in the tomb, securing the justification of every person who repents of their sins and trusts Christ as Lord and Savior. My second assumption trusts that most of the mischaracterizations of Southern Baptist Calvinism are based on misunderstanding or confusion. While this assumption may offend some non-Calvinists, this is certainly not my intention. Simply put, to presuppose many critics of SBC Calvinism are misinformed or confused is better than the alternative, which would be to assume that some Southern Baptists are deliberately misrepresenting others with whom they disagree. I sincerely hope such a sinful approach does not characterize the majority of those who make incorrect statements about Calvinism or vice versa.

I assume that most interested Southern Baptists desire to understand Calvinism even if they reject its conclusions. Undoubtedly many Southern Baptists remain uninterested in the topic, but those individuals who do care about this discussion want to know the facts. When we have accurate information, we are better able to make informed decisions. Finally I assume that the best way to move the conversation forward in a manner beneficial to the entire convention is for all Southern Baptists to represent accurately the beliefs of those with whom they differ. As we do so, we may discover we have more in common than is sometimes apparent. We must understand each other if we are to cooperate as a convention to proclaim the gospel to America and the ends of the earth. The following myths are examined in this spirit of cooperation.

Myth 1. Calvinism Is a Threat to Evangelism

We Southern Baptists pride ourselves on being an evangelistic denomination. The dual emphases of evangelism and missions have been at the heart of the SBC since its founding in 1845 when two of the convention's first acts were the formation of the Foreign and Domestic Mission Boards.[7] Since Arthur Flake's pioneering work during the second quarter of the twentieth century, many Southern Baptist churches have made

---

with a copy of his nearly exhaustive list of publicly available information about Southern Baptist Calvinism over the past quarter century. Brister's Weblog can be accessed at timmybrister.com (accessed November 9, 2007).

[7] *Southern Baptist Convention Annual*, 1845, 14.

evangelism a central component of their Sunday school ministries.[8] Denominational agencies have published numerous curricula dedicated to equipping churches and individuals to share their faith effectively with non-Christians.[9] In recent years denominational leaders like Bobby Welch, Thom Rainer, and Chuck Lawless have called on Southern Baptists to rekindle our zeal for sharing the gospel with all people in the hopes that we can reach more unbelievers and baptize multitudes of new converts.[10] As a rule, Southern Baptists eschew any theology or practice that seems to stifle zeal for the Great Commission.[11] Unfortunately, many Southern Baptists perceive Calvinism to be just such a theology.

Beginning in the mid-1990s, several Baptist state papers claimed that Calvinism is a threat to evangelism. This was largely in response to the 1993 election of R. Albert Mohler Jr. as president of The Southern Baptist Theological Seminary. For example, in an article published in the Texas *Baptist Standard*, Robert Sloan is quoted as claiming that "[Calvinism] is a dagger to the heart of evangelism. The simple historical fact is that it is a deterrent to evangelism."[12] Frank Stagg authored an article for Mississippi's *The Baptist Record* wherein he claims that the type of Calvinism advocated in Southern Seminary's Abstract of Principles "makes missions and evangelism a mere formality, with 'salvation' and

---

[8] See Arthur Flake, *Building a Standard Sunday School* (Nashville: Baptist Sunday School Board, 1934). For a recent argument for adopting Flake's basic approach, see Kenneth S. Hemphill, *Revitalizing the Sunday Morning Dinosaur: A Sunday School Growth Strategy for the 21st Century* (Nashville: Broadman & Holman, 1996).

[9] Some recent examples include Continuous Witnessing Training (CWT), FAITH, and *Share Jesus without Fear*, published by LifeWay Christian Resources, and The NET, produced by the NAMB.

[10] See Norm Miller, "SBC President Bobby Welch to Launch Bus Tour in August," Baptist Press (June 16, 2004), available online at www.bpnews.net/bpnews.asp?id=18492 (accessed November 16, 2007); Thom S. Rainer, "A Resurgence Not Yet Realized: Evangelistic Effectiveness in the Southern Baptist Convention Since 1979," *SBJT* 9, no. 1 (Spring 2005): 54–69; Chuck Lawless, "Why I Love Southern Baptists . . . and Why I Am Concerned," Baptist Press (October 23, 2007), available online at www.bpnews.net/BPFirstPerson.asp?ID=26680 (accessed November 16, 2007).

[11] As Southeastern Baptist Theological Seminary president Danny Akin notes, "Any theology that does not result in a 'hot heart' for lost souls is a theology not worth having." See Daniel L. Akin, "Article V: God's Purpose of Grace," in *Baptist Faith and Message 2000: Critical Issues in America's Largest Protestant Denomination*, ed. Douglas K. Blount and Joseph D. Wooddell (Lanham, MD: Rowman & Littlefield, 2007), 49.

[12] Mark Wingfield, "Who Has a Chance to Get to Heaven: Resurgent Calvinism Spawns New Controversy," *Baptist Standard* (December 7, 1994): 16. Jesse Fletcher and Leon McBeth, who were also cited in the article, argue that Southern Baptists are at their best when they balance the views of Calvinism and Arminianism. Nelson Price echoes Sloan's "dagger" quote in a 2006 article in Georgia's *Christian Index*. See Nelson Price, "Evangelical Calvinism Is an Oxymoron," *Christian Index* (November 23, 2006), available online at http://www.christianindex.org/2780.article (accessed November 14, 2007).

'reprobation' settled before the creation." Furthermore, Stagg argued that Southern Seminary founder James P. Boyce's commitment to missions proves that Boyce held to a "modified" Calvinism, a "hybrid" of Calvinism and Arminianism.[13] A 1997 editorial in Kentucky's *Western Recorder* concedes that SBC Calvinists are missions minded but worries that future Southern Baptists will possess less missionary fervor because "[Calvinist] theology doesn't breed a natural zeal for missions."[14] This particular editorial, and the responses it generated, prompted *Christianity Today* to weigh in on the Calvinism debate in the SBC.[15]

Longtime Southwestern Baptist Theological Seminary church historian William Estep penned a widely read article for the *Baptist Standard* that was arguably the most controversial anti-Calvinism article of the 1990s. Estep claimed that historic Calvinism, when logically followed, is antithetical to missions, arguing, "The Great Commission is meaningless if every person is programmed for salvation or damnation, for evangelism and missionary effort are exercises in futility." Estep warned Southern Baptists to avoid Calvinism because the issue will further divide an already divided denomination.[16] Estep's article provoked a flood of letters to the *Baptist Standard*, many of which were reprinted in subsequent issues of the periodical.[17] In addition, the Summer 1997 issue of *FJ* featured several responses to Estep, including articles by Albert Mohler, Tom Ascol, and Roger Nicole.[18]

This myth continues to be promulgated into the twenty-first century. In a 2000 article in the *Baptist Standard*, evangelist Freddie Gage is quoted as claiming, "There is not a nickel's worth of difference between liberalism, five-point Calvinism [sic] and dead orthodoxy. They are all

---

[13] Frank Stagg, "As the Twig is Bent . . . Theological Institutions and the J. P. Boyce Legacy," *The Baptist Record* (January 5, 1995): 6. The Abstract of Principles is also the foundational confessional document of Southeastern Baptist Theological Seminary.

[14] See Mark Wingfield, "Will Kentucky Churches Buy Calvinism?" *Western Recorder* (September 9, 1997), 5.

[15] Keith Hinson, "Calvinism Resurging among SBC's Young Elites," *Christianity Today* (October 6, 1997), available online at ctlibrary.com/1316 (accessed November 14, 2007). For reactions to Wingfield's original editorial, see Art Toalston, "Editor's Critique of Calvinism Prompts Challenges in Return," Baptist Press (September 19, 1997), available online at www.bpnews.net/bpnews.asp?id=4046 (accessed November 16, 2007); and Tom Ascol, "Doctrinal Integrity Restored at Southern Seminary" in *Western Recorder* (September 23, 1997): 6.

[16] William R. Estep, "Doctrines Lead to 'Dunghill,' Prof Warns," *Baptist Standard* (March 26, 1997): 12.

[17] See "Readers Respond to Story on Calvinism," *Baptist Standard* (April 9, 1997): 4, and "Estep and Calvinism: Against and For," *Baptist Standard* (April 16, 1997): 4.

[18] The entire issue, including a reprint of Estep's original article, is available at www.founders.org/FJ29/article1.html (accessed November 12, 2007).

enemies of soul-winning."[19] That same year current SBC President Frank Page wrote *The Trouble with the Tulip*, wherein he claims that "if one studies the pages of history, one will see that Calvinistic theology (Five Point) has encouraged a slackening of the aggressive evangelistic and missionary heartbeat of the church."[20] In a 2006 editorial in Tennessee's *Baptist and Reflector*, Lonnie Wilkey accused SBC Calvinists of not sharing Jesus' sense of urgency for the lost. He also fears they will cease witnessing, giving to the Cooperative Program, or praying for unbelievers. But in an effort to be "fair," Wilkey admitted that "some" convention Calvinists believe in sharing the gospel with non-Christians.[21] In an article on his ministry's Web site, Nelson Price argues that "Calvinism offers no incentive to go on mission trips, witness to the lost, visit for the church, or appeal for souls to be saved. Without such churches dwindle [*sic*]."[22]

In April 2005, New Orleans Baptist Theological Seminary Provost Steve Lemke delivered a paper at Mid-America Baptist Theological Seminary titled "The Future of Southern Baptists as Evangelicals." Lemke devoted several pages to addressing the potential threat Calvinism poses to Southern Baptist evangelism. The heart of Lemke's critique is a statistical analysis of the baptismal data of 233 churches that claim to be friendly to Founders Ministries. Because these "Founders friendly" churches averaged fewer baptisms and experienced a lower baptismal ration than the "average" Southern Baptist congregation, Lemke concluded that Calvinistic congregations are less evangelistic than other SBC churches.[23] Former SBC President Jerry Vines summarized how many non-Calvinists feel about this issue in a sermon preached at the First Baptist Church of Woodstock in October 2006. Vines flatly contended that if a Calvinist is a soul winner, it is in spite of his theology.[24]

---

[19] Mark Wingfield, "Gage: Baptist Churches Not Reaching 'Pagan' Culture," *Baptist Standard* (April 24, 2000): 10.

[20] Frank Page, *The Trouble with the Tulip: A Closer Examination of the Five Points of Calvinism* (Canton, GA: Riverstone Publishing, 2000), 75.

[21] Lonnie Wilkey, "Calvinists Have No Sense of Urgency—Jesus Did," *Baptist and Reflector* (September 27, 2006): 5.

[22] Nelson Price, "Calvinism," available online at www.nelsonprice.com/index.php/?p=210 (accessed November 15, 2007).

[23] Steve Lemke, "The Future of Southern Baptists as Evangelicals," 16–17. A manuscript of Lemke's address is available at www.nobts.edu/Faculty/ItoR/LemkeSW/Personal/SBCfuture.pdf (accessed November 13, 2007).

[24] The audio version of the sermon is no longer available at First Baptist Woodstock's Web site. A DVD of the sermon can be purchased from Jerry Vines Ministries, available online at www.jerryvines.com/Detail.bok?no=73 (accessed November 14, 2007). This particular sermon is especially important because Florida Baptist Convention executive director John Sullivan ordered a copy mailed to every Baptist pastor in the state. See See Tom Ascol's blog post "Florida Baptist Pastors Sent Anti-Calvinist Propaganda,"

While Southern Baptist Calvinists are not as evangelistic as they should be—which makes them like most Southern Baptists—to claim that SBC Calvinists are not committed to evangelism is incorrect. *Founders Journal* has published numerous articles advocating evangelism, and at times entire issues of the periodical have been devoted to Calvinism's effect on evangelism and/or missions.[25] In the Summer 2001 issue of *FJ*, Tom Ascol authored a lengthy article in response to the charge that Calvinism threatens evangelism. Ascol stated unequivocally that "we should not tolerate any teaching which cuts the nerve of biblical evangelism. The doctrines of grace, rightly understood and applied, have never done that."[26] In a 2003 article, Ascol argued that the work of theological reform and the task of global mission go hand in hand, and Calvinism actually encourages missionary activity.[27]

Southern Baptist Calvinists have argued for their commitment to evangelism in other venues besides *FJ*. Calvinists in the SBC serve as pastors of large churches, work as full-time evangelists, teach evangelism and missions in Southern Baptist seminaries, and author books on evangelism. One of Albert Mohler's first acts as president of Southern Seminary was to establish the Billy Graham School for Missions, Evangelism, and Church Growth in 1994. Mark Dever, pastor of Capitol Hill Baptist Church in Washington DC, has recently written a book on evangelism.[28] The late Ernest Reisinger, who played a key role in establishing Founders Ministries, sums up how many convention Calvinists feel about evangelism when he contends that "Calvinism may kill man-centered evangelism, but true, biblical Calvinism gives evangelism its only proper doctrinal foundation. Furthermore, it guarantees evangelism's success. God saves sinners—that is Calvinism. He does not merely make salvation possible, but actually saves by plan and power."[29] Southern Baptist Calvinists have consistently gone "on record" to affirm their commitment to evangelism and missions.

---

available online at www.founders.org/blog/2007/06/florida-pastors-sent-anti-calvinist.html (accessed November 14, 2007).

[25] *FJ* 5 (Summer 1991): *FJ* 37 (Summer 1999): available online at www.founders.org/FJ37/contents.html; available online at www.founders.org/FJ05/contents.html; *FJ* 33 (Summer 1998): available online at www.founders.org/FJ33/contents.html.

[26] Tom Ascol, "Calvinism, Evangelism, and Founders Ministries," *FJ* 45 (Summer 2001): available online at www.founders.org/FJ45/editorial.html (accessed November 14, 2007).

[27] Tom Ascol, "Reformation and Missions," *FJ* 52 (Spring 2003): available at www.founders.org/FJ52/editorial.html (accessed November 14, 2007).

[28] Mark Dever, *The Gospel and Personal Evangelism* (Wheaton: Crossway, 2007).

[29] Ernest Reisinger, "What Should We Think of Evangelism and Calvinism?" *FJ* 19/20 (Winter/Spring 1995): available online at www.founders.org/FJ19/article5.html (accessed November 14, 2007).

Before proceeding, a word is in order about whether statistical studies like the one Steve Lemke conducted prove anything about evangelism in Calvinistic churches. First, let me say that I share Lemke's concern that many Southern Baptist churches show little passion for evangelism. Churches on both sides of the Calvinism issue must be committed to sharing aggressively the gospel with non-Christians. Nevertheless, at least two major problems with Lemke's methodology remain. First, the study was limited to those churches that choose to align publicly with Founders Ministries, a group with which many SBC Calvinists are not affiliated. Second, Lemke did not survey any churches to inquire about their actual evangelistic activities but instead merely conjectured about evangelism practices based on baptismal statistics. All Lemke's study proves is that Founders-affiliated churches *baptize* fewer people than the "average" SBC church (whatever that means). The baptismal statistics say relatively little about the evangelistic commitment of these Founders-friendly churches and communicates nothing about Calvinistic churches not publicly connected to Founders.

Myth 2. Calvinists Are Against Invitations

A second myth, related to the above misconception, claims that Southern Baptist Calvinists are opposed to invitations. This myth is at least in part the result of semantics; Baptists define the word *invitation* in different ways. By *invitation*, many non-Calvinists mean the common practice of calling for public responses at the end of a corporate worship service or evangelistic event.[30] Many SBC Calvinists prefer to call this practice an "altar call" to distinguish this particular form of invitation from other means of inviting non-Christians to faith in Christ.[31] For many non-Calvinists, a rejection of this type of invitation is considered proof that Calvinists are not committed to urging unbelievers to repent of their sins and trust Christ. For example, in an editorial in the *Baptist Standard*, Presnall Wood argued that James P. Boyce was less evangelistic than his colleague John A. Broadus because the former did not extend an invitation at the end of his sermons.[32] In his aforementioned editorial Lonnie Wilkey claimed that he has "heard of churches that give no invitation

---

[30] For this use of *invitation* and an argument for the practice, see Charles S. Kelley Jr., *How Did They Do It? The Story of Southern Baptist Evangelism* (New Orleans: Insight Press, 1993), 62–69.

[31] For example, see Allen Harrison, "I Thank God for the Call to Preach," *FJ* (Winter 2003): available online at www.founders.org/FJ51/article1.html (accessed November 21, 2007).

[32] Presnall Wood, "Nothing Wrong with 'Whosoever Will,'" *Baptist Standard* (August 16, 1995): 6.

because they believe there is no point because God has decided who will be saved."[33]

Some scholars express concern that some Calvinists reject altar calls. In 1999, while speaking at the Arkansas Baptist Convention's Pastor's Conference, then Southeastern Baptist Theological Seminary President Paige Patterson raised this issue. He noted that "any person who holds to five-point Calvinism will never be in any danger in this convention as long as he does not allow it to lead him to unscriptural conclusions—such as we ought not to give invitations and things like that. When he gets to that point, either implicitly or explicitly, it has now become a hindrance to evangelism and missions."[34] Steve Lemke chastised Midwestern Baptist Theological Seminary for even raising the question about the appropriateness of public invitations in one of its official publications.[35] In a post on his personal Weblog, Liberty Theological Seminary President Ergun Caner claims that there is room in the SBC for "four-point" Calvinists "as long as [Calvinism] does not interfere with the biblical imperative of personal soul winning and *corporate invitations*."[36]

Perhaps it would be helpful to discuss why some Southern Baptist Calvinists are uncomfortable with some forms of public invitations. Some Calvinists fear it is too easy for individuals and churches to confuse responding to an altar call with actual conversion. Historian Bill Leonard argued that the invitation system has transformed the physical manifestation of the conversion experience—typically embodied in walking a church aisle—into a semi-sacramental practice in many SBC churches.[37] This concern that public invitations often devolve into a "practical sacramentalism" leads Jim Elliff, director of Christian Communicator's Worldwide, to encourage churches seriously to reconsider the practice.[38]

---

[33] Wilkey, "Calvinists Have No Sense of Urgency—Jesus Did," 5.

[34] Tammi Reed Ledbetter, "Patterson, Pressler Caution Baptists against Detractions from Evangelism," Baptist Press (November 15, 1999), available online at www.bpnews.net/bpnews.asp?id=2699 (accessed November 19, 2007). In response to a question from the audience about whether Calvinism was compatible with the BFM 2000, Patterson noted, "There's plenty of room under the umbrella for anyone who is anything from a one- to five-point Calvinist."

[35] Lemke, "The Future of Southern Baptists as Evangelicals," 15.

[36] Ergun Caner, "Before You Send Your Letters of Outrage," available online at www.erguncaner.com/site/?p=145 (accessed November 14, 2007). The emphasis in the quote is mine.

[37] Bill J. Leonard, "Southern Baptists and Conversion: An Evangelical Sacramentalism," in *Ties that Bind: Life Together in the Baptist Vision*, ed. Gary A. Furr and Curtis W. Freeman (Macon: Smyth & Helwys, 1994), 9–22, especially 16–17.

[38] Jim Elliff, "Closing with Christ," available online at www.ccwonline.org/closing.html (accessed November 14, 2007).

Tom Nettles contends that the emphasis on public invitations is a result of pragmatism, rooted in the so-called "new measures" of the Second Great Awakening. He argues that the practice represents a departure from the earlier understanding that the entire sermon was intended to press the claims of Christ on lost sinners.[39] He further claims that the invitation system, along with other pragmatically driven approaches to evangelism, is largely responsible for the great disparity between SBC baptismal numbers and actual church membership and attendance.[40] Paul Alexander, writing for IX Marks Ministries, gives nine reasons many Calvinists are uncomfortable with "altar call evangelism." Many of his reasons are concerned with avoiding the appearance that the invitation is a saving event or judging the merits of a worship service based on the number of people who come forward at its conclusion.[41]

Calvinist opinion on the altar call is not uniform. Not all Southern Baptist Calvinists are opposed to extending public invitations when they preach.[42] Some non-Calvinists in the SBC also do not extend public invitations in worship services.[43] Furthermore, while some Southern Baptist Calvinists express reservations about corporate invitations, this should not be equated with a denial that pastors should preach in such a way as to encourage sinners to repent of their sins and trust Christ. Indeed, SBC Calvinists defend evangelistic preaching.[44] Many Calvinists are hesitant about a particular *method* that is popular among many Southern Baptists; rejection of the method should not be confused with a rejection of direct, passionate evangelistic preaching. Disagreement over methods should not be a point of division in the Southern Baptist Convention.[45] What matters is that all of us, Calvinist and non-Calvinist alike, plead with sinners to repent of their sins and trust Christ as Lord and Savior, regardless of our respective convictions on altar calls.

---

[39] Tom Nettles, *Ready for Reformation? Bringing Authentic Reform to Southern Baptist Churches* (Nashville: Broadman & Holman, 2003), 53–60.

[40] Ibid., 60–63.

[41] Paul Alexander, "Altar Call Evangelism," available at www.9marks.org/CC/article/0,,PTID 314526 |CHID598016|CIID1804792,00.html (accessed November 14, 2007).

[42] Mark Coppenger, "*Kairos* and the 'Altar Call,'" *Heartland* (Summer 1999): 8–9.

[43] For example, see Rick Warren, *The Purpose-Driven Church: Growing without Compromising Your Method & Mission* (Grand Rapids: Zondervan, 1995), 302–6.

[44] For example, see Mark Dever, "Evangelistic Expository Preaching," *Give Praise to God: A Vision for Reforming Worship*, ed. Philip Graham Ryken et al. (Phillipsburg, NJ: P&R, 2003), 122–39; and Mark Coppenger, "The Ascent of Lost Man in Southern Baptist Preaching," *FJ* 25 (Summer 1996): available online at www.founders.org/FJ25/article1.html (accessed November 14, 2007).

[45] This is a point that non-Calvinist Danny Akin makes in a recent article. See Daniel L. Akin, "Divine Sovereignty and Human Responsibility: How Should Southern Baptists Respond to the Issue of Calvinism?" *SBC LIFE* (April 2005): available online at www.sbclife.com/Articles/2006/04/sla7.asp (accessed November 14, 2007).

Myth 3. Five-Point Calvinism Is Hyper-Calvinism

A third myth, often coupled with the above, claims that Calvinism is more or less equivalent to hyper-Calvinism. The latter is an aberrant version of Calvinism embracing a number of doctrines that stifle evangelism. According to Timothy George, hyper-Calvinists depart from Calvinism in five areas. (1) Hyper-Calvinists affirm eternal justification, which downplays the need for individual conversion. (2) They deny the free moral agency and responsibility for unbelievers to repent and believe, which turns divine providence into fatalism. (3) They restrict the gospel invitation to the elect, which denies the free offer of the gospel to all people. (4) Hyper-Calvinists teach that non-Christians must be convinced they are among the elect before they have a "warrant" to believe, which undermines salvation by grace through faith. (5) Most importantly, hyper-Calvinists deny the universal love of God to all people, arguing that God loves only the elect and hates the non-elect.[46] Most English Calvinistic Baptists rejected these convictions in the late 1700s, largely because of the leadership of Calvinists like Andrew Fuller, William Carey, and Robert Hall Sr.[47] While many Primitive Baptists embraced hyper-Calvinism in the mid-nineteenth century, the majority of Baptists in the South—including the Calvinists who formed the Southern Baptist Convention in 1845—rejected the system.[48]

Unfortunately, many Southern Baptist non-Calvinists misunderstand hyper-Calvinism. In March 2006, Southwestern Seminary professor Malcolm Yarnell preached a sermon in several venues titled "The Heart of a Baptist." In the sermon Yarnell warned that "hyper-Calvinism is becoming a real problem in the Southern Baptist Convention." He then tied hyper-Calvinism with "a refusal to give an invitation," an issue

---

[46] Timothy George, *Amazing Grace: God's Initiative—Our Response* (Nashville: LifeWay, 2000), 90–91. See also Thomas J. Nettles, *By His Grace and for His Glory: A Historical, Theological, and Practical Study of the Doctrines of Grace in Baptist Life* (Grand Rapids: Baker, 1986; reprint, Lake Charles, LA: Cor Meum Tibi, 2002), 385–91.

[47] See Peter J. Morden, *Offering Christ to the World: Andrew Fuller (1754–1815) and the Revival of Eighteenth-Century Particular Baptist Life*, Studies in Baptist History and Thought (Carlisle, Cumbria, UK, and Waynesboro, GA: Paternoster, 2003); Timothy George, *Faithful Witness: The Life and Mission of William Carey* (Birmingham: New Hope, 1991); Nathan A. Finn, "Robert Hall's Contributions to Evangelical Renewal in the Northamptonshire Baptist Association," *MJT* 6.1 (Fall 2007): 19–34.

[48] See Anthony L. Chute, *A Piety above the Common Standard: Jesse Mercer and the Defense of Evangelistic Calvinism* (Macon: Mercer University Press, 2004), 61–160; and Nettles, *By His Grace and for His Glory*, 161–86; Timothy George, "Southern Baptist Theology: Whence and Whither?" *FJ* 19/20 (Winter/Spring 1995): available online at www.founders.org/FJ19/article2.html (accessed November 14, 2007); Tom J. Nettles, "The Rise and Decline of Calvinism in the Southern Baptist Convention," *FJ* 19/20 (Winter/Spring 1995): available online at www.founders.org/FJ19/article1.html (accessed November 14, 2007).

addressed above. To his credit, despite his reductionistic understanding of hyper-Calvinism, Yarnell acknowledged that "five-point Calvinism is not necessarily hyper-Calvinism."[49] In an article in *The Alabama Baptist*, retired Southwestern Seminary theologian James Leo Garrett addressed traditional hyper-Calvinist doctrines like eternal justification and a refusal to preach the gospel indiscriminately. Unfortunately, Garrett also claimed that belief in unconditional election and the so-called "covenant of redemption" between the Father and Christ are also hyper-Calvinist doctrines.[50] They are not.

Some non-Calvinists more directly equate hyper-Calvinism with Calvinism. In his Mid-America Seminary address, Steve Lemke claimed that Founders Ministries embraces "hard hyper-Calvinism" and argued that the traditional five points of Calvinism, codified by the Synod of Dort, represent hyper-Calvinism.[51] In a sermon preached at Prestonwood Baptist Church in Plano, Texas, Jack Graham argued that the doctrines of grace result in a "hyper theology of Calvinism" that is the "death sentence" for missions and evangelism.[52] Ergun Caner has also confused Calvinism with hyper-Calvinism, both in print and in the pulpit.[53]

Contemporary Southern Baptist Calvinists uniformly reject hyper-Calvinism as a perversion of the doctrines of grace and are regularly frustrated that so many non-Calvinists conflate the two movements. Tom

---

[49] Malcolm B. Yarnell III, "The Heart of a Baptist," 9. The address was published as a White Paper by Southwestern's Center for Theological Research and is available at baptisttheology.org (accessed November 13, 2007).

[50] James Leo Garrett, "Calvinism: What Does It Mean?" *The Alabama Baptist* (August 2, 2007), available online at www.al.com/living/alabamabaptist/index.ssf?/base/living/118581126297920.xml&coll=8 (accessed November 14, 2007). The so-called "covenant of redemption" is a tenet of traditional Reformed theology and is affirmed by many Calvinistic Baptists. The doctrine is also explicitly affirmed in a number of Baptist confessions, including the Second London Confession (1677/1689) and the Philadelphia Confession (1742).

[51] Lemke, "The Future of Southern Baptists as Evangelicals," 13. Lemke slightly backed away from his use of the term "hyper-Calvinism" in a letter posted on Tom Ascol's blog. Lemke wrote, "I also have come to believe that the term 'hyperCalvinism' [sic] is just too controversial and understood to mean too many different things to different people to be very useful in the discussion." See Tom Ascol, "Steve Lemke's Letter and My Response," available at www.founders.org/blog/2005/08/steve-lemkes-letter-and-my-response.html (accessed November 14, 2007).

[52] Jack Graham, "The Truth about Grace," audio available online at resources.christianity.com/details/pbc/19000101/9290F735-33AF-45FC-83A3-2386D0699096.aspx (accessed November 14, 2007).

[53] See Ergun Caner, "Predestined NOT to Be a Hyper-Calvinist," *National Liberty Journal* (June/July 2005). Caner also preached a sermon by the same title at Thomas Road Baptist Church on April 9, 2006. A DVD of Caner's sermon can be purchased from his Web site, www.erguncaner.com (accessed November 14, 2007). See also idem, "Questions on Neo-Calvinism, Part 1," available at www.erguncaner.com/site/?p=138 (accessed November 14, 2007).

Nettles spoke for many convention Calvinists in a 1997 article titled "Are Calvinists Hyper?"

> There is little appreciation of the distinction between Calvinism and hyper-Calvinism in spite of some recent writings, including Timothy George's biography of William Carey, *A Faithful Witness*, which have carefully delineated the differences. Many continue to fail, even in the most appropriate historical context, to give a clear picture of the aggressive evangelical Calvinism that characterized the leaders of the mission movement among English Baptists, American Baptists, and Southern Baptists. Their missionary involvement becomes abstracted from a theological framework and seems to be purely the outcome of guts and zeal or of love for Christ unconnected to any clear views of doctrinal truth. That hyper-Calvinism really is a different theological system from Calvinism is rarely discussed. Hyper-Calvinism is seen as *very serious Calvinism* or "Five-point Calvinism" or the defense of "limited atonement" or "supralapsarianism."[54]

Perhaps Timothy George is correct when he claims that the "ghost" of nineteenth-century hyper-Calvinism still haunts the SBC, leading non-Calvinists to fear that Calvinistic Southern Baptists are always just a few steps away from hyper-Calvinism.[55] Be that as it may, non-Calvinists are wrong when they claim historic, traditional Calvinism is hyper-Calvinism.

Myth 4. Calvinists Deny Free Will

A fourth myth asserts that Calvinists deny human free will. William Estep summarized how many non-Calvinists feel about the Calvinistic understanding of human freedom, arguing that "Calvinism robs the individual of responsibility for his/her own conduct, making a person into a puppet on a string or a robot programmed from birth to death with no will of his/her own."[56] This particular accusation is tricky because *free will* can be defined in a number of ways, and Calvinists have no

---

[54] Tom J. Nettles, "Are Calvinists Hyper?" *FJ* 30 (Fall 1997): available online at www.founders.org/FJ30/article1.html (accessed November 14, 2007).

[55] Timothy George, "Southern Baptist Ghosts," *First Things* 93 (May 1999): 17–24, available online at www.leaderu.com/ftissues/ft9905/articles/george.html (accessed November 14, 2007).

[56] Estep, "Doctrines Lead to 'Dunghill,' Prof Warns," 12. See also Page, *The Trouble with the Tulip*, 43.

single view (nor do non-Calvinists, for that matter). A full treatment of this topic is beyond the scope of this chapter, though a number of fine Calvinistic works address the relationship between divine sovereignty and human responsibility.[57]

This chapter focuses on one aspect of the free-will issue: the accusation that God's saving intention is divorced from human responsibility. This myth comes in two forms, the first claims that God saves people who do not, of their own free will, desire to be saved. The second, and seemingly more common version, argues that God refuses to save individuals who sincerely believe in Christ because they are not numbered among the elect. Non-Calvinists in the SBC have often charged convention Calvinists with the latter.

This stereotype is often tied to a misunderstanding of the Calvinist doctrine of irresistible grace. In a widely disseminated sermon titled "The C-Word," longtime Southwestern Seminary evangelism professor Roy Fish argued that irresistible grace destroys free will: "The 'I' in the TULIP is what is called irresistible grace. That means that people who are going to be saved have no other option. They really don't have a choice. The grace of God cannot be resisted. They cannot resist this special saving grace."[58]

In a 2006 article in Georgia's *Christian Index*, Nelson Price claimed that Calvinists believe God saves and damns people irrespective of their free will in the following illustration:

> A mass of people are gathered at a bus stop marked "Planet Earth." Along comes the Celestial Bus marked "Destination Heaven." It pulls up and stops. The driver, who is God, opens the door, and says, "All destined

---

[57] For example, see D. A. Carson, *Divine Sovereignty and Human Responsibility: Biblical Perspectives in Tension* (Atlanta: John Knox, 1981); Lorraine Boettner, *The Reformed Doctrine of Predestination* (Phillipsburg, PA: P&R, 1932), 208–27; Bruce A. Ware, "Effectual Calling and Grace," in *Still Sovereign: Contemporary Perspectives of Election, Foreknowledge, and Grace*, ed. Thomas R. Schreiner and Bruce A. Ware (Grand Rapids: Baker, 2000), 203–26.

[58] Roy Fish, "The C-Word," a sermon preached at Cottage Hill Baptist Church in Mobile, Alabama, August 11, 1997. A manuscript of the sermon is available online at www.sbc-calvinist.com/cword.htm (accessed November 15, 2007). The manuscript has circulated in at least one state convention. This misunderstanding has also been promulgated in recent days by megachurch pastors Steve Gaines and Jack Graham. See Steve Gaines, "I Believe in Salvation," preached October 16, 2006. The audio of the sermon is no longer available at Bellevue Baptist Church's Web site, but Gaines's sermon outline is available at www.bellevue.org/clientimages/1360 /sermons/notes10-16-05.pdf (accessed November 15, 2007). See also Jack Graham, "The Truth about Grace," wherein Graham argued that irresistible grace means an individual has no choice in her salvation and that God's grace "attacks" a person and "forces" or "coerces" her to believe.

for heaven get on board." A number do. A missionary couple who with zeal have served Christ all their lives start on and God says, "Step aside. You haven't been chosen to ride this bus." A couple of infants start on and God tells them to step aside. Persons who from youth have loved and ministered in Christ's name are told to step aside. As the bus is about to depart and the door is closing God says to those not on board, "Catch the next bus." "No," they plead, "here comes the next bus and it is driven by Satan and marked 'Destination Hell.'"

"Sorry," says God. "I didn't choose to save you. Your love and commitment to Jesus doesn't matter."[59]

Price seems convinced that the Calvinist view of salvation entails God's arbitrarily damning genuine Christians because they are not numbered among the elect. He also claimed that Calvinists believe some infants go to hell, a position a number of Southern Baptist Calvinists have publicly repudiated.[60] In Price's illustration, God's sovereignty and human free will are portrayed as totally incompatible concepts that operate independently of each other.

These examples evidence a misunderstanding of what SBC Calvinists believe about the relationship between divine sovereignty and human responsibility. God neither saves those who do not desire to be saved, nor does He damn those who want to be saved. Ernest Reisinger argued that "no man is saved against his will. No man is pardoned while he hates the thought of forgiveness. No man shall have joy in the Lord if he says, 'I do not wish to rejoice in the Lord. . . .' We are not saved against our will; nor is the will taken away, but the work of the Spirit of God is to change the human will, and so make men willing."[61] Following earlier Baptist theologians like Andrew Fuller, Tom Nettles made a distinction

---

[59] Price, "Evangelical Calvinism Is an Oxymoron."

[60] While some Calvinists do believe not all infants are elect, those SBC Calvinists who have engaged this issue have uniformly argued that all infants are numbered among the elect. For example, see R. Albert Mohler Jr. and Daniel L. Akin, "The Salvation of the 'Little Ones': Do Infants Who Die Go to Heaven?" Available online at albertmohler. com/FidelitasRead.php?article=fidel036 (accessed November 14, 2007). See also Ronald H. Nash, *When a Baby Dies: Answers to Comfort Grieving Parents* (Grand Rapids: Zondervan, 1999).

[61] Ernest Reisinger, "God's Will, Man's Will, and Free Will," *FJ* 25 (Summer 1996): available online at www.founders.org/FJ25/article2.html (accessed November 15, 2007). See also Andy Davis, "Divine Sovereignty and Human Responsibility," preached November 11, 2006 at The Southern Baptist Theological Seminary. An audio recording of the sermon is available at www.sbts.edu/MP3/fall2006/20061107davis.mp3 (accessed November 15, 2007).

between moral and natural ability, arguing that individuals are *naturally* capable of repentance and faith, but because of their captivity to sin, they are *morally* unable to choose Christ. Irresistible grace, or better, effectual calling, is thus God's regeneration of the sinner, making his will compatible with God's saving intention.[62]

In his essay "The Ascent of Lost Man in Southern Baptist Preaching," Mark Coppenger argued that the SBC has increasingly been characterized by a view of human free will that inadequately accounts for bondage to sin. In this setting effectual calling is viewed as doing violence to one's will rather than genuinely freeing the will to pursue God. Coppenger noted,

> While few deny the reality of human free agency (else what sense could we make of the conscious rejection or acceptance of the gospel?), it seems that, today, the "freedom" of the lost has been magnified at the expense of their "bondage." Unlike the founders of the Southern Baptist Convention, some have come to view lost people as discriminating shoppers, whose failure to buy is due to our failure at marketing.[63]

Coppenger and others are simply echoing what SBC Calvinists have historically believed concerning the role of the human will in salvation: effectual calling renders God's sovereignty and human free will compatible. This compatibility is perhaps best stated in the section on "Providence" in the Abstract of Principles: "God from eternity, decrees or permits all things that come to pass, and perpetually upholds, directs and governs all creatures and all events; yet so as not to destroy the free will and responsibility of intelligent creatures."[64] Southern Baptist Calvinists echo Charles Spurgeon, who when asked how he reconciled divine sovereignty and human freedom, allegedly responded, "I do not try to reconcile friends."[65] SBC Calvinists uniformly believe that individuals must choose to trust Christ; we simply differ with non-Calvinists over the role God's sovereignty plays in that choice.

---

[62] Nettles, *By His Grace and For His Glory*, 295. For a recent discussion of Fuller's view of moral versus natural ability, see Gerald L. Priest, "Andrew Fuller, Hyper-Calvinism, and the 'Modern Question,'" in *"At the Pure Fountain of Thy Word": Andrew Fuller as an Apologist*, Studies in Baptist History and Thought, ed. Michael A. G. Haykin (Carlisle, Cumbria, UK, and Waynesboro, GA: Paternoster, 2004), 43–72.

[63] Coppenger, "The Ascent of Lost Man in Southern Baptist Preaching."

[64] The Abstract of Principles, available online at www.founders.org/abstract.html (accessed November 15, 2007).

[65] Quoted in Lewis A. Drummond, "Charles Haddon Spurgeon," *Theologians of the Baptist Tradition*, 122.

Myth 5. Authentic Baptists Are Not Calvinists

From time to time, non-Calvinists argue that Calvinism is a foreign element that was introduced into either the Baptist tradition in general or, more specifically, the Southern Baptist Convention. For example, William Estep argued that although the earliest Baptists were birthed from the English Separatist tradition, which was Calvinistic, even Particular (Calvinistic) Baptists embraced a "modified" Calvinism that presumably softened traditional Calvinism. Estep bluntly stated that "Baptists never have been doctrinaire Calvinists."[66] In their book *God So Loved the World*, Fisher Humphreys and Paul Robertson argued that "traditional Baptists" are not Calvinists, claiming that their book is intended to help traditional Baptists understand Calvinism so they can "relate to [Calvinism] in a Christian way."[67]

Some non-Calvinist scholars argue that Calvinism is a Presbyterian belief, implying that authentic Baptists do not embrace the doctrines of grace. In an article written for *SBC Life*, Malcolm Yarnell claimed that "it could be successfully argued that the Calvinist-Arminian debate is, at root, a Presbyterian argument, not a Baptist one." Despite this claim, Yarnell conceded that Baptists have, in fact, historically debated Calvinism and Arminianism. He admitted, "Early English Baptists were also divided over the debate, with General Baptists identifying more with Arminians and Particular Baptists with Calvinists."[68] In a discussion on Tom Ascol's Weblog, Ergun Caner claims that Calvinistic Baptists embrace what he calls "semi-Presbyterianism." Caner also accuses SBC Calvinists of "killing" churches by preaching sermons on the Presbyterian Westminster Confession of Faith, though he provides no examples of a Southern Baptist preaching from that confession.[69]

Perhaps one reason some scholars are so quick to disassociate Calvinism and the Baptist tradition is because of a desire to identify Baptists with some of the Anabaptist movements, the latter of which have

---

[66] Estep, "Doctrines Lead to 'Dunghill,' Prof Warns," 12.

[67] Fisher Humphreys and Paul E. Robertson, *God So Loved the World: Traditional Baptists and Calvinism* (New Orleans: Insight Press, 2000), 5.

[68] Malcolm B. Yarnell III, "The TULIP of Calvinism in Light of History and the Baptist Faith and Message," *SBC Life* (April 2006), available online at www.sbclife.com/Articles/2006/04/sla8.asp (accessed November 15, 2007). Yarnell also believes some Southern Baptists, presumably Calvinists, "have apparently begun breaking down the biblical walls between Baptists and Presbyterians," though he provides no explanation or examples. See Malcolm Yarnell III, "The Baptist Renaissance at Southwestern," *Southwestern News* 65, no. 2. (Winter 2007): available online at www.swbts.edu/swnews/features/feature8.cfm (accessed November 15, 2007).

[69] See Tom Ascol, "Johnny Hunt to Be Nominated for President of the SBC," available online at www.founders.org/blog/2006/02/johnny-hunt-to-be-nominated-for.html (accessed November 19, 2007).

historically been closer to Arminian theology than Calvinism. Yarnell emphasized theological affinity between Baptists and Anabaptists. In commenting on a new Center for Free Church and Anabaptist Studies at Southwestern Seminary, he contended that Anabaptists are "those often persecuted groups who are identifiably Baptist from a biblical perspective."[70] According to a Baptist Press article, Caner went a step further and identified himself as "a radical reformer in the Anabaptist heritage."[71] The late Estep was a prolific scholar of Anabaptism and perhaps the leading twentieth-century advocate of actual historical continuity between Baptists and Anabaptists.[72]

Southern Baptist Calvinists deny that Calvinism is foreign to the Baptist tradition. Rather, SBC Calvinists (and many non-Calvinist scholars) argue that there have always been Calvinistic Baptists and that Calvinism has at times enjoyed considerable influence within the convention. William Brackney noted that the majority of early Baptists in America adhered to Calvinistic theology.[73] Historians like Tom Nettles and Timothy George have shown that, at the very least, a majority of the *leading* Baptists in the South during the nineteenth-century were Calvinists.[74] Leon McBeth observed that many Southern Baptist Calvinists identify with the Second London Confession, a document originally drafted in seventeenth-century England.[75] Whether Calvinism is biblical is a point worthy of debate, but the influence of Calvinism among Baptists in general and Southern Baptists in particular is a matter of historical record and simply cannot be disputed.

Furthermore, far from being "semi-Presbyterians," Southern Baptist Calvinists have been vocal defenders of Baptist distinctives. Tom Ascol

---

[70] Yarnell, "The Baptist Renaissance at Southwestern."

[71] Ledbetter, "Baptists and Calvinism: Event Was Called Off, but Not the Debate," Baptist Press (October 18, 2006), available online at www.bpnews.net/bpnews.asp?id=24192 (November 16, 2007). In published correspondence with Reformed Baptist theologian James White, Ergun Caner claimed that the Founders Ministries Web site, and more specifically Tom Ascol's Weblog, is a site "where the semi-Presbyterians want to revise our Anabaptist, free church [*sic*] and dissenter heritage." The correspondence between White and Caner is related to a defunct attempt to hold a public debate on the topic of Southern Baptists and Calvinism at Liberty University. The correspondence can be read online at www.aomin.org/ErgunCaner1.html (accessed November 15, 2007).

[72] For example, see William R. Estep, *The Anabaptist Story: An Introduction to Sixteenth-Century Anabaptism* (3d ed.; Grand Rapids: Eerdmans, 1996), 271–303.

[73] William H. Brackney, *Baptists in North America*, Religion in America (Oxford: Blackwell, 2006), 28.

[74] See Nettles, "The Rise and Demise of Calvinism among Southern Baptists"; idem, *By His Grace and for His Glory*, 161–205; George, "Southern Baptist Theology: Whence and Wither?"

[75] H. Leon McBeth, *The Baptist Heritage: Four Centuries of Baptist Witness* (Nashville: Broadman, 1987), 699.

has publicly stated that Founders Ministries and *FJ* are committed to "historic Southern Baptist principles," by which he means Calvinist soteriology and Baptist ecclesiology.[76] Timothy George coedited the Library of Baptist Classics series for Broadman &Holman, which includes a number of volumes dedicated to Baptist convictions.[77] Roughly half of the contributors to the recent book *Why I Am a Baptist* are Calvinists, and Tom Nettles coedited the volume.[78] Nettles has also authored two different works defending believer's baptism by immersion.[79] Fred Malone has also authored two helpful works defending the Baptist understanding of baptism.[80] Thomas Schreiner and Shawn Wright coedited a collection of essays arguing for the Baptist understanding of baptism, with a number of Calvinists contributing to the volume.[81] In a recent article in Southern Seminary's alumni magazine, Greg Wills contested the practice of Baptist churches accepting so-called "alien immersions" and argued that baptism is a prerequisite to the Lord's Supper.[82] Mark Dever and Phil Newton have each authored works defending congregational church government as essential to Baptist ecclesiology.[83] Simply put, Southern

---

[76] For example, see Tom Ascol, "Historic Southern Baptist Principles," *FJ* 9 (Summer 1992), available online at www.founders.org/FJ09/editorial.html (accessed November 15, 2007).

[77] For example, see E. Y. Mullins, *The Axioms of Religion* (Nashville: Broadman & Holman, 1997); Herschel H. Hobbs, *Baptist Why and Why Not Revisited* (Nashville: Broadman & Holman, 1997); B. H. Carroll, *Baptists and Their Doctrines* (Nashville: Broadman & Holman, 1999); J. M. Frost, *Baptist Why and Why Not* (Nashville: Broadman & Holman, 1998); John Albert Broadus, *Baptist Confessions, Covenants, and Catechisms* (Nashville: Broadman & Holman, 1996); James P. Boyce, *Treasures from the Baptist Heritage* (Nashville: Broadman & Holman, 1996).

[78] Tom J. Nettles and Russell D. Moore, *Why I Am a Baptist* (Nashville: Broadman & Holman, 2001).

[79] See Tom J. Nettles, *Believer's Baptism by Immersion*, Foundations of Baptist Heritage (Nashville: The Historical Commission of the Southern Baptist Convention, 1989), and idem, "Baptism of the Professing Regenerate by Immersion," in *Understanding Four Views on Baptism*, ed. John H. Armstrong (Grand Rapids: Zondervan, 2007).

[80] See Fred A. Malone, *A String of Pearls Unstrung: A Theological Journey into Believer's Baptism* (Cape Coral, FL: Founders Press, 1998), available online at www.founders.org/library/malone1/string.html (accessed November 30, 2007), and idem, *The Baptism of Disciples Alone: A Covenantal Argument for Credobaptism Versus Paedobaptism* (Cape Coral, FL: Founders Press, 2003).

[81] See Thomas R. Schreiner and Shawn D. Wright, eds, *Believer's Baptism: Sign of the New Covenant in Christ*, NAC Studies in Bible & Theology (Nashville: B&H, 2006).

[82] Greg Wills, "Are We All Wet or Does Baptism Matter?" *The Tie: Southern Seminary* 75, no. 3 (Fall 2007): 10–12. I have also argued that baptism is prerequisite to Communion. See Nathan A. Finn, "Baptism as a Prerequisite to the Lord's Supper," published by the Center for Theological Research (September 2006): available online at www.baptisttheology.org/papers.cfm (accessed November 15, 2007).

[83] See Mark Dever, *Nine Marks of a Healthy Church* (Wheaton: Crossway, 2000), and Phil Newton, *Elders in Congregational Life: Rediscovering the Biblical Model for Church Leadership* (Grand Rapids: Kregel, 2005).

Baptist Calvinists are both committed Calvinists and authentic Baptists, sharing these convictions with many of our Baptist forebears.

Conclusion: Toward a More Cooperative Future

This chapter has argued that many non-Calvinists in the Southern Baptist Convention have misunderstood some of the convictions of their fellow Southern Baptists who embrace Calvinism. I hope to have helped correct some of the most common misunderstandings about Southern Baptist Calvinists. But the question still remains, is it possible to build bridges between Calvinists and non-Calvinists in the SBC? In closing, I want to propose four commitments that Southern Baptists on both sides of the Calvinism debate must make if we are to work better together in preaching Christ to all people.

First, Southern Baptist Calvinists and non-Calvinists must share a common commitment to the gospel. One way to build on the gains made during the conservative resurgence is for all Southern Baptists to work together to pursue a gospel resurgence that will both revive our churches and reignite our passion for proclaiming the good news to all people. We must heed the words of Timothy George, who warns non-Calvinists to avoid falling into the heresy of Pelagianism and cautions Calvinists against tilting toward the heresy of hyper-Calvinism.[84] The former downplays the power of sin and exalts human freedom, often in a sincere effort to win more people to Christ. The latter quenches a passion for souls and degrades both God's character and human responsibility, often in a sincere effort to be doctrinally pure. If we are to move toward a more cooperative future, we must commit ourselves to being gospel-centered lest we drift toward these and other soul-destroying errors.

Second, both Calvinists and non-Calvinists must share a common commitment to historic Baptist distinctives. The Baptist view of the church is not intrinsic to the gospel, but Baptists believe it is more consistent with the gospel than paedobaptism, open membership, or hierarchical church government. We cannot divorce the gospel from its fruit: baptized Christians whose lives are characterized by a radical commitment to Christian discipleship, a responsible, disciplined church membership, and a zeal for the lost.[85] If we are to move toward a more cooperative future, Southern Baptists on both sides of the Calvinism discussion must

---

[84] David S. Dockery and Timothy George, *Building Bridges* (Nashville: Convention Press, 2007), 49–50.

[85] I am encouraged by recent efforts like "The Fifth Century Initiative," a call from Texas pastor Bart Barber for Southern Baptists to recommit themselves to a gospel-centered Baptist ecclesiology as we get closer to the four hundredth anniversary of the Baptist movement in 2009. The text of "The Fifth Century Initiative" is available online

commit to traditional Baptist principles lest we drift toward errors like paedobaptism, theonomy, or polity structures that are antithetical to congregationalism.

Third, Southern Baptist Calvinists and non-Calvinists must share a common commitment to labor together in the task of the Great Commission. The original constitution of the Southern Baptist Convention claims that Baptists in the South formed a convention for the purpose of "eliciting, combining and directing the energies of the whole denomination in one sacred effort, for the propagation of the Gospel."[86] Simply put, the primary reason we cooperate as a convention is because Southern Baptists believe we can proclaim the good news to more people if we work together. This commitment to interchurch cooperation for missionary endeavors is at the heart of the SBC. If we are to thrive as Southern Baptist Calvinists and non-Calvinists, we must agree to work together in spite of our differences over the doctrines of grace or particular methods. If we are to move toward a more cooperative future, Southern Baptists must never allow our cooperation to be torn asunder by our own internal disputes over Calvinism or any other theological issue over which orthodox, gospel-centered, convictional Southern Baptists might disagree.

Finally, Southern Baptist Calvinists and non-Calvinists must share a common commitment to be humble, irenic, and loving when we attempt to persuade others to embrace our respective positions vis-à-vis the doctrines of grace. This means there are two scenarios we must avoid in our convention. The first is a combative atmosphere between Calvinists and non-Calvinists. God will not use the convention for His purposes if Calvinist Southern Baptists view non-Calvinist Southern Baptists as their enemies, and vice versa. Both Calvinists and non-Calvinists must repent of mischaracterizations, stereotyping, caricatures, and slander that have been perpetrated in our debates over Calvinism. We must commit to engage others with whom we disagree in a winsome, Christlike spirit, or we have no hope of a more cooperative future. Paige Patterson and Albert Mohler modeled this approach in their Calvinism dialog at the 2005 SBC Pastor's Conference in Greensboro, North Carolina.[87]

---

at praisegodbarebones.blogspot.com/2007/08/fifth-century-initiative.html (accessed November 15, 2007).

[86] Cited from the original constitution of the Southern Baptist Convention. A copy of the document is available online at baptiststudiesonline.com/?page_id=24 (accessed November 16, 2007).

[87] See Michael Foust, "Patterson, Mohler: Calvinism Shouldn't Divide SBC," Baptist Press (Junes 13, 2006), available online at www.bpnews.net/bpnews.asp?ID=23457 (accessed November 16, 2007). Danny Akin, Tom Ascol, and Thom Rainer further demonstrated this type of spirit in hosting the conference at which this chapter was originally presented.

The other scenario we must reject is a "naked public square" within the convention concerning Calvinism. A "don't ask, don't tell" policy is no foundation on which to build cooperation. Southern Baptists on both sides of the Calvinism discussion must be free both to hold their convictions and to seek to persuade other Southern Baptists to embrace those convictions. To do anything less is to treat this issue as if it is unimportant—something neither side believes. Furthermore, it devalues our mutual commitment to pursue biblical truth and seek to teach our understanding of that truth to other Christians. The Calvinism issue is not going to go away, so Southern Baptists must be willing to discuss and debate openly the doctrines of grace in an effort to be biblically accurate and perhaps come to a greater theological consensus in the years to come. If we are to move toward a more cooperative future, we must all be committed to defending and commending our particular convictions but not at the expense of either our cooperation with one another or our personal sanctification.

A Southern Baptist Dialogue

Calvinism
Election and Calling

A Molinist View of Election, or How to Be a Consistent Infralapsarian

Ken Keathley
Senior Associate Dean, Professor of Theology
Southeastern Baptist Theological Seminary
Wake Forest, North Carolina

SOUTHEASTERN BAPTIST THEOLOGICAL SEMINARY, where I teach, has a confession of faith called The Abstract of Principles. Written originally for Southern Seminary by Basil Manly Jr., article four of the Abstract states, "God from eternity decrees or permits all things that come to pass and perpetually upholds, directs and governs all creatures and all events; yet so as not in any wise to be the author or approver of sin nor to destroy the free will and responsibility of intelligent creatures."

The article seems self-contradictory. It declares that God's decisions oversee all things, yet at the same time God only *permits* evil, He is not "in any wise" the origin of sin, and His choices do not negate human free will. One model of divine sovereignty and human responsibility which attempts to reconcile all the declarations of the above article is a view called Molinism. This chapter presents the Molinist understanding of election and argues that it provides an alternative for the believer who is convinced that election is a sovereign and gracious choice of God but is unconvinced that this entails accepting the five points of Calvinism.

Two Essential Doctrines: Sovereignty and Permission

The God of the Bible created the world out of nothing—*creatio ex nihilo*—and this truth entails two corollaries: sovereignty and permission. God's sovereignty is His lordship over creation. Divine sovereignty means that God rules and, yes, controls all things.

In his crafting of the Abstract of Principles, Manly was careful to include the concept of permission. Permission is the decision by God to allow something other than Himself to exist. Mere existence seems to be what

God gave to most of creation because most of this immense universe consists simply of physical materials that obey natural laws. He gave a level of freedom, within limits, to certain agents—namely angels and humans. God did not grant us absolute independence or complete autonomy. Using the word *permission* highlights the point that our freedom is a derived freedom. He gave us the ability to choose, and with this ability came the moral responsibility for those choices. The concept of permission means that though God controls all things He does not cause all things.[1] How much freedom did He permit us? Enough freedom to rebel.

Sovereignty and Permission as They Relate to Predestination

The difficult goal before us is to achieve a balanced understanding of both sovereignty and permission, particularly as it pertains to predestination. Those who emphasize sovereignty tend to be Calvinists; those who emphasize permission tend to be Arminians. Extremes exist beyond both sides of the boundaries of Christian doctrine. If one wants to see divine sovereignty emphasized to the point of fatalism, he needs look no further than Islam. The world *Islam* means "submit," and the goal of the devout Muslim is to submit to the irresistible will of Allah.

Opposite of Islam at the other end of the spectrum is process theology. In process thought God is changing and evolving along with the world and needs the world as much as it needs Him. According to the process theologian, evil happens because God is not able to stop it, and the world literally is out of control. Located between the extremes of Islam and process is the biblical truth that God sovereignly rules over creatures which He permitted to have a relative amount of freedom.

The Similarities of Infralapsarian Calvinism and Molinism

Within orthodox Christian beliefs two approaches consciously attempt to do justice to the twin biblical doctrines of divine sovereignty and divine permission by simultaneously affirming both. They are infralapsarian Calvinism and Molinism. Both affirm that God's sovereignty is meticulous and overarching. Both affirm the concept of permission and agree that God did not cause the fall, nor is He the cause of evil, but He permits sin. The real problem is, as always, the problem of evil. As it relates to the issue of election, the question is how humans came to be viewed in the eternal mind of God as sinners in the first place. The

---

[1] Of course, God is the ultimate cause of all that exists. I use "cause" in this instance in the immediate sense that God does not directly cause anything wicked. This chapter argues that, between God and the sinfulness of this world, morally responsible free agents exist. Their choices are the cause of evil, including the evil of rejecting Christ and His salvation.

debate concerning predestination is over the role that permission plays in God's decrees.

Few Christians have a problem with the doctrine of election per se. The Scriptures teach, and our experience confirms, that if God had not first chosen us we would not have chosen Him (John 15:16). God chose us "in Him [Christ], before the foundation of the world" (Eph 1:4),[2] states Paul, while Peter declares that believers are "elect according to the foreknowledge of God the Father" (1 Pet 1:2 NKJV). Election is the clear teaching of Scripture (Rom 8:29).

The question of the reprobate poses a problem. Reprobation is God's decision to reject or pass over certain ones. If God rejects the reprobate because of the reprobate's sin and unbelief, then reprobation is based on God's justice, and His decision poses no moral dilemma. But it would also mean that some aspects of God's decree were conditional rather than unconditional and that in certain ways the free choices of morally responsible creatures affected the eternal decisions of God.

Some Calvinists (following their namesake, John Calvin) cannot accept that there is any conditionality in God's decrees, so they bite the bullet and dismiss permission altogether. They embrace a double predestination in which God chose some and rejected others and then subsequently decreed the fall in order to bring it about. Those who hold this position are called supralapsarians because they understand the decree of election and reprobation as occurring logically prior (*supra*) to the decree to allow the fall (*lapsus*), hence the word *supralapsarianism*.[3]

Most Calvinists blanch at this approach. Reformed theology generally teaches that God first decreed to permit the fall and then from fallen humanity chose certain ones to salvation for reasons known only to Him. This approach is called infralapsarianism (*infra* meaning "after") because it views God's electing choice as occurring logically after He decided to permit the fall.

The crucial concept to the infralapsarian Calvinist model is the notion of permission. God did not cause the fall; He allowed it. God does not predestine the reprobate to hell; He permits the unbeliever to go his own way. Permission is problematic for the Calvinist—particularly to those who hold to determinism—because permission entails conditionality, contingency, and viewing humans as in some sense the origin of their own respective choices. Calvinists such as John Feinberg define God's sovereignty in terms of causal determinism, and this leaves little room

---

[2] Unless otherwise indicated, Scripture quotations are from the HCSB.

[3] Some supralapsarians speak of God's permission, but they generally redefine it in such a way that is not acceptable even to infralapsarians.

for a logically consistent understanding of permission.[4] I am arguing that what Calvinists want to achieve in infralapsarianism, Molinism actually accomplishes. Molinism combines a high view of sovereignty with a robust understanding of permission.

Molinism: Affirming Divine Sovereignty with Genuine Permission

Most Southern Baptists have heard about Calvinism, but not as many are familiar with Molinism. I suspect some who embrace Calvinism do so because they recognize the Bible teaches that God is sovereign and Calvinism is the only theological system of which they are aware that attempts to do justice to God's sovereignty. Calvinism often wins by default, especially when Arminianism is understood to be the alternative.

Arminianism solves the problem of reprobation by presenting God's decision concerning individuals as something entirely passive. God decrees to elect the church as a corporate body, and those individuals who chose Christ are then viewed as the elect while those who reject Him are reprobate. In this respect Arminians view God's decree as the mere ratification of human choices. But the Bible presents God's electing decision as something much more active and decisive.

What is Molinism? Named after its first proponent, Luis Molina (1535–1600), a sixteenth-century Jesuit priest, Molinism holds to a strong notion of God's control and an equally firm affirmation of human freedom.[5] In other words Molinism simultaneously holds to a Calvinistic view of a comprehensive divine sovereignty and to a version of libertarian free will generally associated with Arminianism. As Doug Geivett argues, the fact that Molinism is the one proposal that tries to hold simultaneously to both is a point in its favor, since both "are *prima facie* true."[6]

Molinism teaches that on the issue in question God exercises His sovereignty primarily through His omniscience, and that He infallibly knows what free creatures would do in any given situation. In this way God sovereignly controls all things while humans are also genuinely free. Molinism formulates a radical compatibilism, and for this reason

---

[4] John Feinberg, *No One Else Like Him* (Wheaton: Crossway, 2001), 637: "So, an act is free, though causally determined, if it is what the agent wanted to do."

[5] According to Kirk R. MacGregor (*A Molinist-Anabaptist Systematic Theology* [Lanham, MD: University of America, 2007]), certain Anabaptists such as Balthasar Hubmaier argued for a position similar to Molinism nearly fifty years before Molina published his works.

[6] R. Douglas Geivett, "Divine Providence and the Openness of God: A Response to William Hasker," *Philosophia Christi* 4 (2002): 380.

is often attacked from both sides of the aisle. Calvinists such as Bruce Ware and Richard Muller consider it to be a type of Arminianism, while Roger Olson and Robert Picirilli, (both card-carrying Arminians) reject Molinism for being too Calvinistic.[7] However, Molinism is attractive to many leading Christian philosophers of our day, such as Alvin Plantinga, Thomas Flint, and William Lane Craig; and one of the main reasons is that it demonstrates it is logically possible to affirm divine sovereignty and human freedom in a consistent manner.[8] Even open theist William Hasker, who is no friend to Molinism, admits, "If you are committed to a 'strong' view of providence, according to which, down to the smallest detail, 'things are as they are because God knowingly decided to create such a world,' and yet you also wish to maintain a libertarian conception of free will—if this is what you want, then Molinism is the only game in town."[9]

As a matter of fact, that is exactly what I want because I believe Molinism is faithful to the biblical witness. I suggest that Molinism is the only game in town for anyone who wishes to affirm a consistent formulation of the infralapsarian notion of permission.

Calvin's Supralapsarianism: The Concept of Permission Rejected

Calvin approached the issue of predestination with the premise that "the will of God is the chief and principal cause of all things,"[10] an assumption that left little or no room for permission. Some try to argue that Calvin's successor, Theodore Beza, transformed Calvin's teaching on election into supralapsarianism; but Calvin's work on the subject, a book entitled *Concerning the Eternal Predestination of God*, reveals that Calvin held to double predestination just as firmly as his protégée.[11]

---

[7] See Bruce Ware, *God's Greater Glory* (Wheaton: Crossway, 2004), 25; Richard Muller, *Post-Reformation Reformed Dogmatics*, vol. 3 (Grand Rapids: Baker, 2003), 411–36; Roger Olson, *Arminian Theology* (Downers Grove: IVP, 2006), 194–99; and Robert E. Picirilli, *Grace, Faith, Free Will* (Nashville: Randall House, 2002), 62–63. Wayne Grudem (*Systematic Theology* [Grand Rapids: Zondervan, 1994], 348–49) calls Molinism a type of Arminianism, but says that in many ways it more resembles Calvinism.

[8] Alvin Plantinga, *God, Freedom, and Evil* (Grand Rapids: Eerdmans, 1977); Thomas P. Flint, *Divine Providence: The Molinist Account* (Ithaca: Cornell University Press, 1998); and William Lane Craig, *The Only Wise God* (Grand Rapids: Baker, 1987).

[9] Quoted in Flint, *Divine Providence*, 75.

[10] John Calvin, *Concerning the Eternal Predestination of God*, trans. J. K. S. Reid (Louisville: Westminster John Knox, [1552] 1961), 177.

[11] In addition, J. V. Fesko sets the teachings of Calvin and Beza on reprobation side by side and demonstrates the two men were in agreement on this point. See J. V. Fesko,

In supralapsarianism God's decision to elect and to reprobate is primary. Key to understanding supralapsarianism is to note the distinction it makes between reprobation and damnation.[12] Reprobation is God's rejection of an individual; damnation is God's judgment upon that person for his sins. In this paradigm God does not reject the reprobate because he is a sinner; it is the other way around. The reprobate becomes a sinner because God rejected him. God reprobated certain ones and then decreed the fall in order to actualize His disfavor toward them. Calvin made this clear when he declared that "the highest cause" of reprobation is not sin but "the bare and simple pleasure of God."[13]

If God's decree of double predestination is primary, then its components of election and reprobation have equal ultimacy, a point affirmed repeatedly by modern supralapsarians such as Cornelius Van Til, Herman Hoeksema, and more recently Robert Reymond.[14] God's relationship to both classes of individuals is symmetric. He rejected the reprobate in the same way He chose the elect.[15]

As Bruce Ware, an infralapsarian Calvinist, points out, grace plays no part in the supralapsarian understanding of the initial double decree.[16] This is because when God decided whom He would choose and whom He would reject, humans were not yet viewed in His mind as sinners in need of grace or deserving of judgment. Grace did not logically enter the picture until after God determined to rescue His chosen from the fall. This is why some supralapsarians such as David Engelsma do not hesitate to speak of God's attitude towards the non-elect as one of eternal hatred.[17] In supralapsarianism, sovereign grace gives way to mere sovereignty.

Diversity within the Reformed Tradition: Supra- and Infralapsarianism in Calvin, Dort, and Westminster (Greenville, SC: Reformed Academic, 2001), 138–50.

[12] Calvin, *Concerning the Eternal Predestination of God,* 121. See also Cornelius Van Til, *The Defense of the Faith* (Philadelphia: P&R, 1955), 414–15.

[13] Calvin, *Concerning the Eternal Predestination of God,* 120–21. See also id., *The Epistles of Paul the Apostle to the Romans and to the Thessalonians* (Grand Rapids: Eerdmans, 1960), 190–219.

[14] Van Til, *The Defense of the Faith,* 413; Herman Hoeksema, *Reformed Dogmatics* (Grand Rapids: Reformed Free Publishing, 1966), 161; and Robert Reymond, "A Consistent Supralapsarian Perspective on Election," in *Perspectives on Election: Five Views,* ed. Chad Brand (Nashville: B&H, 2006), 153.

[15] "For first there is certainly a mutual relation between the elect and the reprobate, so that the election spoken of here cannot stand, unless we confess that God separated out from others certain men as seemed good to Him." Calvin, *Concerning the Eternal Predestination of God,* 68–72.

[16] Bruce Ware, "Divine Election to Salvation," in *Perspectives on Election: Five Views,* 56.

[17] "Reprobation is the exact, explicit denial that God loves all men, desires to save all men, and conditionally offers them salvation. Reprobation asserts that God eternally hates

Calvin had no room for permission. Calvin lampooned the notion when he stated:

> It is easy to conclude how foolish and frail is the sup-
> port of divine justice by the suggestion that evils come
> to be not by His will, but merely by His permission.
> Of course, so far as they are evils. . . . I admit they are
> not pleasing to God. But it is quite a frivolous refuge
> to say that God otiosely permits them, when Scripture
> shows Him not only willing but the author of them.[18]

So Calvin makes the breathtaking claim that God is the very "author" of sin, an assertion that subsequent Calvinists reject.

Infralapsarianism:
The Attempt to Blend Calvinism and Permission

Even though Calvin and Beza both advocated supralapsarianism, no major Reformed confession or creed followed their lead. The reason is obvious: supralapsarianism places the origin of sin at God's feet; and as the Canons of Dort declare, the notion that God is the author of sin in any way "at all" is "a blasphemous thought."[19] The Westminster Confession makes a similar declaration.[20]

In Calvin's day a physician in Geneva by the name of Bolsec objected to Calvin's teachings on predestination on the grounds they impugned the character of God. Bolsec was arrested, convicted, and eventually banished from Geneva; and Calvin sought support from Reformers in other Swiss cities for his supralapsarian position. He seemed to have been genuinely surprised when Reformers such as Heinrich Bullinger disagreed with him and argued instead for infralapsarianism.[21] In the subsequent debates between the infralapsarian and the supralapsarian parties, the creeds and the confessions reveal that the Reformed churches universally chose Bullinger over Calvin.

Infralapsarianism refuses to draw out the logical implications of double predestination. The infralapsarian system argues that in some aspects God's sovereign decree is conditional. In addition, this model also argues that in the process of bringing the decree to fruition, some aspects of

---

some men; has immutably decreed their damnation; and has determined to withhold from them Christ, grace, faith, and salvation." David Engelsma, *Hyper-Calvinism and the Call of the Gospel* (Grand Rapids: Reformed Free Publishing, 1994), 58.

[18] Calvin, *Concerning the Eternal Predestination of God*, 176.

[19] Canons of Dort, Art. 15.

[20] Westminster Confession, 3.1

[21] Fesko, *Diversity with the Reformed Tradition*, 135–38.

God's relationship to events—particularly to evil and sinful events—are permissive.

Bruce Ware, arguing for infralapsarianism, declared,

> It seems to me, that the strain in Calvinism that has been reluctant to embrace the "permissive will of God" simply rejects one of the very conceptual tools necessary to account for God's moral innocence in regard to evil. Surely more is needed than just this manner of divine activity. But I don't see how we can proceed if God's sovereign dealings in matters of good and evil are, in fact, symmetrical.[22]

In other words, in order to protect God from the accusation of being the author of evil, we must embrace the notion of permission.

Louis Berkhof concurred with Ware. He pointed out that when the Bible presents God's rejecting a man such a King Saul or a people such as unbelieving Israel, His rejection of them was predicated on their prior rejection of Him.[23] Therefore, election is unconditional but reprobation is conditional. God actively ordains the salvation of the elect, but He only permits the damnation of the reprobate.

Infralapsarianism perceives God to have an asymmetrical relationship with election and reprobation.[24] God first allows all of humanity to fall. Then, viewing all of humanity as justly condemned in their sins, God ordains unconditionally a certain number: these are the elect. God permits humanity to fall; He does not cause them to fall. Infralapsarianism incorporates the historical into the eternal decree. Even supralapsarian Cornelius Van Til stated, "From eternity God rejected men because of the sin that they would do as historical beings."[25] The reprobation decreed in eternity was conditioned by what would occur in time.

Problems with the Infralapsarian Position

Infralapsarianism hinges on the concept of permission, but reconciling permission with the traditional Reformed view of sovereignty is difficult. Calvin declared that "the will of God is the chief and principal cause of all things."[26] If all events are causally determined, what room is there for permission? Some infralapsarian Reformers speak of an "efficacious permission" or a "determinative permission." For

---

[22] Ware, *God's Greater Glory*, 26.
[23] Louis Berkhof, *Systematic Theology*, a new ed. (Grand Rapids: Eerdmans, 1996), 105–17.
[24] Ware, "Divine Election to Salvation," 54–55.
[25] Van Til, *The Defense of the Faith*, 408.
[26] Calvin, *Concerning the Eternal Predestination of God*, 177.

example, Jerome Zanchius, one of the first advocates of infralapsarianism, declared that "God permissively hardens the reprobate with an efficacious permission."[27] Seeing how the term "efficacious permission" is not an oxymoron is a challenge,

To genuinely embrace the concept of permission would require the infralapsarian to abandon some of the key tenets of Reformed theology. Berkhof recognized this when he warned, "Infralapsarianism really wants to explain reprobation as an act of God's justice. It is inclined to deny either explicitly or implicitly that it is an act of the mere good pleasure of God. This really makes the decree of reprobation a conditional decree and leads into the Arminian fold."[28] Infralapsarians have a choice. If the decree to reprobation is conditional, then it is not according to God's mere good pleasure. If it is unconditional, then it is not according to God's permission. Infralapsarianism wants to teach that God damns the reprobate in response to their sins, but this would abandon the classic Reformed view of God's sovereignty, which is why Calvin rejected the concept of permission out of hand.

Second, as many Calvinists concede, the infralapsarian system is rationally inconsistent. Paul Jewett stated that a rational fallacy lies at the heart of the infralapsarian position.[29] He likens infralapsarianism to a pendulum that swings back and forth from the mere foreknowledge position of the Arminians to the pure foreordination position of the supralapsarians. "And so in the end, it seems, there is no consistent position between a mere foreknowledge of the fall, which is Arminianism, and a foreordination of the fall, which (by implication at least) is supralapsarian. For this reason the pendulum of the infralapsarian argument swings now to one side, now to the other."[30]

Third, the concept of permission as presented in the infralapsarian system doesn't solve anything if reprobation is still the result of "God's good pleasure." The Canons of the Synod of Dort state, "Not all, but some only, are elected, while others are passed by in the eternal decree; whom God, out of His sovereign good pleasure, has decreed to leave in the common misery."[31] So even in the infralapsarian system presented by the Synod of Dort, reprobation is not the result of sin but the good pleasure of God.

Supralapsarians like David Engelsma criticize infralapsarianism for its incoherence:

---

[27] Paul Jewett, *Election and Predestination* (Grand Rapids: Eerdmans, 1985), 83–97.
[28] Berkhof, *Systematic Theology*, 123.
[29] Jewett, *Election and Predestination*, 83–97.
[30] Ibid., 96.
[31] Canons of Dort, Article 15.

> If reprobation is the decree not to give a man faith, it is patently false to say that unbelief is the cause of reprobation. That would be the same as to say that my decision not to give a beggar a quarter is due to the beggar's not having a quarter. That reprobation is an unconditional decree is also plain from the fact that if unbelief were the cause of reprobation, all men would have been reprobated, and would not have been elected, for all men are equally unbelieving and disobedient.[32]

In other words, Engelsma was pointing out that if sin is the basis for reprobation, then no one would be elect because all are sinners.

In the final analysis infralapsarianism teaches that reprobation is as much a part of God's decrees as is election. Infralapsarianism and supralapsarianism are simply nuances of the same approach as long as both begin with God's eternal decrees and reject the notion that God would (or even could) grant any type of libertarian choice to responsible creatures.

Conclusions among Calvinists concerning Infralapsarianism

Many supra-Calvinists dismiss the infra- position as incipient Arminianism (one cannot help but smile at Robert Reymond's accusing John Gerstner of being an Arminian),[33] and a number of infralapsarians, such as Louis Berkhof, concede their point.[34] Some Calvinists despair of the enterprise completely. G. C. Berkouwer called the exploration of the decrees a case of "theological trespassing." John Feinberg concluded that "the whole discussion is misguided" and that "this question should not have been asked." John Frame advocated agnosticism.[35] The verdicts of Paul Jewett and Tom Schreiner are in unison. Jewett stated, "In any case, when all is said and done, the problem of reprobation remains unresolved and, it would appear, unresolvable," while Schreiner concluded, "The scandal of the Calvinist system is that ultimately the logical problems posed cannot be fully resolved."[36]

---

[32] Engelsma, *Hyper-Calvinism and the Call of the Gospel*, 57–58.

[33] Reymond, "A Consistent Supralapsarian Perspective on Election," 170–71; also Hoeksema, *Reformed Dogmatics*, 158; Van Til, *Defense of the Faith*, 415–16.

[34] Berkhof, *Systematic Theology*, 118, 121–24.

[35] G. C. Berkouwer, *Divine Election* (Grand Rapids: Eerdmans, 1960), 254; Feinberg, *No One Else Like Him*, 533; John Frame, *The Doctrine of God* (Phillipsburg, NJ: P&R, 2002), 337.

[36] Jewett, *Election and Predestination*, 97; Thomas R. Schreiner, "Does Scripture Teach Prevenient Grace in the Wesleyan Sense?" in *The Grace of God, the Bondage of the Will, Vol 2*, ed. T. R. Schreiner and Bruce A. Ware (Grand Rapids: Baker, 1995), 381.

At this point many infralapsarian Calvinists appeal to mystery, but what we are dealing with is not a mystery but a contradiction. An epistemic paradox and a logical paradox are different.[37] An epistemic paradox results from insufficient information, but a logical paradox indicates an error either in one's starting assumptions or his reasoning processes. The decretal Calvinist cannot accept his own conclusions. This means that something is wrong somewhere.

This situation is not like contemplating the Trinity or the incarnation, where one encounters transcendent truths in which he can go no further. The dilemma for the Calvinist is that he cannot take his starting assumptions to their logical conclusions. John Gerstner warned his fellow Calvinists that in its formulation of the relationship of God's decree to sin, Reformed theology "hovers" over "the abyss of blasphemy."[38] To their credit, Calvinists by and large do not take the plunge (with a few unfortunate exceptions). All these problems indicate that it is questionable whether one should use the doctrine of election as a control belief when considering issues such as the extent of the atonement.

Molinism: Simultaneously Affirming Both Sovereignty and Permission

Let's go back to our two control beliefs. It may not make the Arminian happy, but let's affirm that God sovereignly controls all things.[39] Charles Spurgeon preached,

> I believe that every particle of dust that dances in the sunbeam does not move an atom more or less than God wishes,—that every particle of spray that dashes against the steamboat has its orbit as well as the sun in the heavens,—that the chaff from the hand of the winnower is steered as surely as the stars in their courses,—that the creeping of an aphis over a rosebud is as much fixed as the march of the devastating pestilence, and the fall of sere leaves from the poplar is

---

[37] David Ciocchi, "Reconciling Divine Sovereignty and Human Freedom," *JETS* 37:3 (1994), 397.

[38] John Gerstner, "Augustine, Luther, Calvin and Edwards on the Bondage of the Will," in *The Grace of God, the Bondage of the Will, Vol 2*, 281.

[39] Flint, *Divine Providence*, 12–21; Olson stated that Molinism's affirmation of God's control of all things is the reason most Arminians reject it. Olson, *Arminian Theology*, 194–99.

as fully ordained as the tumbling of an avalanche. He
who believes in God must believe this truth.[40]

With Spurgeon let's also declare our confidence in God's intricate
providence.

The Calvinist may be displeased, but let's understand *permission* the
way the dictionary defines it: "permission is the giving of an opportunity or a possibility to another." This is the way permission is normally
understood. Permission entails that God has granted at least some type of
libertarian choice to the moral causal agents He created.[41]

Molinism simultaneously affirms meticulous, divine sovereignty and
genuine human freedom. How does it do this? In short, Molinism argues
that God is able to exercise His sovereignty primarily by His omniscience.
In this way God controls all things but is not the determinative cause of
all things. How is this possible? The distinctive feature to Molinism is its
contention that God's knowledge of all things can be understood in three
logical layers or moments. Molinism is particularly noted for its view
that God can infallibly assure the choices of free creatures by using what
it calls God's middle knowledge.

The Three Moments in Molinism

Decretal theology (i.e. supra- and infralapsarianism) attempts to discern the logical order of God's decrees. Molinism, on the other hand,
posits that there is only one decree (a point that has scriptural support
and that many Reformed scholars recognize)[42] but attempts to discern
the logical order of God's knowledge. Rather than attempting to explore
the "layers" of God's decree, Molinism explores the "layers" of God's
omniscience. Decretal Calvinism perceives logical moments in God's
will; Molinism perceives logical moments in God's *knowledge*.[43]

---

[40] C. H. Spurgeon, "God's Providence," *The Metropolitan Tabernacle Pulpit* (Pasadena:
Pilgrim Pub., [1908] 1978), 502. My attention was directed to this sermon by an unpublished paper by Thomas McCall.

[41] Most Molinists hold to what can be called "soft libertarianism." Soft libertarianism
holds to agent causation and argues that the ultimate responsibility for a person's decisions rests on that individual, which indicates in a profound way that he is in some way
the origin of his choices. Two excellent defenses of libertarianism are Robert Kane,
The Significance of Free Will (Oxford: Oxford University Press, 1998) and Timothy
O'Connor, *Persons and Causes: The Metaphysics of Free Will* (Oxford: Oxford University Press, 2000). It may come as a surprise to some Calvinists that libertarians by and
large do not view free will as "the absolute ability to choose the contrary" or as "the
freedom of indifference."

[42] Berkhof, *Systematic Theology*, 102; Feinberg, *No One Else Like Him*, 533–36.

[43] These moments are logical moments, not chronological moments. Nothing temporal is
implied with the use of the word *moment*.

Discerning moments in God's knowledge is not unique to Molinism. Reformed theologians generally agree with Molinists that God's knowledge can be understood in terms of moments or aspects. For example Louis Berkhof recognizes two moments of divine omniscience: God's natural knowledge and his free knowledge.[44] By His nature, God knows all things, so this aspect of His knowledge is labeled natural knowledge. This natural knowledge contains all truths that are necessarily true in the actual world (for example, "a triangle is a three-sided object" or "God cannot die") and all necessary truths in all possible worlds (for example, "what the world would be like if you or I had never been born"). So God's natural knowledge contains all necessary truths.

When we consider God's natural knowledge of possible or hypothetical truths, things get a little complicated. A possible state of affairs, i.e., something that is hypothetically true is called a *counterfactual*, a state of affairs that does not obtain. A counterfactual is a statement contrary to fact which has truth content.[45] The Bible recognizes counterfactuals, and biblical writers used them often. For example, Paul said that "if Christ has not been raised . . . [then we] are still in [our] sins" (1 Cor 15:17). That is a counterfactual state of affairs that gloriously does not obtain.[46]

An illustration of counterfactuals that is fairly easy to understand is the premise of the Christmas movie *It's a Wonderful Life*. Jimmy Stewart's character, George Bailey, is shown what the world would have been like had he never been born. Molinists label these complex scenarios made up of counterfactuals as *possible worlds*. Just contemplating the notion that God knows not only all actual truths but also all possible truths staggers our finite minds, but accomplishing this presents no burden to our omniscient God.

As stated earlier, Berkhof recognized a second moment in God's knowledge—His free knowledge. He defined God's free knowledge as "the knowledge of everything about this particular world." Out of all the possible worlds He could have created, God freely chose this one. This world is the product of God's free choice, which is why His knowledge of it is called His free knowledge.

Reformed theologians (such as Berkhof) acknowledge that God's knowledge has at least two moments: His natural knowledge and His free knowledge. Molinists would also agree with Berkhof's assertion that "the decree of God bears the closest relation to the divine knowledge."[47]

---

[44] Berkhof, *Systematic Theology*, 102; Hoeksema, *Reformed Dogmatics*, 157.

[45] Or, more precisely, a counterfactual is a proposition rather than a statement.

[46] Some other Scriptural examples of counterfactuals are 1 Sam 23:6–10; Jer 38:17–18; and 1 Cor 2:8. Jesus often made use of counterfactual knowledge as seen in Matt 11:23; 17:27; 26:24; John 15:22,24; 18:36; and 21:6, to list a few.

[47] Berkhof, *Systematic Theology*, 102.

That is, God brings about His sovereign will primarily by using His omniscience. What about all the possible choices of genuinely free creatures? Where are these counterfactuals located in the realm of God's knowledge? Here is where the Molinist's concept of middle knowledge enters the picture.

As Thomas Flint explained it, God's knowledge of counterfactuals of creaturely freedom cannot be part of His natural knowledge because God's natural knowledge is made of what is necessarily true. Nor can these counterfactuals belong to God's free knowledge since they are only hypothetical and not actual. Molinists argue that God possesses a third type of knowledge, located "between" God's natural knowledge and His free knowledge (hence the label *middle knowledge*).[48] The divine natural knowledge is populated with truths that are true due to God's nature, and God's free knowledge is populated with that which is true due to God's will, but middle knowledge is of truths in which the decisions of free creatures are the truth makers.[49] This is what a robust concept of permission entails.

Armed with these three conceptual tools, Molinism argues that God accomplishes His sovereign will via His omniscience. First, God knows everything that *could* happen. This first moment is His *natural knowledge*, where God knows everything due to His omniscient nature. Second, from the set of infinite possibilities, God also knows which scenarios *would* result in persons' freely responding in the way He desires. This crucial moment of knowledge is between the first and third moment, hence the term *middle knowledge*. From the repertoire of available options provided by His middle knowledge, God freely and sovereignly chooses which one He will bring to pass. This results in God's third moment of knowledge, which is His foreknowledge of what certainly *will* occur.[50] The third moment is God's *free knowledge* because it is determined by His free and sovereign choice.

By utilizing these three phases of knowledge, God predestines all events, yet not in such a way that violates genuine human freedom and choice. God meticulously "sets the table" so that humans freely choose what he had predetermined. An example of this could be Simon Peter's denial of the Lord. The Lord predicted Peter would deny him and by use of middle knowledge ordained the scenario that infallibly guaranteed

---

[48] Flint, *Divine Providence*, 42–43.

[49] Ibid., 46–50.

[50] The verbs *could, would,* and *will* highlight the distinctions in the moments of God's knowledge. From knowledge of what *could* happen (first moment), God knows which ones *would* bring about His desired result (second moment), and He chooses one possibility which means He knows it *will* come about (third moment).

Peter would do so. However, God did not make or cause Peter to do as he did.

The Advantages of the Molinist Approach

The Molinist approach has a number of advantages over both Calvinism and Arminianism, which I want to list briefly. First, *Molinism affirms the genuine desire on the part of God for all to be saved in a way that is problematic for Calvinism.* God has a universal salvific will even though not all, maybe not even most, will repent and believe the gospel. Historically, Calvinists have struggled with this question. Most have either denied God's desire for all to be saved, or else they claimed that God has a secret will which trumps His revealed will.

Molinism fits well with the biblical teaching that God universally loves the world (John 3:16) and yet Christ has a particular love for the Church (Eph 5:25). William Lane Craig suggests that God "chose a world having an optimal balance between the number of the saved and the number of the damned."[51] In other words, God has created a world with a maximal ratio of the number of saved to those lost. The Bible teaches that God genuinely desires all to be saved, and even though many perish, still His will is done. Molinism better addresses this apparent paradox.

An illustration may be helpful here. Before the Normandy invasion General Dwight Eisenhower was told by many of his advisors that casualties might exceed 70 percent. The actual human toll was terrible but thankfully not that high. Eisenhower gave the order for the invasion to proceed, but he would have been quick to tell you he genuinely desired that none of his men should perish. Molinism understands God's will for all to be saved to operate in a similar fashion, though we recognize all analogies break down eventually.

To try to explain the Calvinist view of God's salvific will, John Piper and Bruce Ware also used illustrations of leaders—George Washington and Winston Churchill, respectively—who were forced to make similarly difficult decisions.[52] Their illustrations work against their position because a key component of the Calvinist doctrine of election is that the reprobate are passed over because of "God's good pleasure." Molinism better fits the biblical description of the two wills of God (or the two aspects of God's will)—His antecedent and consequent wills. The Molinist can affirm without qualification that God is "not willing

---

[51] William Lane Craig, "'No Other Name': A Middle Knowledge Perspective on the Exclusivity of Salvation through Christ," *Faith and Philosophy* 6:2 (April 1989): 185.

[52] John Piper, "Are There Two Wills in God? Divine Election and God's Desire for All to Be Saved," in *The Grace of God, the Bondage of the Will, Vol. 1,* 122–24; and Bruce Ware, "Divine Election to Salvation," 33–34.

that any should perish but that all should come to repentance" (2 Pet 3:9 NKJV).

Second, *Molinism provides a better model for understanding how simultaneously God's decree of election is unconditional while His rejection of the unbeliever is conditional.* God's omniscient foreknowledge is the Achilles' heel for most Arminian presentations of election. If God has exhaustive knowledge of all future events, then conditional election does not really remove the unconditional nature of God's decisions. If God knows that a certain man will freely accept the gospel while that man's brother freely will not, and yet God decides to create both of them anyway, then this is a mysterious, sovereign, and unconditional determination on the part of God.

Some Arminians recognize this dilemma and opt for open theism instead. In open theism, God does not know how an individual will respond to the gospel. He creates a person and hopes for the best. The open theist sees God as an actuary working the odds and understands God's sovereignty as an exercise in risk management.

Molinism provides a much better answer. Why does the reprobate exist? Because of God's sovereign will. Why is he reprobated? Because of his own unbelief. When God made the sovereign choice to bring this particular world into existence, He rendered certain but did not cause the destruction of certain ones who would reject God's overtures of grace. According to Molinism, our free choice determines how we would respond in any given setting, but God decides the setting in which we actually find ourselves. As Craig stated, "It is up to God whether we find ourselves in a world in which we are predestined, but it is up to us whether we are predestined in the world in which we find ourselves."[53]

In other words, the Molinist paradigm explains how it is possible for there to be a decree of election without a corresponding decree of reprobation, which is in fact the biblical witness. One of the strongest motivations for the infralapsarian position is the conviction that God did not ordain the reprobate to hell in the same way He ordained the elect to salvation. The Molinist model presents an asymmetric relationship between God and the two classes of people, the elect and the reprobate, in a manner that infralapsarianism cannot. This is a great advantage to Molinism.

The third point is the converse to the previous one: *in the Molinist system, unlike Arminianism, God is the author of salvation who actively elects certain ones.* In Arminianism God employs only a passive foreknowledge (in open theism God elects no individuals at all). Molinists contend that God uses His exhaustive foreknowledge in an active,

---

[53] See Craig, "No Other Name," 172–88.

sovereign way. God determines the world in which we live. Whether I exist at all, have the opportunity to respond to the gospel, or am placed in a setting where I would be graciously enabled to believe are sovereign decisions made by Him. The Molinist affirms that the elect are saved by God's good pleasure. The distinctive difference between Calvinism and Molinism is that Calvinism sees God accomplishing His will through His omnipotent power while Molinism understands God's using His omniscient knowledge.

The fourth point expands the third point: *Molinism has a more robust and scriptural understanding of the role God's foreknowledge plays in election than does either Calvinism or Arminianism.* The Bible repeatedly states that "those He foreknew he also predestined" (Rom 8:29) and that the saints are "chosen according to the foreknowledge of God the Father" (1 Pet 1:1–2 NKJV). Calvinists generally claim that in these instances God's foreknowledge should be understood as His "forelove." This seems to be a classic case of special pleading. Arminians contend that what is foreknown by God is merely the believer's faith. Molinism rejects both explanations.

In the Calvinist understanding of foreknowledge and predetermination, the future is the product of the will of God. The Calvinist view clearly presents God as sovereign, but He also appears to be the cause of sin. In the Arminian formulation God looks forward into a future made by the decisions of free creatures and then makes His plans accordingly. The Arminian model emphasizes that God is a loving Father, but unfortunately His will has nothing to do with much that happens.

By contrast Molinism contends that God actively uses His foreknowledge. Among the many possibilities populated by the choices of free creatures, God freely and sovereignly decided which world to bring into existence. This view fits well with the biblical simultaneous affirmation of both foreknowledge and predetermination (Acts 2:23). Some Calvinists such as J. I. Packer and D. A. Carson affirm both, but they call their view the antinomy or paradox position because they know it cannot be reconciled with either the supra- or infralapsarian models.[54] Molinism is the one position that can radically affirm both with logical consistency.

In his book *Hyper-Calvinism and the Call of the Gospel*, supralapsarian Calvinist David Engelsma denies that the gospel is offered to everyone who hears it. He contends that no one who adheres to five-point Calvinism and to reprobation according to God's inscrutable decree can consistently hold to a "well-meant offer." He claims that his position is

---

[54] J. I. Packer, *Evangelism and the Sovereignty of God* (Downers Grove: IVP, 1961); and D. A. Carson, *Divine Sovereignty and Human Responsibility* (Atlanta: John Knox, 1981).

not hyper-Calvinism but consistent Calvinism. I believe Engelsma is in fact a hyper-Calvinist, but his argument highlights the problem Reformed theology has with affirming that the gospel is presented to every hearer in good faith. By contrast, Molinism has no difficulty in holding that the offer of the gospel is sincere and well meant. This is another decided advantage to the Molinist view.

Fifth, *Molinism provides a better model for understanding the biblical tension between divine sovereignty and human responsibility*. With both the Calvinist and Arminian scenarios, at times one gets the distinct impression that whole classes of passages are being shoehorned in order to fit the respective theological systems or that some passages are not interpreted so much as they are explained away. By contrast, when the Molinist assembles his theological paradigm, fewer biblical spare parts are left over.

For example, consider Jesus' condemnation of the cities of Chorazin, Bethsaida and Capernaum for failing to repent, and then His subsequent prayer and invitation (Matt 11:20–28). In this way, our Lord brings human responsibility immediately alongside divine sovereignty, a coupling that occurs throughout Scripture.[55] Jesus first denounces the unrepentant:

> Woe to you, Chorazin! Woe to you, Bethsaida! For if the miracles that were done in you had been done in Tyre and Sidon, they would have repented in sackcloth and ashes long ago! ... And you, Capernaum, will you be exalted to heaven? You will go down to Hades. For if the miracles that were done in you had been done in Sodom, it would have remained until today" (vv. 21,23).

Jesus places the blame at their feet. They should have responded but they did not.

But in a turnabout that affirms the unimpeded sovereignty of God, Jesus then praises the Father:

> At that time Jesus said, "I praise You, Father, Lord of heaven and earth, because You have hidden these things from the wise and learned and revealed them to infants. Yes, Father, because this was Your good pleasure" (vv. 25–26).

By so praying, Jesus reveals that God's sovereign will is still being accomplished. Despite appearances to the contrary, God was in complete control.

---

[55] E.g., Gen 50:20; Isa 10:5–19; or Acts 2:23; 3:17–21; 4:24–28; 13:48–14:1.

Arminians tend to focus on vv. 20–24 with its emphasis on human responsibility, while Calvinists give prominence to the stress on divine sovereignty in vv. 25–27. But how can Jesus' warning and prayer both be true? And if God's will is somehow being done through their unbelief, how can Jesus conclude with an invitation to "Come to Me, all of you who are weary and burdened, and I will give you rest" (v. 28)? How can his offer be sincere?

Molinists point to Jesus' use of counterfactual knowledge to find a solution. Jesus highlights the guilt of the surrounding cities by contrasting their opportunity with that of some of the most evil cities of the Old Testament. Jesus knows how His message would have been received by the wicked inhabitants of Tyre, Sidon, or even Sodom, and He expresses this knowledge counterfactually. *If* they had had the opportunity that Israel had received, *then* they would have repented (vv. 21,23). Jesus indicates counterfactual knowledge of the choices they would have made had they been given the chance.

One might ask at this point why the citizens of Sodom, Tyre, and Sidon were not given the same opportunity the inhabitants of the Galilee region were given. Jesus teaches us that God's good and sovereign plan necessitated otherwise (vv. 25–27). Think again of Eisenhower's order for the invasion of Normandy, for the analogy applies here also. God desires the salvation of all, and is accomplishing the work of redemption in a maximal way, but this does not guarantee nor require that everyone have an optimal opportunity. Besides, Jesus clearly indicates that the responsibility for unbelief rests on the unbeliever, regardless of the level of opportunity, because he could have repented.

Molinism argues that, as the text indicates, God used his middle knowledge to accomplish His will despite (and even through) the unbelief of Israel. Since Molinism affirms the reality of both human agency (vv. 20–24) and divine agency (vv. 25–27), it holds that God is meticulously achieving His will and that Jesus' offer is in good faith when He invites all to freely come to Him. Like so many other passages, Matt 11:20–28 simultaneously teaches human choice and divine sovereignty. Molinism is in the unique position of not having to bludgeon one truth into submission for the sake of the other.

Sixth, *Molinism places mystery where it should be located, i.e., in God's infinite attributes rather than in His character.* Critics of Molinism, particularly open theists, contend that Molinism fails to give an adequate explanation of how God infallibly knows what choices free creatures are going to make. This is generally known as "the grounding objection" because it questions whether Molinism provides any grounds or basis for God's middle knowledge.

Molinists generally reply by arguing that God innately knows all things by virtue of His omniscience and that for God to have infallible knowledge of all things is simply in His nature. The Molinist advocate affirms but may not be able to explain to everyone's satisfaction that God has exhaustive foreknowledge of what creatures with libertarian freedom will do.[56]

If Molinists have to appeal to mystery at this point, they do so at a better and more reasonable point. I'd rather have the Molinist difficulty of not being able to explain how God's omniscience operates than the Calvinist difficulty of explaining how God is not the author of sin. In other words, Molinism's difficulties are with God's infinite attributes rather than His holy and righteous character. Implicit in the grounding objection is the denial that God has the ability to create creatures with libertarian freedom (of the morally significant kind). This places a surprising constraint on the scope of God's sovereignty. The Molinist embraces a richer conception of God's sovereignty since God exercises meticulous providence despite the existence of free creatures![57]

One of the things we understand least about God is how His infinite attributes operate—His omniscience, omnipotence, and omnipresence. Why place the mystery of reprobation in God's character? Molinists do not claim to know God's purposes exhaustively, but among the things most clearly revealed about God are His holiness, righteousness, and goodness. Would we not rather place the mystery within the transcendent, infinite, inexhaustible omniscience of God than the revealed character and purposes of God?

Seventh, *Molinism has a valid concept of permission that does not have to resort to special pleading.* In infralapsarian Calvinism, what exactly does *permission* mean? Not much. Many within Reformed theology acknowledge that the language of permission is used merely to make Calvinism seem to be less harsh. John Frame stated, "Evidently, the Reformed use *permit* mainly as a more delicate term than cause."[58] Berkhof concurred, saying that infralapsarians speak of a permissive decree because it sounds "more . . . tender."[59] This opens Reformed theology to the accusation of using the term in a misleading manner because, as Frame pointed out, in the final analysis Calvinism sees permission as

---

[56] For a response to the grounding objection, see William Lane Craig, "Middle Knowledge, Truth-Makers, and the 'Grounding Objection'," *Faith and Philosophy* 18:3 (2001): 337–52.

[57] I want to thank Doug Geivett for his insights and help with this paragraph.

[58] Frame, *The Doctrine of God*, 178.

[59] Berkhof, *Systematic Theology*, 124.

just another "form of ordination, a form of causation."[60] In Molinism, *permit* means "permit."

One of the interesting developments in recent days is the appearance of "middle knowledge Calvinism." Bruce Ware, John Frame, and Terrance Tiessen are among the Reformed theologians who are trying to incorporate the insights of Molinism into infralapsarian Calvinism.[61] They do so for the express purpose of using the concept of permission in a quasi-Molinist manner because they recognize the problems with the Calvinist formulation of the decrees. However, the concept of middle knowledge is superfluous in any system that holds to causal determinism.

Sometimes Molinism is described as inconsistent Calvinism, but one could argue that it is the other way around. Perhaps infralapsarian Calvinism is inconsistent Molinism. To my infralapsarian brothers, I say, in regard to the concept of permission, Molinists have simply taken the steps you want to take or at least you want to appear to have taken. If you wish to be consistent, you have a choice: either supralapsarianism or Molinism.

Conclusion

I am thankful for the contributions that Calvinists are making to Southern Baptist life. They are right to call Southern Baptists away from pragmatic methodologies and reaffirm that salvation is a sovereign work of God. However, the decretal approach to election taken by Calvinism seems to create more problems than it solves.

Molinism does not provide an explanation as to why God created a world in which it was possible for sin to enter, but it is not necessary to do so. Molinism is a defense not a theodicy. A theodicy is an attempt to explain *why* God ordained the world He did. A defense is much more modest. A defense simply attempts to demonstrate that it is *logically consistent* to believe that a good and sovereign God can purpose to create a world like ours. Molinism accomplishes this.

If one is going to do justice to the doctrine of God, he must affirm both God's sovereignty and His permission. Molinism presents a forceful affirmation of both.

---

[60] Frame, *The Doctrine of God*, 178.

[61] For example, see Terrance Tiessen, "Why Calvinists Should Believe in Divine Middle Knowledge, although They Reject Molinism," *WTJ* 69 (2007): 345–66.

Election and Calling:
A Biblical Theological Study

Greg Welty
Assistant Professor of Philosophy
Southwestern Baptist Theological Seminary
Fort Worth, Texas

ACCORDING TO MY SEMINARY PRESIDENT, Dr. Paige Patterson, "If one wishes to know what most Baptists believed during the formative days of the Southern Baptist Convention, he will discover it in this volume," that is, in J. L. Dagg's *Manual of Theology*.[1] He continues by saying that "every pastor, professor, and seminary student should avail himself of the opportunity to become acquainted with one of the most sublime of our Baptist fathers." I commend him to you as well, with the admission that there's not much in this chapter that you won't be able to find in Dagg, in particular in his exposition of the "Sovereignty of Grace" (Book Seventh, Chapter IV).

My plan is simple. I want to defend both unconditional election and effectual calling, by first defining these doctrines, then expounding some proof texts, and finally interacting with some criticisms. Like so many, I lament the growing tensions within the convention on a number of fronts, but I see honest and respectful dialogue as one key way to promote unity. We should not try to paper over differences in theology but build bridges of communication. In fact, I'm convinced that we have a signal opportunity—as professors, pastors, and colaborers in Christ's kingdom—to set an important example of how Southern Baptists can and ought to dialogue about their differences without rancor or ill will.

---

[1] J. L. Dagg, *Manual of Theology* (South Carolina: Southern Baptist Publication Society, 1857; Harrisonburg, VA: Gano Books, 1990). The citation is from the inside back cover of the 1990 reprint.

Unconditional Election

What is unconditional election?

Unconditional election is both an assertion and a denial. The "election" part is the assertion, and the "unconditional" part is the denial. Unconditional election asserts that God elects or chooses us for salvation, but it denies that this choice is on the basis of works or foreseen faith.

An assertion (or positive claim): God graciously chooses us for salvation

The positive claim that God graciously chooses us for salvation is largely uncontroversial among Christians in general, including Southern Baptists. Who would deny that God is a God who chooses kings for office, nations for service, and sinners for salvation? Even a casual perusal of a Bible concordance reveals that the words *elect, choose, foreordain*, and *predestine* are firmly embedded in the sacred text. Indeed, they are there by divine design for our instruction and our comfort. On this much we all agree: the blessings of God's salvation are only available to sinners, and only come to sinners, by God's choice. As Ken Keathley put it, "Election is the gracious decision of God by which he chooses certain ones to be the recipients of salvation."[2] And as BFM 2000 puts it:

> Election is the gracious purpose of God, according to
> which He regenerates, justifies, sanctifies, and glorifies
> sinners. It is consistent with the free agency of man,
> and comprehends all the means in connection with the
> end. It is the glorious display of God's sovereign good-
> ness, and is infinitely wise, holy, and unchangeable. It
> excludes boasting and promotes humility.[3]

It seems that Southern Baptists unite around this positive claim as a matter of common confession.

A denial (or negative claim): God's choice is not on the basis of foreseen faith or good works

Clearly then, the controversy between Calvinists and non-Calvinists over unconditional election is not the Calvinists' assertion that God elects some for salvation since non-Calvinists believe this too. Rather, the controversy is over the Calvinists' negative claim, namely, the denial

---

[2] Ken Keathley, "The Work of God: Salvation," in *A Theology for the Church*, ed. Daniel L. Akin (Nashville: B&H Academic, 2007), 707.

[3] Available at www.sbc.net/bfm/bfm2000.asp (accessed November 19, 2007). The citation is from section V.

that divine election unto salvation is on the basis of works or foreseen faith.[4] But why should anyone, biblically or theologically speaking, so forcefully deny, as Calvinists do deny, that election is conditioned upon something foreseen in us?

Why believe in unconditional election?

Ephesians 1:3–11

Several texts appear to teach, or at least strongly imply, unconditional election. Probably the most well-known is Eph 1:3–11. At least three things leap out at us from this text:

Election is eternal. God is a God who "chose us in Him before the foundation of the world" (v. 4).[5] God's action of election does not await our fulfillment of certain conditions. According to Paul, God's activity of choosing a people for Himself was an accomplished fact before we were born, indeed, before there was even a world. This fact all by itself should fill us with astonishment and awe. If you are a Christian, from all eternity God had you in mind and marked you out for a peculiar destiny.

Election is personal. According to Paul, God did not choose abstract categories or hypothetical conditionals and then say, "I thus choose you, O abstract category or hypothetical conditional! Whoever ends up having faith in Christ will end up being saved, and I choose that that's the way it's going to be. Whoever is in category A will end up being in category B as well." Interesting theory, but far from the thought of the apostle Paul. God elects people, not categories or conditions. Paul said, "He chose us" (v. 4), not that He chose a category. Paul said, "He predestined us" (v. 5), not that He predestined a conditional to be true. Paul said, "We have . . . been predestined" (v. 11). This is a matter of simple grammar, it seems to me, a matter of noting that personal pronouns occur throughout this text and that those pronouns refer to us, such that we are the direct objects of God's choosing activity, not some abstract category.[6]

Election is grounded in God's will. Specifically, election is grounded in God's will to love us, His will to be gracious to us, and His will to fulfill His purpose for us. Far from some cold, analytical move on God's part, "in love He predestined us to adoption as sons through Jesus Christ

---

[4] As Keathley puts it, unconditional election means that "there is no consideration of any foreseen merit or faith on the part of the elect" (Keathley, "The Word of God: Salvation," 708).

[5] Unless otherwise indicated, Scripture quotations are from the NASB.

[6] Likewise for the other things Paul noted, such as the fact that God "has blessed *us* with every spiritual blessing" (v. 3), that "He freely bestowed on *us*" his grace (v. 6), and that "*we* have obtained an inheritance" (v. 11). Throughout this passage the various divine activities are directed specifically to persons, not abstract categories or conditionals.

to Himself" (vv. 4–5). "To the praise of the glory of His grace" (v. 6) He so predestined us, indeed, "according to the riches of His grace" (v. 7).

In this passage *our will and what we do with it* is never mentioned as the basis of God's choice. In fact, Paul repeatedly and emphatically draws our attention to *God's* will as the foundation of our salvation. "He predestined us to adoption as sons," not according to (or on the basis of) our will to choose Him but "according to the kind intention of His will" (v. 5). What is relevant in explaining the divine gift of salvation is "the mystery of His will" and "His kind intention" toward us (v. 9), not the mystery of our will or our kind intention toward Him.[7] Paul said, "He chose us" (v. 4), and God chose us not because we were holy enough to make the right choice for Him but so "that we *would be* holy and blameless before Him" (v. 4). In other words, election is unto holiness, not because of holiness.

Verse 11 is especially clear that election is grounded in God's will: "having been predestined according to His purpose who works all things after the counsel of His will" (v. 11). In other words, God is a certain kind of God—a God "who works all things after the counsel of His will," and "according to the purpose" of *that* kind of God we have "been predestined." Thus, Paul understood and accounted for the spiritual predestination of individuals in light of the broader, more general truth that God "works [*energeō*] all things [not just some things] after the counsel [*boulē,* "decision, purpose, plan, intention"] of His will" (v. 11). Our particular predestination to salvation is just part of a larger purpose that embraces all events. Unconditional election is not some perplexing anomaly in our portrait of God, something to be explained away or passed over in embarrassment. Rather, in verse 11 Paul sees it as a natural consequence of his larger doctrine of God and His providence.

Surely, then, the notion that election is conditioned upon something in the creature cuts across the grain of this entire passage. To review my three points, Paul is teaching us that from eternity past God chose certain persons for salvation, and He did so on no other basis than that He willed to be loving and gracious toward them in this way. This and this alone accounts for Paul's repeated insistence that salvation is "to the praise of the glory of His grace" (v. 6), "according to the riches of His grace" (v. 7), and "to the praise of His glory" (vv. 12,14).

Romans 9

The doctrine of unconditional election is confirmed when we turn to Romans 9. Although we do not have time to examine the chapter in full, at least three things are evident from the text:

---

[7] The latter just doesn't seem to play any explanatory role at all as to why God chose us to be saved.

First, *Paul here addresses matters of spiritual salvation*, not merely election to temporal service or historical privilege. As Tom Schreiner put it:

> When Paul speaks of the anguish in his heart and his desire to be accursed because of his fellow Israelites (Rom 9:1–3), the reason he feels this way is not because Israel is merely losing out on temporal blessings. Distress torments his heart because his kinsmen from Israel were not saved. Paul is almost willing "to be separated from Christ" (9:3) because his fellow Israelites are separated from Christ.[8]

Clearly, matters of eternal and spiritual significance were at stake in the unbelief of Israel, and Paul aimed to reconcile this with the promise and faithfulness of God.

Indeed, if Paul was only talking about temporary, earthly blessings or mere historical privilege in Romans 9, why would the entire chapter be filled with the kind of language that Paul characteristically employs everywhere else to speak of *salvation and damnation?*—"accursed," "election," "works," "unrighteousness," "mercy," "compassion," "wrath," "destruction," "saved," "righteousness," "righteousness of faith," "by faith," "by the works of the law," "whoever believes on Him will not be put to shame," and so on. Surely mere historical destiny is not in view.

Rather, Paul was using historical examples to make a point about spiritual salvation, about the present-day *spiritual* status of his kinsmen according to the flesh. In effect, by talking about Isaac and Ishmael, Jacob and Esau, Moses and Pharaoh, Paul was building a case for a consistent *modus operandi* of God throughout history and then explaining the present salvation of only a remnant of Israel in terms of a divine pattern that has been revealed from the beginning.

Second, Paul revealed that *God's own purpose and will have always been the ultimate reason He chooses some and passes over others*. God said to Rebekah, "The older will serve the younger" (v. 12), and He said this, "though the twins were not yet born and had not done anything good or bad" (v. 11a). Why would God do such a thing? Paul said: "So that God's purpose according to His choice would stand, not because of works but because of Him who calls" (v. 11b). The reason God distinguished between Jacob and Esau and elevated Jacob to a privilege higher than that which he would otherwise have obtained, was "God's purpose according to His choice," that is, "because of Him who calls."

---

[8] Thomas R. Schreiner, "Does Romans 9 Teach Individual Election unto Salvation? Some Exegetical and Theological Reflections," *JETS* 36 (1993): 27.

Again, when God decided to give Moses the inestimable privilege of seeing the divine glory and goodness on Mt. Sinai, "He says to Moses, 'I will have mercy on whom I have mercy, and I will have compassion on whom I have compassion'" (v. 15). This is not an uninformative tautology but a divinely instituted stopping point to all inquiry when it comes to grounding the selectivity of divine grace. The stopping point is God's will, and we can reach no higher, nor should we want to do so.[9] It is as if God were to say, "This is how I have always dispensed My blessings. It is a matter of My will to be merciful, compassionate, and gracious, and there's an end on it." Salvation is ultimately a gift from above, bestowed by sovereign prerogative, not something owed to the creature or conditioned on the creature. It is not, "I will have mercy on who responds to Me," but, "I will have mercy on whom I have mercy, and that in turn will explain all else."

Again, God said to Pharaoh, "For this very purpose I raised you up, to demonstrate My power in you, and that My name might be proclaimed throughout the whole earth" (v. 17). And what is Paul's divinely inspired inference from God's *modus operandi*, as he surveys the historical record of God's dealings with Isaac and Ishmael in the desert, with Jacob and Esau in the womb, with Moses on the mount and Pharaoh on the throne? "So then He has mercy on whom He desires [*thelei*, "to desire, want, will"], and He hardens whom He desires [*thelei*]" (v. 18). Once more, whether hardening continues as a form of divinely intended judgment or mercy breaks through with divine power and secures divine blessing, it is all traced back to the divine will (*thelei*), and no further.

Third, *Paul clearly denies that God's saving purposes are conditioned on how we use our will*. Probably the clearest text here is v. 16: "So then it does not depend on the man who wills or the man who runs, but on God who has mercy." God's electing purposes are not some sort of divine ratifying of human willing ("the man who wills") or human effort ("the man who runs"). God's electing purposes are not dependent on these things at all.

This is not to say that divine election has no place for human willing or effort in history. Nor is it to say that divine election is unrelated to our

---

[9] Clearly the surrounding context of Exod 33:19 (which Paul cites here in Rom 9:15) makes no suggestion there was anything *in Moses* that warranted God's revealing His glory on that occasion. Indeed, "The Lord said to Moses, 'I will also do this thing of which you have spoken; for you have found favor in My sight, and I have known you by name'" (Exod 33:17 emphasis added). God does not say, l: "for you have found favor in My sight," not, "for I have found you to be favorable." The Hebrew expression for "find favor" refers to receiving a *gift*, not a *reward* (see *NIDOTTE*, 2:203–6). And again: "for… I have known you by name," not, "for you have made yourself renowned." The reason for God's mercy and compassion on that occasion was the Lord's own purpose and will.

willing and working. It is simply to say that divine election is not *on the basis of* our willing and efforts. As Paul taught the Ephesians, election is *unto* holiness (1:4), and *that* certainly involves our will and our efforts. So our willing for God and our effort on behalf of God are important to God. As Paul commanded the Philippians, "Work out your salvation with fear and trembling" (2:12). Nevertheless, the fundamental point remains: the fact *that* what we will and work is ultimately due to God's working in our lives: "For it is God who is at work in you, both to will and to work for His good pleasure" (2:13). The doctrine of unconditional election traces this all the way back to the eternal and gracious purpose of God in our lives.

Paul's response to the imaginary objector of Rom 2:14 and 19 corroborates this interpretation. In response to the teaching on Jacob and Esau, the objector asks, "What shall we say then? There is no injustice with God, is there?" (v. 14a). And in response to the teaching on Pharaoh, the objector asks, "Why does He still find fault? For who resists His will?" (v. 19). Paul's response is, "May it never be!" (v. 14b), and, "Who are you, O man, who answers back to God?" (v. 20a). If election were conditional, Paul would have every reason to say, "Wait, you've misunderstood my teaching. God's choice of men ultimately hinges on men's choice for God, so it's all fair in the end. We can resist God's will, and if God foreknows that, He wouldn't choose us to begin with. God's choice of Jacob was really based on Jacob's future choice for God. So of course there's no injustice here; God just saw the future and ratified Jacob's choice." No, in the face of the repeated accusation of injustice on the part of God, Paul does nothing to blunt the edge of his teaching about unconditional, divine selectivity in matters of grace.[10]

What are some objections to unconditional election?

The Bible teaches that election is on the basis of our foreseen faith

Some have argued that there are scriptural texts which clearly contradict unconditional election, the so-called "foreknowledge" texts. For instance, Rom 8:29 says, "For those whom He foreknew, He also predestined to become conformed to the image of His Son, so that He would be the firstborn among many brethren." So there's something prior

---

[10] As D. J. Moo puts it, "If Paul had assumed that faith was the basis for God's election, he would have pointed this out when he raised the question in v. 14 about the fairness of God's election. All he would have needed to say at that point was 'of course God is not unjust in choosing Jacob and rejecting Esau, for his choosing took into account the faith of one and the unbelief of the other.' Paul's silence on this point is telling." D. J. Moo, *The Epistle to the Romans,* NICNT (Grand Rapids: Eerdmans, 1996), 583.

Beyond Eph 1 and Rom 9, additional Scriptures pertaining to unconditional election include Acts 13:48; 1 Thess 5:9; and 2 Tim 1:9.

to predestination, namely, foreknowledge. Likewise with 1 Pet 1:1–2, which speaks of those "who are chosen according to the foreknowledge of God the Father, by the sanctifying work of the Spirit, to obey Jesus Christ and be sprinkled with His blood." So God makes a choice, but it is a choice "according to the foreknowledge of God the Father." Given this, what could be clearer than that God predestines us on the basis of His foreknowledge of how we will in fact respond to Him (or, alternatively, how we would respond if He were to give us His gospel)?

Well, not so fast. The proposed interpretation is neither necessary nor plausible. It's certainly not necessary because neither text says that God elects us on the basis of *foreseen faith*. In fact, neither text even *mentions* faith as something foreseen at all, much less that election is based on it.[11] Rather, in the "foreknew passages" (Rom 8:29; 1 Pet 1:2), what is said to be foreknown are *people*, not faith or works. What Rom 8:29 says is: "*Those* whom He foreknew, He also predestined." It is *persons* who are said to be foreknown, not their acts of faith specifically. First Peter 1:1–2 is more ambiguous; it just mentions "foreknowledge" without clarifying whether the object of that foreknowledge is persons, or their faith, or their works, or anything else about them.

Not only is the "foreseen faith" interpretation unnecessary (from a textual point of view), but it is also implausible, for it would cut against the grain of everything we've already seen in Ephesians 1 and Romans 9. Instead of responding to the imaginary objector, "Who are you, O man, who answers back to God?" (Rom 9:20), Paul could have said, "What's the matter, didn't you read Rom 8:29? I already told you: all this is based on foreseen faith. Human choices ultimately determine salvation, not God's will." But of course Paul does not say this, though that reply would be ready at hand in Romans 9 if in fact Rom 8:29 is speaking of foreseen acts of faith. In addition, there seems little reason for Paul to say in Rom 9:16, "So then it does not depend on the man who wills or the man who runs, but on God who has mercy" if in Rom 8:29 he had just taught that election *does* depend on the man who wills. I think a principle of hermeneutical charity is relevant here: it is not only implausible but uncharitable to interpret Paul in a way that introduces palpable contradiction into his thought, and that in the space of two chapters, especially if said interpretation is textually unnecessary in the first place.

Those familiar with the Calvinist debate at this point are probably well aware of how Calvinists take these two texts. *Knowledge* in Scripture

---

[11] Obviously, God *does* foresee our faith, as He does all else. The question is whether in these passages Paul and Peter are even referring to foreseen acts of faith, much less grounding election in these foreseen acts. I suggest there is little textual evidence for either of these possibilities.

often denotes not bare cognition or awareness but a personal relationship entered into by choice. For instance, God said through the prophet Amos, "Hear this word which the Lord has spoken against you, sons of Israel, against the entire family which He brought up from the land of Egypt: 'You only have I chosen [lit. "known," *yāda'*] among all the families of the earth; Therefore I will punish you for all your iniquities'" (Amos 3:1–2). Clearly when God said that Israel was the only family on earth He had known, He didn't mean that He was unaware of all the other nations. What He meant is that Israel was the only nation *with whom He had entered into a specific covenant relationship* (which is why the NASB and NIV translate *yāda'* in this text as "chosen").

Likewise, Jesus warned religious hypocrites that on the last day, "I will declare to them, 'I never knew you; depart from Me, you who practice lawlessness'" (Matt 7:23). In saying He never "knew" them, Jesus was not saying that He was cognitively unaware of them (as though afflicted with a case of divine amnesia). What He was saying is that He never had a saving relationship with them, despite their many words and outward deeds. It is this kind of intimate, personal, committed relationship that Calvinists suggest is being spoken of in these and other biblical texts (see Gen 4:1; Exod 2:25; Hos 13:4–5), and in Rom 8:29 and 1 Pet 1:2 as well. God foreknows individuals, which is to say He *foreloves* them; and in virtue of that special, distinguishing love, He marks them out for a peculiar destiny: conformity to the image of His Son (Rom 8:29) and obedience to Jesus Christ and sprinkling by His blood (1 Pet 1:2).[12]

In the end, the Calvinistic interpretation of the "foreknowledge" texts is much more plausible because the background to the New Testament doctrine of election is surely God's election of Israel in the Old Testament, and there it is clear that God's election *is* according to foreloving. That is, the Lord chose them *because* "the Lord loved you"

---

[12] To be sure, these texts do not *explicitly* say "whom God foreloved" or "chosen according to foreloving," even as they do not explicitly say "those whose faith God foreknew" or "chosen according to foreseen faith." Both Calvinists and non-Calvinists need to admit that neither interpretation is textually necessary. Still, as seen above, in Scripture "knowledge" *does* often have the connotation of purposed, intimate relationship, whereas there seems to be little to no biblical example of "knowledge" standing in for "knowledge of foreseen faith."

Furthermore, in response to Arminian author Jack Cottrell, the Calvinist interpretation does not render Paul's statement redundant, as if Paul were saying, "Those whom God has chosen, he has also chosen." Rather, the idea is that to those whom God has foreloved he has purposed a particular destiny as well, namely, being conformed to the image of God's Son. The particular destiny (conformity to Christ) is grounded in a prior, distinguishing love. There's nothing uninformative here; Rom 8:29 offers us a genuine explanation of why one follows from the other, rather than a case of divine stuttering. See Keathley, "The Work of God," 717, who cites Cottrell as raising this objection.

(Deut 7:6–8; 10:15–16). Ask an Old Testament Jew or a New Testament Christian why he was elected by God, and the answer is going to be the same: "Not because of anything in ourselves, but because God chose to set His love upon us."[13]

Arguments for unconditional election confuse faith with good works

J. L. Dagg cited several texts which make clear that "election is of grace, and not of works" (e.g., Eph 2:8–9; Rom 11:6; 9:11; 2 Tim 1:9). From this Dagg inferred, "It necessarily follows, that election is not on the ground of foreseen faith or obedience."[14] But although this is a popular argument among Calvinists, it does seem a bit quick. A non-Calvinist who believes in conditional election might accuse Dagg of treating saving faith as if it were a meritorious work, thus forgetting the obvious Pauline contrast between faith and good works. The advocate of conditional election might say, "God chooses us on the basis of foreseen faith, but I would never say that our foreseen faith constitutes *merit* before God, as if it is some kind of good work deserving of a reward. It isn't. It's faith, and Paul regularly *contrasts* faith and works in his teaching on justification (Rom 3:28; 4:2,5; 5:1; Gal 2:16). The simple exercise of faith is the antithesis of relying on good works. So I can agree that God does not choose us based on foreseen *merit*, but I continue to hold that God chooses us on the basis of foreseen *faith*. And that's because the merit of works and the presence of faith are two very different things."

Indeed, Arminian Donald M. Lake makes this point in his contribution to the Clark Pinnock anthology, saying, "Calvinists never seem to be able to see this fundamental distinction unfortunately!"[15] In short, election based on foreseen faith is *not* the same thing as election on the basis of good works, so Bible texts denying the latter should not be construed as denying the former. Thus, typical Calvinist arguments for unconditional election rest upon a confusion of Pauline categories, or so it would seem.

---

[13] The New Testament texts on election do not just drop from heaven fully formed in a historical fashion; they occur as part of the climax of God's redemptive plan in history, a plan which reaches back to the beginning of the Old Testament revelation. It would be odd to suppose that Paul's doctrine of election had little to do with how God elected His people in the past. Indeed, in Rom 9–11 Paul inferred many truths about salvific election from God's pattern of historical election. In each case, "it does not depend on the man who wills or the man who runs, but on God who has mercy" (Rom 9:16). If God had grounded His choice of Israel in His "foreseeing" Israel's future faith, then—given the subsequent history of Israel—that would have been a poor choice indeed.

[14] Dagg, *Manual of Theology*, 312. Dagg cited his various Scripture texts on p. 311.

[15] Donald M. Lake, "He Died for All: The Universal Dimensions of the Atonement," in *Grace Unlimited*, ed. Clark Pinnock (Minneapolis: Bethany, 1975), 43. I found this citation in D. A. Carson, *Exegetical Fallacies*, 2d ed. (Grand Rapids: Baker, 1996), 121.

However, appearances here are deceiving. I agree that Calvinists need to make their case more clearly at this point. They need to affirm wholeheartedly Paul's contrast between faith and works and then press the point that unconditional election is the only way to *account for* this Pauline contrast. After all, if our faith ultimately originates from us and is not a gift of God given to us by the gracious choice of God, then why *wouldn't* it be as meritorious as any other work done in obedience to God? The exercise of faith is said to be something that pleases God (Heb 11:6), the gospel summons to repentance and faith is a command of God (Matt 11:28; Acts 17:30), Scripture says that God will punish all those who do not obey the gospel of God (2 Thess 1:8), and unbelief is a form of disobedience (Heb 3:18–19). So faith is a divine command directed to us and therefore a divinely imposed obligation resting upon us. If our obedience to that command were ultimately from us, why wouldn't we take credit for it? An *independently exercised* faith would be meritorious. The only way Paul could consistently sustain this contrast between faith and works is by presupposing that faith is fully a work of grace.[16] As D. A. Carson put it, if five prisoners accept a pardon and five reject it, those who accept "are distinguishable from those who reject the offer solely on the basis of their own decision to accept the pardon. The only thing that separates them from those who are carted off to prison is the wisdom of their own choice. That becomes a legitimate boast. By contrast, in the Calvinistic scheme, the sole determining factor is God's elective grace."[17]

Another way to put it is to say that our salvation is not "to the praise of the glory of His grace" (Eph 1:6) if it ultimately depends on our choice. For in that case *we* made the ultimate difference between our being saved or not saved. So why shouldn't we get some of the credit? God's grace was insufficient to save us since that grace didn't ensure our choice for Him.[18]

---

[16] Notice here the intimate connection between the two main topics of this paper. Faith is the gift of God (effectual calling) given to us by the gracious choice of God (unconditional election).

[17] Carson, *Exegetical Fallacies*, 121–22.

[18] According to BFM 2000, election "excludes boasting and promotes humility" (section V). But as I have just argued, conditional election at least *appears* to do neither, though I make this point gently and with respect for those who disagree. Unconditional election is, for me, the only way to make sense of this part of the BFM's claim about election, though I would not insist that my interpretation is the only acceptable one. (Requiring belief in alleged implications of a confessional document, beyond the explicit statements of the document itself, immediately defeats the purpose of a confessional document, which by nature is a *consensus* document that leaves at least some matters purposefully vague for the sake of unity. If the authors and revisers of the BFM 2000 really intended to include unconditional election, it would be stated explicitly.)

If God unconditionally chooses us for salvation, we don't really choose Him, which is clearly unbiblical

Yes, it is clearly unbiblical to say that humans don't choose God. Indeed, humans *must* choose God (in Christ) for salvation, and we ought to be clear and unambiguous about the importance of this choice, especially when we preach the gospel. If there is no personal response to our Savior's summons to repentance and faith, then there is no salvation. Men and women must believe in Christ—they must choose Christ—for salvation. And the faithful preaching of the gospel, including its demands for a response, is a vital and powerful means in the hands of God toward eliciting such a choice (Rom 1:16; 10:8–17; Jas 1:18; 1 Pet 1:23–25).

Thankfully Calvinists don't subscribe to an untenable dichotomy between divine choices and human choices. As with so much else in the Bible, the truth is not an either/or, but a both/and. The apostle John said, "We love, because He first loved us" (1 John 4:19). Here is the dual fact of choice: there is divine choice *and* human choice. Beyond this dual fact of divine and human choice is a clear implication of asymmetry: we love *because* He first loved us. That is, God's love is the prior and determining factor in our love for Him.

In fact, Jesus Himself highlighted this asymmetry and went so far as to say to His disciples, *"You did not choose Me but I chose you*, and appointed you that you would go and bear fruit, and that your fruit would remain, so that whatever you ask of the Father in My name He may give to you" (John 15:16). Now, of course, humanly speaking the disciples *did* choose to follow Jesus; the Gospels are replete with various accounts of their choices to follow Him. Jesus is not denying this evident truth. The point of His mild hyperbole is clear: Jesus' choice of His disciples was such a significant and determining factor in their subsequent life experience that in comparison it was *as if* the disciples did not choose Him. Jesus was saying: My choice of you is the *reason* for all else![19]

---

[19] This biblically endorsed asymmetry pretty much spells disaster for so-called "concurrence" views of election, according to which divine choice and human choice are on a logical par, such that neither is logically prior to the other. Clearly, God's choice to love us *was* logically prior to His knowledge of our love for Him, since Scripture says the latter depends on the former. In general, appealing to divine simplicity or timelessness to ground concurrence views proves far too much, for it would imply that *no* choice in God is logically prior to His knowledge of earthly events, which seems a bit much. For instance, surely God knew the Red Sea would be parted *because* God chose to part the Red Sea; it's not the other way around! For a brief discussion (and endorsement) of concurrence views, see Keathley, "The Work of God," 718–23. For a helpful criticism of concurrence views, see Roger E. Olson, *Arminian Theology: Myths and Realities* (Downers Grove, IL: InterVarsity Press, 2006), 68–69.

Moral and Practical Objections of Various Kinds

In this broad category I place objections that can be summarized in this way: If unconditional election is true, then it turns God into a wholly arbitrary, morally reprehensible, insincere tyrant whose existence renders all evangelistic efforts to be null and void. We could call this the "Shrek" objection—Calvinism turns God into an ogre.[20]

My overarching strategy here is one I dub "Calvinistic telekinesis." The critic fires his argument arrows at the proponent of unconditional election only to find these same arrows turning back 180 degrees and seeking *him* out instead. Less colorfully, I submit that each of the following criticisms, if sound, proves far too much: they prove we have reason to reject *orthodox theism*, Calvinistic or not. Each of these objections would apply to *anyone* who holds that (1) God exists, (2) God is infallibly omniscient about the future, and (3) God is a purposeful Creator (that is, He creates in order to realize intelligent and wise goals of some sort). Since these beliefs are held in common among evangelical Calvinists *and* non-Calvinists, the objections about to be discussed cannot be used to adjudicate the Calvinist/non-Calvinist debate. These objections are better seen as matters for intramural discussion among the family of faith rather than reasons to reject Calvinism in favor of some other view.[21]

If election is unconditional, then it must be arbitrary, random, and therefore lacking in wisdom

Not at all, and here it's clear the critic is involved in a non sequitur of some sort. It does not follow from the fact that God's reason is not grounded in the creature or that we are ignorant of God's reasons, that therefore God doesn't *have* a reason for His choice. The issue here is parallel to that of creation. Why did God create Earth with its particular size, with its particular distribution of chemical elements, with its particular number of fellow planets in the solar system? Why did God create us such that we are capable of seeing the range of colors we see and no more or less? To be honest, I have no idea (and neither do you). Presumably, God had lots of options here, on these and an infinite number of other details. But does it follow from our ignorance as to *why*

---

[20] Shrek was, cinematically speaking, rather nice overall, but you get the idea. Perhaps Tolkien's Balrog is more apt.

[21] Logicians among us might suggest that I am falling prey to the *tu quoque*, or "you too," fallacy. On this view, I am saying to my critics, "Your criticism doesn't work, because it applies to you too." And this *would* be a fallacy since the fact that a *critic* is inconsistent doesn't do anything to show that *the view being criticized* is consistent. But this isn't what I'm doing. I'm not saying, "Your criticism doesn't work," but rather, "Your criticism cannot be used to judge or prefer one view over the other since it applies to *both* views." And that seems right, as I am about to argue.

God created as He did, that therefore God's act of creation was arbitrary, random, and lacking wisdom? Of course not.

The same is true with respect to the particularities of providence. Why did God choose Abraham from Ur of the Chaldees, rather than Joe Ashurnapel from Babylon? Why did God have the disciples catch 153 fish rather than 154 (John 21:11)? To these and similar questions, I don't have the slightest clue. Does it follow from my ignorance that therefore God didn't *have* a reason? No. All that follows is that I am ignorant.

The same is true with respect to election. Why does God choose this one for salvation and pass over that one? In general, because of His love and His justice, respectively. But why did His love result in *that* particular choice of *that* particular person? I don't know. It doesn't follow from the Calvinistic claim (that God does not elect according to foreseen faith or merit) that therefore God has *no* reason for choosing to do what He does. For all we know, God *does* have a reason (perhaps a very complex reason, involving a multitude of greater goods) for choosing as He does. All the Calvinist is saying is that, whatever that reason might be, it has nothing to do with the foreseen faith or merit of the sinner who is chosen and predestined to heaven.

For a philosopher the fallacy in this criticism is easy to spot. It illegitimately makes inferences from epistemology to metaphysics—in this case, from our lack of *knowledge* of reality to a lack in reality itself. In general, it doesn't follow from the fact that I don't know God's reason for something (or from the fact that God's reason isn't ___) that therefore God doesn't *have* any reasons. Advocates of unconditional election can continue to affirm that election "is the glorious display of God's sovereign goodness, and is infinitely wise, holy, and unchangeable" (BFM 2000, section 5).[22]

If election is unconditional, then God is to blame for people being in hell.

The idea here is that there's something morally reprehensible in the idea of God's even passing over some for salvation when He could have saved all. If salvation depends on man's free will, then presumably it's not God's fault that some perish eternally in hell. It's the fault of those on whom salvation depends, namely, men with free will. But, non-Calvinists argue, if salvation depends (ultimately) on God's unconditional election,

---

[22] This is relevant to reprobation, since reprobation is simply the indirect result of God's decree to elect some to heaven. Why did God pass over some and leave them in their sins? I don't know, specifically. I'm happy to confess that I'm an ignorant Calvinist on this point, but my ignorance is hardly a good argument for the conclusion that God's decision was "arbitrary." Nothing at all follows about the "arbitrariness" of God's decision, from the fact that I am largely ignorant of God's reasons.

then it *is* God's fault that some are not saved, for it was within His power to save all. If salvation *ultimately* depends on God's choice, then it is *ultimately* God's fault that hell has a single person in it.

Once again, if this argument works, it proves too much and attacks both Calvinist *and* non-Calvinist views. As long as God is both omniscient and omnipotent, similar difficult questions can be asked about God's acts of *creation* and *providence*, quite apart from matters of election.

For example, given God's foreknowledge, God creates at least some people whom He knows will never come to faith. Thus, He knows they will end up in hell if they are created. Knowing this, God creates them. Why would He do a thing like that? Why create people whom He knows will end up in hell when it was in His power not to create them? Why would God deliberately and knowingly create individuals that He infallibly knows will never come to Him? I don't know. But does the fact that I don't have an answer mean I should ditch the doctrine of divine omniscience? I don't think so.[23]

Or again, clearly it is an evident fact of history that multitudes of people are born, live, and die without ever hearing the gospel, even though it would be a trivial thing for divine omnipotence to directly reveal the gospel message to them. Again, why would God not ensure they get the gospel message when He could do so? I don't know, but does it follow that I should deny divine omnipotence? Of course not.

It's hard to tell, then, why the non-Calvinist position should be advertised as a moral *improvement* over the Calvinist position. When someone says that the Calvinist position implies that God not only elected some to heaven but also (in virtue of that same act) condemned others to damnation, he is describing his own position as well. It's just that for the non-Calvinist, the lost are damned passively by God's acts of creation and providence rather than by the decree of election. While these are perplexing issues, the problem raised for the Calvinistic view of reprobation can also be raised for any (reasonably orthodox) alternative view.[24]

---

[23] "If God knows that a certain person will freely accept the gospel while that person's brother freely will not, and yet God decides to create both of them anyway, then this is a mysterious, sovereign, and unconditional determination on the part of God" (Keathley, "The Work of God," 718). Thus, anyone who affirms the BFM 2000, and is therefore not an open theist, in effect affirms a "passive decree" of reprobation anyway. On open theism, see Bruce A. Ware, *God's Lesser Glory* (Wheaton: Crossway, 2000); James Beilby and Paul Eddy, eds. *Divine Foreknowledge: Four Views* (Downers Grove, IL: InterVarsity, 2001).

[24] Dagg pointed out that "unless it can be shown that the election of grace lessens the number of the saved, no objection can lie against it, on the ground of its relation to God's benevolence" (*Manual of Theology*, 320). To be sure, given unconditional election, only some will be saved. But if election were conditioned rather on foreseen faith, would it follow that *more* people would be saved? Not at all; for all we know *fewer* people would

The bottom line is that the language of "fault" or "blame" is entirely inapplicable here to begin with. There is no "fault" in God if He passes over some for salvation—whether by election, creation, or providence—for He did not owe salvation to any. God is not defaulting on some sort of obligation to humanity if He does not secure the salvation of all. If salvation is in fact by God's grace, then it cannot be something God is obligated to provide.[25]

If election is unconditional, then God's gospel offer of salvation is insincere

If God has elected only some to salvation, then how can God sincerely offer salvation to those whom He has already passed over? Is God sincerely hoping that His decree is impotent? Is He sincerely hoping that a contradiction is true: that He both has and has not passed over some for salvation? The criticism here is that unconditional election makes the gospel offer insincere, if not meaningless, for multitudes of those to whom it comes.

Precisely parallel questions can be raised for the non-Calvinist. Presumably, God infallibly knows who will and who will not come to faith, and He has known this from all eternity. How can God sincerely offer salvation to those whom He knows will never accept it? Is God sincerely hoping that His infallible foreknowledge is mistaken? Is He sincerely hoping that a contradiction is true: that He both does and does not know what their response will be? Thus, if unconditional election makes the gospel offer insincere, then so does infallible foreknowledge.[26]

---

be saved (or none), if left to themselves apart from the gift of faith according to gracious election.

[25] Just to clarify my own views: unconditional election is not the "mirror image" of reprobation in every respect. Asymmetries here must be maintained. Unconditional election is independent of merit (sinners do not deserve heaven on account of their works); reprobation is not independent of merit (sinners do deserve the judgment they receive in hell). Unconditional election involves God's causal activity (God chooses to work faith in the hearts of the elect); reprobation does not involve any direct causal intervention on the part of God (He doesn't have to *do* anything at all; He simply passes over sinners and leaves them in their sin). "The Reformed view teaches that God positively or actively intervenes in the lives of the elect to insure their salvation. The rest of mankind God leaves to themselves. He does not create unbelief in their hearts. That unbelief is already there. He does not coerce them to sin. They sin by their own choices. In the Calvinist view the decree of election is positive; the decree of reprobation is negative" (R. C. Sproul, *Chosen by God* [Carol Stream, IL: Tyndale, 1994], 142–43).

[26] Likewise for the perseverance of the saints, a doctrine to which all Southern Baptists are also committed (BFM 2000, section 5). If God knows that all believers *shall* persevere to the end by His grace and thus He knows that their salvation is secure, then how can He be "sincere" in commanding them to persevere and not to fall away? And yet Scripture is filled with such commands (Heb 2:1; 4:11,14; 10:23,36).

In addition, Dagg argued that "in truth, there is no ground whatever for this charge of insincerity."[27] If in every case in which men refuse to come to Christ, they are sent to hell, then God's warning of judgment *was* sincere. "God proves His sincerity, by holding them to the obligation, and condemning their unbelief."[28] And if in every case in which men come to Christ, they are heaven-bound, then God's promise of blessing *was* sincere. "He promises salvation to all who believe in Christ; and he proves His sincerity, by fulfilling His promise in every instance."[29] In effect, Dagg was asking, "What more do you want in a doctrine of sincerity?" If God promised judgment on unbelief, and then didn't bring it, *that* would be insincere. And if God promised heaven on belief in Christ and then didn't bring it, *that* would be insincere. God *always* keeps His word, and in that respect He is as sincere as anyone could possibly be. God does not warn and promise and then turn around and say, "Oops, sorry, I was just joking! That's not really true. Unbelievers will go to heaven, and believers will go to hell, despite what I said." So either the charge of insincerity applies to the Calvinist and non-Calvinist views alike, or (as Dagg argued) it is fundamentally misguided to begin with.

If election is unconditional, then there's no reason to evangelize

If God has determined from the beginning who will be saved, then why evangelize? Whoever will be saved will be saved, and whoever won't, won't. No one can do anything now to make God's decree other than it is. So advocates of unconditional election should just sit home and do nothing rather than reach the world for Christ.

As the reader no doubt expects, the problem here is that even if this argument had a chance of being sound, it would prove too much. In fact, if it were sound, it would exclude conditional election as well. After all, if God has infallible foreknowledge about the future, then He has already known from eternity who shall come to faith and who will not. So what would stop an advocate of conditional election from saying, "God knows who will come to faith, and thus it's certain they *will* come to faith, for God cannot be mistaken in His foreknowledge. But if it has been certain from eternity (since God has known it from eternity), then why should I do anything to reach the lost? God already knows they're going to be saved, He's known this from eternity, and there's nothing we can do to make His knowledge other than what it is."

This argument, however, has no chance of being sound in either context, for it overlooks the fact that God is a God of *means* as well as ends. God

---

[27] *Manual of Theology*, 319.
[28] Ibid.
[29] Ibid.

uses responsible human effort to bring His purposes to pass in history. If God has ordained not only x, but x-shall-come-about-by-way-of-y, then doing y is important, nay vital, in bringing x to pass. Indeed, apart from y, x wouldn't come to pass! For all I know, God has ordained that I shall be the one who shall call many to faith in my lifetime. If so, I'd better get busy! In fact, the Scriptures present election as a *motivation for* vigorous effort on behalf of Christ's kingdom: "For this reason I endure all things for the sake of those who are chosen, so that they also may obtain the salvation which is in Christ Jesus and with it eternal glory" (2 Tim 2:10).

I conclude that these four moral/practical objections are a grab bag of "family problems," questions that the entire community of orthodox believers must work on and strive to answer. That is because they are applicable to both Calvinism *and* any reasonably orthodox alternatives to Calvinism. These are not special problems for the Calvinist alone, problems which can be cited as a means of preferring one view to the other. For the most part, the fact that *we believe in God* is sufficient to generate most of these questions. I think the identification of red herrings like these can have a salutary effect on future discussion. It frees us up to focus on the actual biblical materials and the best way to interpret them without being distracted by these extraneous (because irrelevant) questions. It does no good to raise a point as a means of adjudicating between A and B, if that point tells against *both* A and B.

Effectual Calling

What is effectual calling?

In transitioning now from unconditional election to effectual calling, we move from God's *planning* of salvation in eternity past to God's *bringing about* that salvation in the historical present. Of course, God does many things in order to accomplish salvation on our behalf and apply salvation to our hearts: He sent Christ to die on behalf of sinners, justifies us, adopts us into His family, sanctifies us, enables us to persevere to the end, and brings us into glory forever after. But the one aspect of salvation on which I want to now focus is "effectual calling." Effectual calling makes two assertions: God calls sinners to Himself (He both invites and commands them to repent of their sins and place their faith in Christ), and there is a call of God which is effectual (because it explains why we exercise both repentance and faith). As will be seen, each assertion carries with it a crucial distinction.

God calls sinners to Himself (not just the outer call but also the inner call)

Advocates of effectual calling are clear that God calls sinners to Himself for salvation. However, they make a distinction between the "outer call" (which goes to all to whom the gospel is preached and which may not result in faith and repentance) and the "inner call" (which goes to the elect alone and conveys the gift of faith and repentance).

God's call is effectual (not just a necessary but also a sufficient condition)

In addition, advocates of effectual calling stress that the "inner call" is the means God uses to work faith and repentance in the heart. It is effectual because it *does something* in the life of the sinner. However, here Calvinists make a distinction between something being *necessary* for faith and repentance and something being *sufficient* for faith and repentance, and they insist that the effectual call belongs in the latter category, not merely in the former.

Most evangelicals have little problem with saying that God's work of grace on the human heart is *necessary* if we are to repent and believe the gospel. For instance, (classic) Arminians typically hold to a doctrine of universal, prevenient grace, a work of God's Spirit which goes to all human beings and is required to enable otherwise depraved men and women to believe the gospel. On this view prevenient grace gives us back our free will that we lost in Adam. Then it is ultimately up to us how we use that free will (we can use it to either accept or reject the offer of salvation).[30] The real controversy between Calvinists and non-Calvinists is whether God's work of grace upon the human heart is *sufficient*, in any individual case, to bring someone to repentance and faith.[31] Dagg offers a useful summary:

---

[30] Roger Olson speaks of the "gift of God through prevenient grace—grace that precedes and enables the first stirrings of a good will toward God" (*Arminian Theology,* 20). "Prevenient grace is simply the convicting, calling, enlightening and enabling grace of God that goes before conversion and makes repentance and faith possible" (p. 35). "From the Arminian perspective prevenient grace restores free will so that humans, for the first time, have the ability to do otherwise—namely, respond in faith to the grace of God or resist it in unrepentance and disbelief" (p. 76).

[31] Since the terminology of "necessary" and "sufficient" is teleological in character (necessary *for what?* sufficient for *what?*), its context of usage must always be specified to avoid confusion. For instance, Keathley speaks of "sufficient overcoming grace" and contrasts this with "limited irresistible grace" ("The Work of God," 724–25). However, what he means by "sufficient" is different from what I (and most Calvinists) mean by "sufficient" when speaking of effectual calling. For Keathley, sufficient overcoming grace is "the convicting and enabling work of the Holy Spirit accompanying the preaching of the gospel"; nevertheless, "God's grace can be successfully resisted" (p.

> Besides the call which is external, and often ineffectual, there is another, which is internal and effectual. This always produces repentance and faith, and therefore secures salvation. . . . It is not true of all who receive the external call, that they are predestined to life, justified, and saved. Whenever these blessings are represented as belonging to the called, the internal and effectual call must be meant.[32]

Now I want to sketch the biblical and theological basis for effectual calling, and defend it from a few objections.

Why believe in effectual calling?

A Distinction between the Outer Call and the Inner Call

Several texts appear to teach or at least strongly imply a distinction between the outer call and the inner call. In His parable of the wedding feast (Matt 22:1–14), Jesus contrasts those who were invited to the feast but did not come (vv. 3–8) with those who were actually "gathered together" by the king's slaves so that they filled the wedding hall (vv. 9–10). Jesus seems to contrast these two groups: "For many are called, but few are chosen" (v. 14). The first group received the outer call or invitation, which was resisted; but the second group responded to the summons: they were "gathered together." Thus, the word "called" (the adjective *klētos,* related to the verb *kaleō,* "call") envisioned in verse 14 is an outward call to all, a call that can and often is successfully resisted by those to whom it comes.[33]

Another usage of the term *kaleō,* "call," appears in the epistles: the inward, effectual call. For instance, Paul said that "these whom He predestined, He also called; and these whom He called, He also justified; and these whom He justified, He also glorified" (Rom 8:30). Here "called"

---

726). In other words, paradoxically, Keathley's "sufficient overcoming grace" is not sufficient to overcome all resistance on the part of the sinner (although it is necessary). By way of contrast, the view Keathley terms "limited irresistible grace" is closer to the view I am defending, since "this work always accomplishes the task of drawing his chosen to himself" (p. 725). That is, it is sufficient to overcome the sinner's resistance. (I do not intend this as a criticism of Keathley, just a clarification of my own view in light of his terminology.)

[32] Dagg, *Manual of Theology,* 332.

[33] Likewise, in Luke's recounting of a similar parable, the master's command to the slave was, "Go out into the highways and along the hedges, and compel them to come in, that my house may be filled. For I tell you, none of those men who were invited shall taste of my dinner" (Luke 14:23–24). Again we see two distinct groups who are recipients of two different calls: those who were merely invited did not make it to the meal, whereas those who were *compelled* to attend presumably did so.

refers to the inner, effectual call, for according to Paul everyone who receives *this* call is also justified and glorified. (The repetition of the near demonstrative pronoun *toutous,* "these," indicates that the same group of people is the object of each divine activity in the series, so that whoever is the recipient of one blessing is thereby the recipient of the rest as well.)

Paul told the Corinthians, "We preach Christ crucified, to Jews a stumbling block and to Gentiles foolishness, but to those who are the called, both Jews and Greeks, Christ the power of God and the wisdom of God" (1 Cor 1:23–24). "The called" here are set in contrast to those Jews who heard the message but stumbled at it as well as Gentiles who heard the message and regarded it as foolishness. Clearly for Paul "the called" are not those who merely hear the gospel but those who in fact embrace it. They are called *effectually.*

Likewise, Peter exhorted his readers to pursue various qualities of Christian character, as a means to "be all the more diligent to make certain about His calling and choosing you" (2 Pet 1:10). Clearly Peter was not asking his readers to make sure they heard the gospel outwardly and verbally. Rather, he was using "calling" in its inward, effectual sense: make certain that *you are a believer.*

Finally, Jude said that he was writing his epistle "to those who are the called, beloved in God the Father, and kept for Jesus Christ" (Jude 1). This certainly seems to imply that there is a sense in which "the called" are those who are in fact saved—that is, not only "beloved in God the Father," but also "kept for Jesus Christ," which certainly is not the same group of people who merely hear the gospel outwardly.

God's work of grace in calling a sinner to Himself is sufficient for that person to come to faith

Beyond this biblical distinction between the outer call and the inner call are quite a few texts which teach that God's work of grace in calling a sinner to Himself is *sufficient* for that person to come to faith. It ensures the presence of faith and repentance because these gracious gifts of the Spirit of God are in fact *conveyed* by the effectual call.

For instance, Paul told the Philippians that to them "it has been *granted* [*charizomai,* "to give graciously"] for Christ's sake, not only to believe in Him, but also to suffer for His sake" (Phil 1:29). Here faith itself, not just suffering, is said to be a gift of God.

Likewise, Luke recorded the reply of Peter and the apostles to the Sanhedrin: "He is the one whom God exalted to His right hand as a Prince and a Savior, to *grant* [*didōmi,* "to give"] repentance to Israel, and forgiveness of sins" (Acts 5:31). So both faith and repentance are granted as gifts by the risen and exalted Savior. This view is confirmed by Paul's instruction to Timothy that he should gently correct "those who are in opposition, if perhaps God may *grant* [*didōmi*] them repentance leading to the knowledge of the truth" (2 Tim 2:25; see also Acts 11:18).

Indeed, for Lydia, "the Lord opened her heart to respond to the things spoken by Paul" (Acts 16:14), and for the Gentiles more generally, "as many as had been *appointed* [*tassō*, "to order, determine, put in place"] to eternal life believed" (Acts 13:48). God's effectual work in bringing a sinner to Himself is also likened to a resurrection from the dead: "Even when we were dead in our transgressions, [He] made us alive together with Christ" (Eph 2:5). His work is also compared to something we clearly did not accomplish by our own power or on our own initiative, namely, being born: "according to His great mercy [He] has caused us to be born again to a living hope" (1 Pet 1:3). And this birth was "not of blood nor of the will of the flesh nor of the will of man, but of God" (John 1:12–13). In the end, "by His doing you are in Christ Jesus" (1 Cor 1:30).[34]

John 6

Perhaps the most discussed and, I believe, the most persuasive passage in support of effectual calling is John 6. Note especially these verses:

> Jesus said to them, "I am the bread of life; he who comes to Me will not hunger, and he who believes in Me will never thirst" (v. 35).

> "All that the Father gives [*didōmi*] Me will come to Me, and the one who comes to Me I will certainly not cast out" (v. 37).

> "This is the will of Him who sent Me, that of all that He has given [*didōmi*] Me I lose nothing, but raise it up on the last day" (v. 39).

> "No one can come to Me unless the Father who sent Me draws [*elkō*, "to pull, draw, attract"] him; and I will raise him up on the last day. It is written in the prophets, 'AND THEY SHALL ALL BE TAUGHT OF GOD.'

---

[34] The reader will have to forgive my offering a catena of uninterpreted Scripture texts, but I do think these are most naturally interpreted as supporting my overall thesis that God's regenerating work in our lives not only makes possible but in fact *secures* the intended blessing: faith, repentance, and new life in Christ. Meanings of Greek words here and elsewhere are from *A Greek-English Lexicon of the New Testament and other Early Christian Literature* (BDAG), rev. and ed. Fredrick W. Danker (3d ed.; Chicago: University of Chicago Press, 2000).

This edition is an electronic version of the print edition published by the University of Chicago Press.

Everyone who has heard and learned from the Father, comes to Me" (vv. 44–45).

"But there are some of you who do not believe." For Jesus knew from the beginning who they were who did not believe, and who it was that would betray Him (v. 64).

And He was saying, "For this reason I have said to you, that no one can come to Me unless it has been granted [*didōmi*] him from the Father" (v. 65).

First, in verse 35 Jesus makes coming to Christ ("He who comes to Me") parallel to believing in Christ ("he who believes in Me"), which strongly indicates that they are in fact the same thing. Coming to Christ amounts to exercising saving faith in Christ.

Second, in verse 44 Jesus teaches that no one can exercise saving faith unless God specifically "draws" that person to do so. In fact, according to verse 65, no one can exercise saving faith unless "it" (the faith, the coming to Christ) has been "granted" by God.

Is this really a proof of effectual calling? Many non-Calvinists have responded to John 6 by arguing that these texts only prove that the Spirit's work of "drawing" is *necessary* for men to come to Christ, not that it is *sufficient*. Why can't someone agree that no one can come to Jesus except the Father draws him but also maintain that the Father draws everyone equally, all the time? Thus, the Spirit's work is *needed* if someone is going to come to faith but that work certainly doesn't *ensure* a particular outcome. The drawing of the Spirit is universal, not selective.

The problem with this approach is that it is exegetically implausible. In particular, verses 64–65 reveal that it is precisely in terms of a distinction which the Father makes—in whom He grants to come to Jesus—that Jesus explains the unbelief of those who rejected Him. But this explanation (which is the explanation Jesus gives) couldn't *be* the explanation if the Father drew everyone equally. In verse 65 Jesus began His explanation of the unbelief of the "some" of verse 64 with "therefore" (*dia touto*, "because of this"). His point is that the *reason* these Jews "do not believe" is that it was not granted to them by the Father. This couldn't be the case if the non-Calvinist were correct in supposing that God drew everyone equally by the universal drawing of His Spirit. How can the Father draw everyone equally if the *selectivity* of such drawing explains Jewish unbelief (according to Jesus)?[35]

---

[35] "The only point that Jesus can sensibly be making by His statement in 6:65 is that those resistant to Him do not believe because they are not so drawn by the Father. He surely is not saying to people who are drawn by the Father that only those drawn by the Father can come. This would do nothing to explain what the context of this passage

I conclude that the drawing of men and women by God's Spirit is not only necessary but sufficient for their coming to Christ: those who are "drawn" do in fact exercise saving faith. It secures this outcome by the power of God. The doctrine of unconditional election seems to confirm this view. That men and women come to faith is ultimately the outcome of an eternal, divine plan that it shall be so. In this chapter Jesus teaches that there is a people whom the Father has given to Christ, and this people *shall* come to Christ: "All that the Father gives Me shall come to Me, and the one who comes to Me I will certainly not cast out" (v. 37). In fact, this verse seems to teach unconditional election ("All that the *Father* gives to Me"), effectual calling ("*shall* come to Me"), and perseverance of the saints ("and the one who comes to Me I will *certainly not* cast out").[36]

What are some objections to effectual calling?

Regeneration cannot "precede" faith because they occur simultaneously in Christian experience

Calvinists typically hold that the exercise of faith and the reality of regeneration are simultaneous, chronologically speaking. They happen at the same time. As Keathley put it, "At the moment a person believes, he is also regenerated."[37] Both Calvinists and non-Calvinists can agree about this simultaneity.

But this chronological simultaneity surely does not preclude there being a logical asymmetry, such that one thing logically depends on the other. In everyday life, quite apart from theological matters, we recognize that something can logically depend on something else, and not vice versa, even if both happen together. When Socrates drank the hemlock and died, Xanthippe became a widow. Presumably, these two

---

demands: why His opponents remain in their unbelief" (Bruce Ware, "Effectual Calling and Grace," in *Still Sovereign: Contemporary Perspectives on Election, Foreknowledge, and Grace,* ed. Thomas Schreiner and Bruce Ware [Grand Rapids: Baker, 2000], 219). I highly recommend Ware's entire discussion of John 6 (pp. 212–20).

[36] Does the BFM 2000 teach effectual calling in the sense I am defending? It seems to me that section IV. A. of that document (about "regeneration") is compatible with my view: "Regeneration, or the new birth, is a work of God's grace whereby believers become new creatures in Christ Jesus. It is a change of heart wrought by the Holy Spirit through conviction of sin, to which the sinner responds in repentance toward God and faith in the Lord Jesus Christ. Repentance and faith are inseparable experiences of grace." But it is also ambiguous, such that both proponents and rejecters of effectual calling can endorse that section. It all depends on whether the antecedent of "to which the sinner responds" is "conviction of sin" or "a change of heart wrought by the Holy Spirit." Reasonable people can disagree on the best interpretation here, so perhaps the best view is that the BFM 2000 neither rejects nor requires the doctrine of effectual calling.

[37] Keathley, "The Work of God," 705.

events were simultaneous: Socrates' dying and Xanthippe's becoming a widow. And yet clearly one event *explains* the other. *Because* Socrates died, Xanthippe became a widow. It would be absurd to think that it was the other way around: that because Xanthippe became a widow Socrates died. Clearly one event has logical priority over the other and, therefore, explains the other, even if both happen together with no chronological gap whatsoever.

So it is, Calvinists claim, with respect to regeneration and faith. Regeneration precedes faith not chronologically but logically. It explains why we have faith in the first place.[38]

The Scriptures teach that God's grace is often resisted

Stephen told the Sanhedrin, "You men who are stiff-necked and uncircumcised in heart and ears are always resisting the Holy Spirit; you are doing just as your fathers did" (Acts 7:51). But if men "are always resisting the Holy Spirit," then God's grace is not "irresistible" (as Calvinists often put it), and so the doctrine of effectual calling seems unbiblical.

In reply, to be sure, men *do* reject God's grace again and again. Indeed, the Calvinistic doctrine of an outer, external call describes a call that can and often is successfully resisted by those to whom it comes (see the previous discussion of Matt 22:1–14). But the question is whether a man can successfully resist when God's individual purpose toward that man is to draw him to Himself? The Calvinistic doctrine of effectual calling was never meant to preclude the phenomenon of all men resisting God (see Rom 1:18). Rather, it precludes the notion that, once God has set His purpose of saving grace upon a person (so that he is made willing by God's grace), that person can somehow *continue* successfully to resist. This the doctrine of effectual calling denies.

Effectual calling is a form of coercion

Calvinists typically conjoin their doctrine of effectual calling with a doctrine of total depravity, which holds that unbelievers would never *want* to come to faith—indeed, *cannot* come to faith—apart from God's effectual call in their lives. (Indeed, the doctrine of effectual calling is often *motivated* by way of the biblical materials in support of total depravity.[39])

---

[38] Of course, this defense of the *coherence* of the Calvinist doctrine is no proof that the doctrine is *true*; for that, see the earlier presentation of the relevant biblical materials. But hopefully it does clear up some misconceptions about what it means to say that regeneration, which is implied in effectual calling, precedes faith. No chronological priority need be implied. No one can be a regenerate unbeliever, just as Socrates could not die without making his wife Xanthippe a widow.

[39] E.g., Rom 6:6–7; 8:7–8; 1 Cor 2:14; 2 Cor 4:3–4; Eph 2:1; 4:17–19; Col 1:21; 2:13; Titus 1:15–16. Bruce Demarest explains, "Sin has corrupted every aspect of their being:

If it is true that we would never come to God on our own and if effectual calling not only makes possible but confers the twin gifts of repentance and faith, then is this not a form of coercion, of forcing someone both to choose and to act against His will? Does not conversion, Calvinistically construed, do violence to the will of man? Here we are with all of our sinful desires, rebelling against God, and God unilaterally changes our nature so that we choose Him. He goes against our will, which is to say, He coerces us.

Two brief replies are in order. First, is coercion always bad? To be sure, if coercion were the *central and pervasive* element in human-human and divine-human relationships, that would tend to undermine the integrity of those personal bonds. No relationship would be attractive or desirable if it proceeded *primarily* by way of coercion. Nevertheless, in some contexts coercion is not only acceptable but praiseworthy. If a neighbor's house were on fire and yet there he sat, enamored with some trifling pastime as the burning walls began to collapse on all sides, surely I would be regarded as a hero if I snatched him up and removed him from danger, all without the consent of his will. He might even come to his senses later and thank me for engaging in such decisive effort on his behalf. Why can't this be an acceptable analogy for what God does on our behalf in effectual calling and regeneration? Would the redeemed in heaven really say, "Nice place you've got here, God, but why didn't you respect my will and let me slide into hell? Not sure I can have a real relationship with you."

Second, it's not clear that the Calvinistic view *is* a form of coercion anyway. Since freedom from coercion means having the freedom to do what you want to do, then yes, if you do something even though you did not want to do it, that would be coercion. But at no stage in the Calvinistic pre-conversion/conversion/postconversion story is the sinner forced to *do* anything he does not *want* to do. Rather, God (mysteriously, no doubt) changes our wants. We go from wanting our idols and sins to wanting God and righteousness. But wants are not actions. So regeneration does not produce any actions that go against our wills. Instead, regeneration is a matter of God's *renewing* the will so that the whole person delights in God and is inclined to find Him wholly attractive, to prefer Him above all else. And with that renewed will, we choose in accordance with it, and we choose Christ. At every stage in this story,

mind, will, emotions, relationships, and actions. By virtue of their anti-God bias and predilection to sin, the unregenerate, apart from grace, are incapable of turning to God, pleasing God, and saving themselves. . . . Left to their own resources, sinners degenerate from bad to worse (Rom 1:26–32). This grim human condition, widely attested by revelation and life experience, constitutes the stage for the display of God's marvelous grace" (*The Cross and Salvation* [Wheaton: Crossway, 1997], 75).

we are doing what we want to do. And so at every stage in this story, we are free from coercion. It is never a matter of God's making someone act *contrary to* his will.[40]

Effectual calling carries with it all the problems of unconditional election

Yes, and these problems can be dispensed with in the same way as before. For instance, Keathley said:

> The problem with this view [i.e., irresistible grace or effectual calling] is that it freely accepts the notion that God offers salvation from eternal damnation while at the same time withholding the ability to accept it. The irresistible grace position ensures a purely gracious salvation but does so at a high cost. The logical conclusion is that those who reject the gospel remain lost because God wants them lost.[41]

If this argument is a good one, then we have another "logical conclusion" on our hands, one that applies whether we're Calvinists or not: those who never hear the gospel remain lost because God wants them lost. After all, God could easily *get them* the gospel (He's omnipotent). In fact, the problem looks *worse* in this case: it's not just that God won't do what would be sufficient for their salvation (as in the case of effectual calling); it's that God won't even do what would be *necessary* for their salvation (get them the gospel). If this state of affairs is not a reason to reject the non-Calvinist view, why would it be a reason to reject the Calvinist view?[42]

Conclusion

In conclusion, you may wonder if I have any advice for Southern Baptists who are engaged in the so-called Calvinist-Arminian debate. Yes, I do. To my non-Calvinist brothers, I say: Please consider the arguments I have given and reflect carefully upon the Scriptures I have brought to your attention. May the Lord give you insight into all of this.

---

[40] The 1689 Second London Baptist Confession of Faith makes this point rather well: "effectually drawing them to Jesus Christ; yet so as they come most freely, being made willing by his Grace." Available at www.ccel.org/creeds/bcf/bcfc10.htm (accessed November 19, 2007). The citation is from section X.1.

[41] Keathley, "The Work of God," 725.

[42] In general, effectual calling does not seem to raise any difficulties that are not already raised against unconditional election, including the moral/pragmatic objections already considered under that heading.

To my fellow Calvinists I will be a bit more blunt. There is a distinction between *esse* and *bene esse*, that is, between a doctrine's being part of the essence of the gospel (its *esse*) and a doctrine's being part of the well-being of the gospel (its *bene esse*). In light of this, I find the popular Spurgeon quote to be unhelpful, that "Calvinism is the gospel." I understand what Spurgeon was trying to say, but I think it can be both misleading and unhelpful, to the extent that I never use that quote myself. It's just not worth it, for it usually generates more heat than light. Surely we don't want to get someone to think that he has to believe in all the traditional points of Calvinism if he is going to believe the gospel, and yet that is exactly what that quote can convey if it is tossed around loosely. Most of the evangelical non-Calvinists I know may not believe in the five points of Calvinism, but they do believe in the five *solas* of the Reformation; and even if you think that is inconsistent, God never sent a man to hell for being inconsistent but only for his sins.[43]

Far better simply to give the arguments for Calvinism as best you can and pray that the Lord blesses your efforts. I would counsel my fellow Calvinists in the SBC not to say, "Arminianism denies the essence of the gospel," but rather, "Calvinism promotes the well-being of the gospel by bringing out for God's people all the more clearly how grace is really grace." Non-Calvinists may disagree even with this latter statement, but at least they'll know what our motives are: to magnify the greatness of God's grace, not to draw the circle of fellowship more narrowly than Christ Himself has drawn it.

---

[43] If it is a sin to be inconsistent, God have mercy on us all!

A Southern Baptist Dialogue

Calvinism

Working Together to Make Christ Known

Answering the Call to a Great Commission Resurgence

Daniel L. Akin
President, Southeastern Baptist Theological Seminary
Wake Forest, North Carolina

IN JUNE 1985 SOUTHERN BAPTISTS gathered in Dallas, Texas for their annual Convention. It would be the largest gathering of a Protestant denomination in history. More than 45,000 messengers met as the "Battle for the Bible" reached a feverish pitch. The future of the Southern Baptist Convention was as yet undecided.

On Monday night prior to the Convention's two day meeting, Dr. W. A. Criswell, in his 58th year in the ministry, closed out the two day pastors conference. The date was June 10, 1985. The title of his address was "Whether We Live or Die." His message was historic. Dr. Criswell well understood the urgency of the hour and what was at stake. He knew our denomination was at a crossroads and that the decisions we would make in the coming years would chart our course and impact the health of our convention. He was convinced that we had before us two options: one road would lead to life and usefulness for the kingdom of God. The other would lead to decline and eventually to death. Much was on the line.

Southern Baptists may be facing a similar scenario a little more than 20 years later. The context is different, but once again we are confronted with important issues that cannot be ignored. These issues must not be caricatured or misrepresented. We must face them squarely, honestly, and most of all biblically and theologically. Only then will we discover if we can truly walk together.

The dawn of a new century confronts the church of Jesus Christ with significant new challenges. This is true nationally and on a global scale. Southern Baptists in particular have entered a zone of generational transition that is exciting, but also uncertain. The previous generation had leaders who were loved and respected, trusted and followed. Today there is a tremendous void, if not a vacuum of such respected leaders. Southern Baptists are in the middle of something of a leadership crisis. The death of Adrian Rogers is the symbolic moment that signaled a new day in terms of leadership in the Southern Baptist Convention. God may not raise up a single individual whose larger-than-life personality captures our devotion. That may be best. What is clear, however, is that we need godly men who can help us move forward in concert for the glory of God, the building of the church, and the evangelization of the nations. We need men of character and substance, vision and wisdom, humility and conviction. We desperately need leaders who can guide us and challenge us. Such leaders will not demand leadership, for true leadership is not demanded. It is given. It is given by those who believe and trust men they believe can lead them to do greater things for the glory of God.

We need men with a vision for what can be called "A Great Commission Resurgence." Early in 2007 several of us began talking about such a movement. Building on the conservative resurgence that was initiated in 1979, we believe the time has come for us to focus on the great task the Lord Jesus left us as He ascended back into heaven (Acts 1:8). Fulfilling the task will in no way leave behind or neglect an equal commitment to a faithful biblical theology. In fact, it will naturally grow out of that kind of theology. A true and genuine Great Commission resurgence will of necessity be wed to a strong and healthy theology. Such a theology will have definite and non-negotiable parameters. However, it will avoid a suffocating system that paralyzes our passion to be aggressive in our personal witness and to take the gospel around the globe.

With this preamble before us, I want to raise and attempt to answer two questions: (1) *Why* should we come together in a Great Commission resurgence? And (2) *How* can we come together in a Great Commission resurgence? Some may question the wisdom or even the appropriateness of my raising these questions at a conference on Calvinism. If you happen to fall into that camp, you will, I pray, lend your ear to my brief proposal. This meeting is exactly the place where a Great Commission resurgence should receive a hearty and unanimous "amen!"

Why Should We Come Together in a Great Commission Resurgence?

I will purposefully limit my observations to what I believe are seven compelling reasons we should unite in this task, though the list could easily be expanded.

1. We agree on a common confession of faith to guide us, BFM 2000. This statement is not perfect or exhaustive. However, it is sufficient to provide a theological consensus for our cooperation in obeying the Great Commission. Some of us may confess more than what is found in BFM 2000. I certainly do. However, we will not confess less than what this document affirms. Further, in the context of Calvinism, we will not require more or less than this statement affirms from any direction or perspective. The tent here is big enough for all of us.

2. We agree on the inerrancy, infallibility, and sufficiency of the Bible. Though the precise terms of "inerrancy" and "infallibility" do not appear in article I on "the Scriptures," the affirmative that "all Scripture is totally true and trustworthy" equates to the same. This common commitment separates us from the liberal and neoorthodox theologies that have drained the spiritual life and vitality out of the mainline denominations. Some would say the battle for the Bible has been won and it is time to move on. I would warn against this viewpoint. The battle over the Word of God did not begin in 1979 but in the garden of Eden. The battle for biblical authority will never be completely and finally won until Christ returns in power and glory. Each generation of believers must reaffirm its commitment to Holy Scripture as its sole and sufficient source of authority in all matters.

3. We agree on the necessity of a regenerate church. Southern Baptists may have faltered and stumbled over this at their annual meetings in 2006 and 2007, but I believe we will soon get this right as a convention body. Why am I optimistic on this point? First, because it is biblical. Second, because historically a regenerate church has always been a characteristic of Baptist theology. Now it is evident we have some serious work to do in this area. Some of the conversations and discussions in recent years concerning this doctrinal distinctive have been shallow and sloppy theologically. However, let us lead the way in educating our people to think more biblically about this vital doctrine. Derisive comments and condescending attitudes toward those who, as of yet, do not see the issue clearly, will be of little value. Let's shepherd them in the right theological direction.

4. We agree on the exclusivity of the gospel. Article IV of BFM 2000 on salvation is clear: "There is no salvation apart from faith in Jesus Christ as Lord." The heresies of soteriological universalism and inclusivism are not welcome in Southern Baptist life. They are ruled out of bounds by the witness of Jesus (John 14:6), Peter (Acts 4:12), and Paul (1 Tim 2:5). Our agreement on this theological tenet should serve as a major motivation for a revived devotion to the Great Commission. People are lost—eternally lost—without Christ. He came, by His own confession, "to seek and save that which was lost" (Luke 19:10 KJV). How can we who call Him Lord do less? Charles Spurgeon gets in our business when he says, "Someone asked will the heathen who have never heard the Gospel be saved? It is more a question with me whether we—

who have the Gospel and fail to give it to those who have not—can be saved."

5. We agree on the sinfulness and lostness of humanity apart from Christ. We are of one mind that humans are born in a sinful state. Some see our state as sinners to be a more severe condition than do others. Yet none of us believes that we come into this world with a neutral or positive moral inclination. No, we are sinners both by nature and by choice. All aspects of our being are infected with the disease of sin. As a result no one seeks after God apart from the initiating work of the Holy Spirit. Our sinfulness does not destroy God's image in us, but it is certainly and clearly defaced and damaged. Some of us again may confess more than this, but none of us will confess less.

6. We agree that salvation is by grace alone through faith alone in Christ alone. Salvation is a free gift in which human works plays no part. In our doctrine of salvation, we should start with God and not with man. We all can agree on this. The Bible affirms that salvation is from the Lord (Jonah 2:9) and by grace we are saved through faith. This salvation is not from yourselves; it is God's gift—not from works, so that no one can boast (Eph 2:8–9). The Bible teaches that salvation is God's work. He is the author and finisher of our faith (Heb 12:2). He takes the initiative. He is the true Seeker. The Bible also teaches that we must respond and that we are responsible to repent and exercise faith in Christ. A clear biblical balance must be maintained.

We therefore should affirm the truth of both God's sovereignty and human free will. The Abstract of Principles was the founding confession for The Southern Baptist Theological Seminary. It was penned by Basil Manly Jr. in 1859. Manly was a classic Calvinist, and yet Article IV on providence reveals a healthy, theological balance in our Baptist forefather. Manly wrote,

> God from eternity decrees or permits all things that come to pass, and perpetually upholds, directs and governs all creatures and all events; yet so as not in any wise to be author or approver of sin nor to destroy *the freewill and responsibility* of intelligent creatures. (emphasis mine)

The Bible teaches that God predestines and elects persons to salvation, but that He does so in such a way as to do no violence to their free will and responsibility to repent from sin and believe the gospel. Will we have differences among us in how we nuance this issue? No doubt! Is there a tension here? Yes. Is there divine mystery? Absolutely! Do not let this reality be a discouragement. This is what Paul felt when, at the end of his magnificent treatment of this subject in Romans 9–11, he concludes with a doxology of praise: "Oh the depth of the riches both of the wisdom and the knowledge of God! How unsearchable His judgments and untraceable His ways" (Rom 11:33 HCSB). It is a challenge to fathom the depths of this doctrine. In humility we should gladly and readily acknowledge that, and we also should show respect toward those who do not line up on the issue exactly as we do. Let us listen to one another. Let us learn from one another.

7. We agree that the Great Commission is a divinely mandated assignment given to the church by the Lord Jesus and that it is a task we are to give ourselves to until the end of the age. The modern missionary movement was launched by a Baptist. It was also launched by a Calvinist. His name is William Carey. He represents the best and healthiest stream of the Calvinist tradition and one I can enthusiastically embrace. Carey did not receive universal support in his desire to get the gospel to the "heathen" as they were called in his day. Another tributary of Calvinism was resolute in its opposition to the aspirations of young William. This type of Calvinism was of no value in Carey's day. It is of no value in our day. Significant headway can be made if in heart and confession it can be said, "I am a Carey Calvinist" or "I am a Judson Calvinist" or "I am a Spurgeon Calvinist." I am a Calvinist who embraces with my whole being our Lord's command to take the gospel across the street and around the world. Anything less puts a person outside the camp of Southern Baptists. It is to deny our heritage and misunderstand our identity. It is to neglect Christ's command, disobey His last words, and miss the promised blessing that attends all who take up this holy assignment.

Now lest I be viewed as unfairly picking on my Calvinist brethren, let me quickly add that too many non-Calvinists talk the talk but do not walk the walk. They do not put their money where their mouth is. Few, if any, answer the call to take the gospel to the nations from their churches; and their slick worship services, cute gimmicks, and selling an unrecognizable Christianity are equally tragic and distasteful. We all have much to repent of when it comes to not our *verbal agreement* about the Great Commission, but our *obeying* the Great Commission. After all, I have never met a Southern Baptist who says "I am a non-Great Commission Christian." They would never say this is who they are. They just live like this is who they are.

Here then are seven major areas of confessional and ideological agreement. Here are theological and practical truths that faithful Southern Baptists can embrace—Calvinist and non-Calvinist alike. The argument has been made for why we should come together. Let me now address the second question we must consider.

How Can We Come Together in a Great Commission Resurgence?

I have had a singular and unique privilege in my Christian and Southern Baptist pilgrimage. I am the better for it. On the one hand, I served alongside Dr. Paige Patterson for nine years and studied under him for three years. He was my preaching professor and preached my ordination sermon. He is my father in the ministry and a self-professed non-Calvinist. On the other hand, I also served beside Dr. Al Mohler for almost eight years at The Southern Baptist Theological Seminary. I helped him build the wonderful faculty of our mother seminary. He is one of my closest and best friends.

During those 17 years never did I find myself in a theological quandary. I never felt any pressure to compromise personal convictions. My theology is not identical or in lockstep with either Dr. Patterson or Dr. Mohler. However, though our theology is not *identical*, it is wonderfully and happily *compatible*. On the essential, nonnegotiables of orthodox Christianity and Baptist theology, we see eye to eye with no disagreement—not one. That agreement did not, however, prevent many hours of spirited discussion on numerous issues. On more than a few occasions, we discussed and sometimes debated issues like total depravity, unconditional election, particular redemption and effectual calling. We had healthy conversations about the timing of the rapture (never its *truth*), plurality of elders, cessationism of spiritual gifts, the best way to interpret Genesis 1, and the pros and cons of Calvin, Luther, the Anabaptists, Wesley, Whitefield, Edwards, Owen, Gill, Mullins, and Conner. We talked about the best form of apologetics and, if I remember correctly, we landed in three different camps.

Still, we worked together very well At least that was my perspective. How did we do it? How can we do it as Southern Baptists? I put forward five propositions for our careful, even prayerful, consideration. I will state them in the form of theological and practical axioms I hope we all can embrace.

1. We need a sound theology, not a soft theology or a straightjacket theology. Our agreement on the BFM 2000 is an asset, not a weakness. It is a plus and not a minus. If I were to pen my own confession, it would not look exactly like the BFM 2000. But then I do not want or need people exactly like me in order to work together for the proclamation of the gospel of Jesus Christ and the building of His church. Our confession is a solid foundation for a sound theology that avoids the pitfalls and quick-sand of a straightjacket theology. Do we want or need a theology that rules out of bounds open theism, universalism and inclusivism, faulty perspectives on the atonement, gender-role confusion, works salvation, apostasy of true believers, infant baptism, and noncongregational ecclesiologies, just to name a few? Yes we do. These theological errors have never characterized who we are, and they have no place in our denomination today. Inerrancy is not up for debate. The deity of Jesus and His sinless life are not up for debate. The triune nature of God as Father, Son, and Holy Spirit is not up for debate. The perfect atoning work of Christ as a penal substitute for sinners is not up for debate. Salvation by grace alone through faith alone in Christ alone is not up for debate. A regenerate church should not be up for debate. Believer's baptism by immersion should not be up for debate. The glorious, historical, and personal return of Jesus Christ is not up for debate. The reality of an eternal heaven and an eternal hell are not up for debate. There is nothing soft about this kind of theology, and we must avoid a soft theology at all cost.

On the other hand, we must also be on guard against a straightjacket theology that would bind us and potentially suffocate us. For clarity sake let me illustrate. I have Calvinist friends who say they hope and pray for the day when all of our seminaries have presidents and faculties that are five-point Calvinists. They dream of a denomination that looks exactly like the Baptist participants in "Together for the Gospel" and John MacArthur's Shepherd's Conference. Let me quickly note that most of these men are friends of mine who have spoken at the seminaries I have served. I intend to invite each of them to grace the campus of Southeastern again in the future. Is this my vision for the future of the Southern Baptist Convention? No, it is not.

I also have friends who pray Calvinism will just go away. The first question they ask me when I mention a pastor or professor is not "Does he have a private prayer language?" but "Is he a Calvinist?" They believe conferences like this are ill-advised and of no real value. They would mandate, if they could, that there would be no classic Calvinists in our seminaries, and they would never, under any circumstances, support a five-point Calvinist for an office in the Southern Baptist Convention. They would even hint that one's position on Calvinism should be a litmus test for appointment as a missionary. Is this my vision for the future of the Southern Baptist Convention? No, it is not. Both perspectives are too extreme and will weaken our denomination. Both perspectives also ignore a major stream in our historical identity. We are better than this. At least, I pray that we are.

The BFM 2000 is a well-constructed canopy under which varying perspectives on the issue of Calvinism can peacefully and helpfully co-exist. Is there a place for differing positions on the issues of election, the extent of the atonement and calling, as well as the details of how we do missions, evangelism, and give the invitation? I am convinced that the answer is yes.

Furthermore, I believe we will be the better for it theologically and practically as we engage one another in respectful and serious conversation. As one who considers himself to be a compatibilist, affirming the majestic mystery of both divine sovereignty and human responsibility, I have been challenged and strengthened in my own theological understanding by those less reformed than I am as well as those more reformed. Because of our passionate commitments to the glory of God, the lordship of Christ, biblical authority, salvation by grace through faith, and the Great Commission, we should be able work in wonderful harmony with one another.

2. We need to let a biblical theology drive and determine our systematic theology. Any theological system must guard against becoming a master rather than a servant to the biblical revelation. It runs the risk of squeezing the biblical text to fit its necessary parameters and thus making the Bible say what it actually does not say. This is true of any system of theology, whether it is Calvinism or Arminianism, dispensationalism or covenant theology; Roman Catholicism, Greek Orthodoxy, or even Evangelicalism.

The safeguard that will keep us from falling into this theological trap is to let a biblical theology drive, determine, and dictate our systematic theology. We must have a text-driven theological system. This will enable us to avoid those theological ghettos that may espouse a nice, neat theological system, but that do so at the expense of a wholesome, well-rounded, and comprehensive theology. Will this force us to live with some tension in our system? The answer, of course, is yes. That, however, is a small price to pay for biblical fidelity in exegesis and theological balance in our system.

When John MacArthur was at Southern Seminary during my service there, he was asked about predestination, election, and prayer. His response was quite interesting: "I do not let my Reformed theology get in the way of my prayers for the salvation of my children and grandchildren. I pray and ask God to save each and every one of them." I appreciate the pastoral sensitivity, personal concern, and theological balance in his perspective. The same spirit was evident in the heart of Charles Spurgeon, who is such a worthy model for all of us in this discussion.

Charles Spurgeon was a five-point Calvinist. This is not debatable. Yet he was also a passionate evangelist and soul winner. On August 1, 1858, he preached a sermon entitled "Sovereign Grace and Man's Responsibility." The words of wisdom that flowed from his mouth that day could only come from a capable pastor/theologian with a shepherd's heart and a love for the lost. Here are words we all should embrace:

> I see one place, God presiding over all in providence; and yet I see and I cannot help seeing, that man acts as he pleases, and that God has left his actions to his own will, in great measure. Now, if I were to declare that man was so free to act, that there was no precedence of God over his actions, I should be driven very near to Atheism; and if, on the other hand, I declare that God so overrules all things, as that man is not free enough to be responsible, I am driven at once into Antinomianism or fatalism. That God predestines, and that man is responsible, are two things that few can see. They are believed to be inconsistent and contradictory; but they are not. It is just the fault of our weak judgment. Two truths cannot be contradictory to each other. If, then, I find taught in one place that everything is fore-ordained, that is true; and if I find in another place that man is responsible for all his actions, that is true; and it is my folly that leads me to imagine that two truths can ever contradict each other. These two truths, I do not believe, can ever be welded into one upon any human anvil, but one they shall be in eternity: they are two lines that are so nearly parallel, that the mind that shall pursue them farthest, will never discover that they converge; but they do converge, and they will meet somewhere in eternity, close to the throne of God, whence all truth doth spring....You ask me to reconcile the two. I answer, they do not want any reconcilement; I never tried to reconcile them to myself, because I could never see a discrepancy.... Both are true; no two truths can be inconsistent with each other; and what you have to do is to believe them both.

3. We need a revival of authentic expository preaching that will lead us to be genuine people of the book. Our denomination has suffered, and suffered terribly, because of the absence of true and authentic biblical exposition. Seduced by the sirens of modernity, we have jetti-soned the faithful and consistent proclamation of the Word of God. Many of us thought the conservative resurgence would provide healing to this malady that plagues the body of Christ like a cancer. Tragically, this has not been the case.

Unfortunately we have a generation of preachers, good and godly men, who believe themselves to be expositors when what they do in the pulpit betrays their confession. Too much of our SBC preaching sounds like the classic liberal Harry Emerson Fosdick who used the pulpit as a counseling office and a self-help seminar. Our seminaries clearly share in the responsibility of our current plight, though the speed at which so many of our preachers flee to the newest homiletical fads bespeaks an even greater spiritual and theological problem.

In the days ahead we must aggressively pursue a pulpit agenda of what I would call *engaging theological exposition*. We must wed sub-stance and style, content and delivery. We must teach the whole counsel of Scripture book by book, chapter by chapter, verse by verse and word by word. We must honor the text and its context, recognizing that the Holy Spirit of God gave us the Scriptures as we have them. To rearrange and manipulate the text of Scripture is to correct the Holy Spirit and play the fool.

Authentic exposition will bring biblical balance to our theology and force us to engage the tough doctrines of Scripture. It will also cultivate a pastoral perspective that results in a love for the Savior's sheep and the lost.

Authentic exposition will also help us recapture the truth of Luke 24 that all of the Bible testifies to Christ. It will pursue its holy assign-ment in light of the grand redemptive story of Scripture. Moralistic and self-help preaching will be set aside as weak and wholly inadequate in building healthy churches and healthy doctrine. Rather, we will preach the Bible in such a way that Jesus is always seen as the hero and Savior of sinners who cannot save themselves. We will not preach the Old Testament like a Jewish rabbi, nor will we preach any text like a sancti-fied Dr. Phil or Tony Robbins. We will bind our mind, heart, and soul to the text of Scripture in a sacred commitment characterized by a fidelity that is reflected in the covenant of marriage itself. Worship the Bible? Never? Love and honor the Bible? Always, both in what we say about it and in how we handle it.

4. We need the balance of a Great Commission theology. In 1 Cor 11:1 the apostle Paul makes a remarkable statement: "Imitate me, just as I also imitate Christ" (NKJV). That is exactly what we need to do as we join in an unbreakable and permanent union the twin disciplines of theology and missions. The greatest missionary and theologian who ever lived was Jesus. The greatest Christian missionary and theologian who ever lived was Paul. The Son of God came down from heaven on missionary assignment "to seek and to save that which was lost" (Luke 19:10 KJV). He came to show us the Father (John 1:18) and to reveal how all of Scripture is fulfilled in Him (Luke 24). No man ever spoke or taught like our Lord. He saw no dichotomy between being a passionate evangelist and a committed theologian, and neither should we.

Paul was no different, for he sought to imitate Christ in all he did. Therefore he could write Romans and Galatians, Ephesians and Philippians, Colossians and the Pastorals. He could also spend his energy and give his life in at least four missionary journeys (three recorded in Acts) because he knew that without a preacher, people will not hear, and without hearing, people will not be saved (Romans 10).

I run the risk of caricature and stereotype, but let me take the risk anyway. Some of my semi-Arminian friends (I do not think there are any consistent, self-conscious Arminians in the SBC) need to become better and more careful theologians. They need to study theology themselves as lifelong learners, and they need to teach theology to their people. We do our Lord and our people a tremendous disservice with an anemic, soundbite, dumbed-down theological diet. No wonder so many starving souls are running to the banquet tables of Piper, MacArthur, Begg, and others of a Reformed orientation. I urge ministers to quit whining about first, second, and third John (Calvin, MacArthur, and Piper) and raise the theological bar in their churches, teaching the content and theology of the biblical epistles of 1, 2, and 3 John. I urge ministers to train and equip their flock so that they can engage "the doctrines of grace" and other theological issues intelligently and graciously.

In contrast, some of my hyper-active Calvinist friends (I do not think there are many, if any, consistent, self-conscious, hyper-Calvinists in the SBC) need to get out of their study and onto the mission fields. They need to hit the streets and become hot-hearted evangelists for Jesus Christ, and not John Calvin. In 2007 I traveled to six countries visiting and ministering to our International Church Planting students. My wife Charlotte and I saw the lostness of the world up close and personal. In the summer and fall of 2007, I immersed myself in missionary biographies, spending time with William Carey, Adoniram Judson, Bill Wallace, and Lottie Moon. I discovered something very interesting. All four, including Lottie Moon and Bill Wallace, as best I can tell held a strong view of God's sovereignty. However, none of them wore this doctrine on their sleeves or on their chest as a badge of honor. They were too busy trusting in the providence of a sovereign God and pursuing the souls of lost men and women to get sidetracked by theological debates that can lead us down a dead end street. We spend our time talking and arguing, while they spent their time going and telling. Is your theology leading you to go to the nations with the gospel of Jesus Christ? Are you building, where you serve, a Great Commission church? Do you pine for the salvation of the lost with the same zeal that you pine for theology? Good missionaries will be good theologians, and good theologians will be good missionaries. John Piper recently said all true Calvinists will be missionaries. He's right. A strong view of God's sovereignty should lead to courage and obedience in evangelism and missions.

5. We need to love and respect one another as brothers and sisters in Christ even though we are not in complete agreement on every point of theology. One of our problems has been semi-Arminians with an attitude and Calvinists with a chip on their shoulder. The shrill rhetoric, sloppy history and theology, and unchristian words and actions on both sides of this issue have resulted in a number of unnecessary situations. Misrepresentations of our brothers and sisters' positions on this issue have prevented healthy and honest conversations. Hidden agendas have divided churches and fractured fellowships. False caricatures have made for cute sound bites, but they lack Christian charity and integrity. All in all, the cause of Christ and the well-being of His body have been damaged.

When Dr. Adrian Rogers died in November 2005, many of us wept in sorrow at the loss of this great man to the church, and especially to Southern Baptists. However, not everyone felt this way. On the day of his death, my son Jonathan was teaching at Boyce College on the campus of Southern Seminary. During their time of prayer, he shared with his class the home-going of Dr. Rogers. Later, after class, a student approached him and said he could see that Jonathan was grieving over Dr. Rogers's death. But then he said, "Don't you think the death of Adrian Rogers is a great thing for the cause of Calvinism in the SBC?" Jonathan was speechless, and so was I when he told me. We must not forget that if it were not for Adrian Rogers, we would not be here today, and the SBC would not be discussing Calvinism, but homosexuality, universalism, and feminism.

However, the pendulum does not swing only in one direction. Comparing Calvinists to Muslims, accusing them of fatalism, and stating that there is no such thing as an evangelistic Calvinist is either ignorant or dishonest or both. I am not sure which is worse. Are there nonevangelistic Calvinists? Of course, the answer is yes, and they should be ashamed of themselves. They fail to represent the best and healthiest stream of that tradition. But are there non-evangelistic semi-Arminians who are derelict in sharing their faith and building a Great Commission church? Absolutely. Southern Baptists are continuing to experience a decline in baptisms. And yet the overwhelming majority of our churches are not pastored by five-point Calvinists. Could it be that the real problem is not Calvinism but a lack of love for Christ, the shortage of a vigorous and healthy theology, and the abundance of agendas for church life that push to the back row the reaching of the lost, both at home and across the globe? Could it be that our lack of demonstrable and evidential love for one another on numerous levels has compromised and wounded our witness? Let us not forget that it is not by a perfect theology that the world will know we are Christians. It is by the way we love one another. Approximately six months before he died, I had lunch with Adrian Rogers in Memphis. We talked about the current state of the SBC, the conflict and confusion which were showing up at every turn. With his typical wisdom and insight he gave an analogy that captured perfectly where we are and why we are here. During the conservative resurgence, Bible believing Southern Baptists stood shoulder to shoulder as we faced an enemy, theological liberalism, that would destroy us if given the chance. Minor differences in theology and methodology did not trouble us because our attention was directed towards our common enemy. Today, we do not find ourselves shoulder to shoulder on the battlefield. Now we are in the barracks looking face-to-face into one another's eyes. Because many of us are in the habit of fighting, we are now fighting not the real enemy, but one another. The real enemy is Satan, the world, and the flesh. We need to get back on the battlefield and engage once again our real opponent and adversary. Dr. Rogers was right. We need to be shoulder to shoulder, back on the battlefield, with the sword of the Spirit and the unconquerable gospel of Jesus Christ. That is where the real enemy is located. That is where the real war is going on.

Conclusion

The modern missionary movement was birthed out of evangelical Calvinism, both in Great Britain with William Carey and in America with Adoniram Judson. Both drank from the well of David Brainerd. He drew nourishment from Jonathan Edwards. Would it not be a remarkable providence of our sovereign God if a conference on Calvinism was the genesis and spark of a Great Commission Resurgence among Southern Baptists? Wedding a healthy, well-informed, and robust theology to a consuming passion for the evangelization of the nations, we come together as never before to carry out the final command given by King Jesus. Our Baptist fellowship is big enough, in all the right ways, to have room for William Carey, Andrew Fuller, Luther Rice, Adoniram Judson, Charles Spurgeon, John L. Dagg, Basil Manly Sr. and Jr., Lottie Moon, and Annie Armstrong. It is big enough to include Al Mohler and Paige Patterson, Voddie Baucham and J. D. Greer, Adrian Rogers and Timothy George, Jerry Vines and Mark Dever, W. A. Criswell and Hershel Hobbs, Buddy Gray and Johnny Hunt, Andy Davis and Steve Gaines, Danny Akin and Tom Ascol. We may not agree on everything, but we agree on more than enough to work together for our Lord Jesus in fulfilling the Great Commission. Will we live or will we die? Will we come together for life or fracture apart in death? I make my choice for life. It is my hope and my prayer that you will join me.

Working Together to Make Christ Known: Considerations for the Future

Tom Ascol
Senior Pastor, Grace Bible Church
Executive Director, Founders Ministries
Cape Coral, Florida

THE CHAPTERS IN THIS BOOK have helped clarify many of the points of unity as well as points of tension that exist between so-called Calvinists and non-Calvinists within the Southern Baptist Convention (SBC) of churches. Obviously, much more could be said; but what has been addressed provides a hopeful model for serious, theological dialogue and points the way forward into what I trust will be further efforts to encourage and challenge one another to follow Christ more carefully.

Without this kind of open and honest dialogue, I despair of the future of the SBC. Despite all our impressive statistics and favorable recognition in the evangelical world, we stand in need of ongoing doctrinal and spiritual renewal. Our devotion to the authority of God's Word must be matched with a similar commitment to its sufficiency, or else we risk undermining the positive gains secured by the conservative resurgence.

Such reformation will not be experienced without the kind of humility that is willing to be challenged and, where necessary, corrected by the Word that we love and hold dear. That is one of the functions of genuine Christian fellowship. Where such fellowship is broken or even hindered, we are robbed of one of our primary means not only of growing in grace but also of advancing the cause of our Lord and Savior, Jesus Christ.

Southern Baptists and cooperation go together like airplanes and aerodynamics. The more care that is given to the latter, the more useful are the former. Cooperation is part of the Southern Baptist Convention's DNA. The charter of the convention, established in 1845, states the reason for its formation as being "for the purpose of eliciting, combining, and directing the energies of the Baptist denomination of Christians, for the propagation of the gospel."[1]

In other words, the SBC was formed to help Baptists work together to make Christ known. Over the last 162 years, the combined energies of Southern Baptists have been blessed of God to propagate the gospel throughout the United States and among more than a thousand people groups of the world. Yet the present needs and future potential far exceeds all our past accomplishments, which makes the rising challenges and threats to our cooperative unity all the more serious.

Calvinism is arguably the most important issue that confronts Southern Baptists in the early years of the twenty-first century, but it is far from the only one, nor is it necessarily the most volatile. It is important because it is substantive both theologically and historically. No one can argue that the doctrines of sovereign grace did not occupy at least a major part of the theological foundation of the SBC.[2] Many of our earliest denominational leaders, educators, and pastors were firmly convinced that these doctrines are imminently biblical. Our confessional history also bears witness to the prominence of Calvinism in our denominational heritage.

Additionally, it is evident that a growing number of modern Southern Baptists are becoming convinced that the doctrines of grace are taught in God's Word.[3] As other chapters indicate, this development has been met with mixed reviews by denominational leaders, pastors, and laypersons throughout the SBC. Furthermore, it is sadly but unmistakably clear that some have used the doctrines of grace as a license to engage in ungracious conduct.

All this underscores the challenge that faces Southern Baptists who are genuinely interested in working together to make Jesus Christ known

---

[1] www.sbc.net/aboutus/legal/default.asp.

[2] Of course, many argue that Calvinism was the theological consensus of the founders of the SBC. Timothy George notes, "The *Philadelphia Confession of Faith* was transplanted to the Charleston Baptist Association in South Carolina. It soon became the most widely accepted, definitive confession among Baptists in America both North and South. Each of the 293 "delegates," as they were then called, who gathered in Augusta to organize the SBC in 1845, belonged to congregations and associations which had adopted the *Philadelphia/Charleston Confession of Faith* as their own." (Timothy and Denise George, general editors, *Baptist Confessions, Covenants, and Catechisms* [Nashville: Broadman & Holman, 1996], 11.) George goes on to note the prominent influence which this confession had on early Southern Baptist theological education: "When James P. Boyce was considering a suitable confessional standard for Southern Baptists' first seminary, he originally planned to use the Philadelphia/Charleston Confession of Faith as the doctrinal basis for this new institution. When he became convinced that a briefer, more succinct summary of doctrine would be more useful for this purpose, he commissioned Basil Manly Jr. to draft an Abstract of Principles based on the Philadelphia/Charleston standard." (Ibid.)

[3] See the chapter by Ed Stetzer in this volume.

to our unbelieving world. Mere denominational affiliation can no longer sustain such cooperation (if it ever could). If Southern Baptists are going to work together in any kind of meaningful way, we must find common ground on which we can stand while linking arms.

In light of that, I would like to propose an agenda that can, I believe, lead us in our quest for such common ground. As you might have guessed, my proposal has five points. Call it "the five points of bridge building," if you will. The first three points are doctrinal and definitional. The last two are ethical and convictional.

Al Mohler has proposed the work of "theological triage" as a tool to help us think about the relative importance of various doctrinal issues.[4] While no Christian is free to dismiss any teaching of God's Word as unimportant, we must recognize that some truths are foundational to others and are, therefore, more important than others in the establishment and maintenance of genuine Christian unity.

In that spirit I suggest that there are three doctrinal issues that we must address and on which we must come to a large measure of agreement if we hope to establish a foundation for working together in any legitimate way to make Christ known. I pose them in the form of questions.

1. What is the gospel?
2. What is a Christian?
3. What is a church?

No doubt many will be tempted to scoff at asking such basic questions. After all, don't we all know the answers to these questions? Should making an issue of these elementary subjects be seen as offensive or at least a waste of time?

Obviously, I am convinced that we can no longer assume that we do agree on these most basic biblical teachings. In fact, I fear that because we have so long assumed that we know the answers to these questions we are in many ways losing the gospel, misrepresenting what it means to be a Christian and promoting religious societies that have little to do with what the New Testament calls a church.

What Is the Gospel?

The Greek word for gospel, *euaggelion*, occurs more than 70 times in the New Testament. It means simply, "good news." The gospel is news. It is a message. It is the news of God's work in providing salvation for sinners through His Son, Jesus Christ.

---

[4] www.albertmohler.com/commentary_read.php?cdate=2004-05-20.

The content of the gospel is this: *who* Jesus Christ is, *what* He has done, and *why* that matters. The gospel answers those three questions. In other words, the gospel is all about Christ. To preach the gospel is to preach Christ. He is the content of our message.

Listen to the way the apostle Paul simply and forcefully makes this point in 1 Cor 15:1–4:

> Moreover, brethren, I declare to you the gospel which I preached to you, which also you received and in which you stand, by which also you are saved, if you hold fast that word which I preached to you—unless you believed in vain. For I delivered to you first of all that which I also received: that Christ died for our sins according to the Scriptures, and that He was buried, and that He rose again the third day according to the Scriptures.[5]

When Paul said, "Christ," he was referring to the man Jesus Christ who was born of the virgin Mary in fulfillment of Old Testament prophecy. He is the Messiah sent from God, the eternal Son of God, fully man and fully divine. There is no gospel apart from the person of Jesus Christ.

Paul went on to elaborate the work of Christ—what He has done. Specifically, he cited Jesus' death, burial, and resurrection. He died "for our sins." This is a reference to the atoning work of Christ on the cross—His substitutionary sacrifice in behalf of sinners, His taking upon Himself the wrath of God that was due to our sins so that in Him we might have forgiveness.

This is the essence of the message—the good news that Jesus commissions us to proclaim. This is the data. These are the facts. Without them, there is no gospel. Fail to speak of Jesus Christ, and you have failed to preach the gospel.

The gospel is not merely a set of facts to be recounted. After all, it would not take long to do that, and yet we find the apostles and early churches giving days, months, and years—indeed their whole lives—to proclaiming the gospel of Jesus Christ. There is far more to the gospel than just a set of facts, more than just a message. Rather, it is a message so radical, so reality altering, that to believe it changes your whole life. In that sense, we could see the gospel is a worldview.

Believing the gospel affects every area of your life. This is what makes it a worldview. It is like a pair of corrective glasses that enables you to see the world the way it really is.

---

[5] Unless otherwise indicated, Scripture quotations are from the NKJV.

In this sense the gospel is both exclusive and inclusive. It is *sui generis* in that there is no other message that has the power to bring fallen people into a saving relationship with the Creator. It is the metanarrative of the Bible and indeed of all history because it gives meaning to life.

The gospel is an exclusive message

The gospel of Jesus Christ is the only message we are to preach. Paul made this abundantly clear in his first letter to the Corinthians. Consider the language that he uses to describe his ministry among them.

> For the message of the cross is foolishness to those who are perishing, but to us who are being saved it is the power of God. For it is written: "I will destroy the wisdom of the wise, and bring to nothing the understanding of the prudent." Where is the wise? Where is the scribe? Where is the disputer of this age? Has not God made foolish the wisdom of this world? For since, in the wisdom of God, the world through wisdom did not know God, it pleased God through the foolishness of the message preached to save those who believe. For Jews request a sign, and Greeks seek after wisdom; but we preach Christ crucified, to the Jews a stumbling block and to the Greeks foolishness, but to those who are called, both Jews and Greeks, Christ the power of God and the wisdom of God. Because the foolishness of God is wiser than men, and the weakness of God is stronger than men (1 Cor 1:18–25).

He was unwilling to omit or even amend the simple message of Christ crucified because he was convinced that it alone is the power and wisdom of God to those who believe it. He makes an even more radical statement in the next chapter of that letter.

> And I, brethren, when I came to you, did not come with excellence of speech or of wisdom declaring to you the testimony of God. For I determined not to know anything among you except Jesus Christ and Him crucified. I was with you in weakness, in fear, and in much trembling. And my speech and my preaching were not with persuasive words of human wisdom, but in demonstration of the Spirit and of power, that your faith should not be in the wisdom of men but in the power of God (1 Cor 2:1–5).

If we are going to be apostolic in our preaching, then we must, like Paul, recognize the centrality of the gospel and determine "not to know anything . . . except Jesus Christ and Him crucified" in all our proclamation. Spurgeon understood this and so admonished his fellow pastors, "Give the people Christ, and nothing but Christ. Satiate them, even though some of them should say that you also nauseate them with the gospel."[6]

Neither Paul nor Spurgeon advocated a reductionist approach to preaching. To preach the gospel exclusively does not mean that all we do is recite gospel data in our sermons. Nor does it mean that all we ever talk about is Jesus. Rather, it means that we recognize that all saving knowledge is wrapped up in or extends from Jesus Christ crucified. Therefore, no part of divine revelation can be adequately preached until it is preached in its proper relationship to Christ.

This sheds light on true expository preaching. Jesus said to the Jews of His day, "You search the Scriptures, for in them you think you have eternal life; and these are they which testify of Me" (John 5:39). Luke describes His instruction to the two disciples on the road to Emmaus this way: "And beginning at Moses and all the Prophets, He expounded to them in all the Scriptures the things concerning Himself" (Lk 24:27). To the rest of His disciples, He said, "These are the words which I spoke to you while I was still with you, that all things must be fulfilled which were written in the Law of Moses and the Prophets and the Psalms concerning Me" (Lk 24:44).

Do you see the implication that this has for preaching? If the whole Bible is about Jesus, then no part of the Bible can be rightly preached unless Christ is preached from it. Therefore, all biblical preaching must be Christological, which is another way of saying that all biblical preaching must be gospel preaching. If a sermon can be well received in a synagogue or by a gathering of Mormons or Jehovah's Witnesses, it is not a Christian sermon.

The gospel is an all-inclusive message

The metanarrative of the gospel informs not only all biblical revelation but also all human experience. All the stories within redemptive history serve to make known the one, overarching story of what God has done for sinners in the person and work of Jesus Christ. All our teaching and living must be governed and guided by the gospel of Christ. This means that all theology and all ethics must be grounded in who Jesus is and what He has done.

---

[6] Charles H. Spurgeon, *An All-Round Ministry* (Pasadena, TX: Pilgrim Publications, 1973), 117.

I love systematic theology and believe not only that it is a legitimate discipline but also that it is a necessary one for effective Christian ministry.[7] One of the dangers of systematic theology, however, is that it can easily be approached in a way that is detached from the Gospel. While we divide theology into separate categories to facilitate study, we must always remember that Christology is the main heading of all. Paul gives us an example of how to do this in Col 1:15–18 where he treats the doctrines of God, creation, and church in their relationship to the person and work of Jesus Christ. Keeping the gospel central will prevent our doctrinal studies and preaching from devolving into mere intellectualism or doctrinaire treatments of biblical subjects.

Again, listen to Spurgeon on this point:

> Again, the theme of a minister should be Christ Jesus in opposition to mere doctrine. Some of my good brethren are always preaching doctrine. Well, they are right in so doing, but I would not care myself to have as the characteristic of my preaching, doctrine only. I would rather have it said, "He dwelt much upon the person of Christ, and seemed best pleased when he began to tell about the atonement and the sacrifice. He was not ashamed of the doctrines, he was not afraid of threatening, but he seemed as if he preached the threatening with tears in his eyes, and the doctrine solemnly as God's own word; but when he preached of Jesus his tongue was loosed, and his heart was at liberty." Brethren, there are some men who preach the doctrine only, who are an injury, I believe, to God's church rather than a benefit. I know of men who have set themselves up as umpires over all spirits. They are the men. Wisdom will die with them. If they were once taken away the great standard of truth would be removed. We do not wonder that they hate the Pope, two of a trade never agree, for they are far more popish than he, they being themselves infallible. I am afraid that very much of the soundness of this age, is but a mere sound, and is not real; does not enter into the core of the heart, nor affect the being. Brethren, we should rather preach Christ than election. We love election, we love predestination, we love the great doctrines of God's word,

---

[7] See my "Systematic Theology and Preaching" in *FJ* 4 (Spring 1991): available online at founders.org/FJ04/editorial.html and "The Pastor as Theologian" in *FJ* 43 (Winter 2001) available at founders.org/FJ43/contents.html.

but we had rather preach Christ than preach these. We desire to put Christ over the head of the doctrine, we make the doctrine the throne for Christ to sit on, but we dare not put Christ at the bottom, and then press him down, and overload him with the doctrines of his own word.[8]

All ethical concerns must also be seen as deriving from the gospel of Jesus Christ. No bare list of principles or precepts can rightly lay claim to the description of Christian ethics. The gospel keeps admonitions to live holy lives from the emptiness of moralism. The apostles based all their practical teaching on the person and work of Jesus.

For example, they taught sexual purity not as bare precept but as a necessary expression of devotion to Jesus Christ who "has loved us and given Himself for us" (Eph 5:2, see vv. 3–6) and because God's people do not belong to themselves but have been "bought at a price" (1 Cor 6:20; see vv. 15–20). Similarly, faithfulness in marriage was taught not as a mere moral or beneficial duty but as a calling to dramatize the gospel through a living parable where the wife gets to play the one rescued and the husband portrays the one who gets killed in order to rescue (Eph 5:22–26).[9] Even something as apparently "unspiritual" as giving is grounded in who Jesus is and what He has done. "For you know the grace of our Lord Jesus Christ, that though He was rich, yet for your sakes He became poor, that you through His poverty might become rich" (2 Cor 8:9).

Such gospel reasoning extends across the ethical spectrum in the writings of the apostles. Because they understood the content, exclusivity, and inclusiveness of the message of Christ, all their doctrinal and ethical teaching was based on and extends from the gospel.

What Is a Christian?

The 2000 Baptist Faith and Message (BFM 2000) gives a whole article (IV) to the nature of salvation. Its statements are helpful in answering the question, What is a Christian?

Salvation involves the redemption of the whole man, and is offered freely to all who accept Jesus Christ as Lord and Saviour, who by His own blood obtained eternal redemption for the believer. In its broadest sense salvation includes regeneration, justification,

---

[8] Charles Spurgeon, "Christ Lifted Up," *New Park Street Pulpit*, vol. 3, 260.
[9] I am indebted to Voddie Baucham for this language.

sanctification, and glorification. There is no salvation apart from personal faith in Jesus Christ as Lord.

A. Regeneration, or the new birth, is a work of God's grace whereby believers become new creatures in Christ Jesus. It is a change of heart wrought by the Holy Spirit through conviction of sin, to which the sinner responds in repentance toward God and faith in the Lord Jesus Christ. Repentance and faith are inseparable experiences of grace. Repentance is a genuine turning from sin toward God. Faith is the acceptance of Jesus Christ and commitment of the entire personality to Him as Lord and Saviour.

B. Justification is God's gracious and full acquittal upon principles of His righteousness of all sinners who repent and believe in Christ. Justification brings the believer unto a relationship of peace and favor with God.

C. Sanctification is the experience, beginning in regeneration, by which the believer is set apart to God's purposes, and is enabled to progress toward moral and spiritual maturity through the presence and power of the Holy Spirit dwelling in him. Growth in grace should continue throughout the regenerate person's life.

D. Glorification is the culmination of salvation and is the final blessed and abiding state of the redeemed.

These four aspects of salvation occur in accordance with God's gracious purpose in election. As article V of the BFM 2000 states:

Election is the gracious purpose of God, according to which He regenerates, justifies, sanctifies, and glorifies sinners. It is consistent with the free agency of man, and comprehends all the means in connection with the end. It is the glorious display of God's sovereign goodness, and is infinitely wise, holy, and unchangeable. It excludes boasting and promotes humility.

What the BFM 2000 summarizes is the biblical teaching on the blessings of the new covenant. First announced in Jeremiah 31, these blessings are repeated in Heb 8:8–12 and 10:16–17. In short, they are the blessings of God's work *for* us and God's work *in* us. Because of Jesus Christ, Christians have their record permanently wiped clean and their inner life irrevocably renewed. Thus they are both justified and regenerated.

269

This does not happen apart from personal repentance and faith; but where true repentance and faith exist, Christians find not only the promise of a right standing before God in justification but also a new life in regeneration. Justification is God's declaration, and it changes a sinner's status before His law. A gracious work takes place outside the sinner and is received by faith alone in Christ alone. Regeneration, as the BFM 2000 says, is a change of heart wrought by the Holy Spirit. It is a gracious work that takes place within the sinner, changing his nature. These two works are distinct but inseparable. One's status before God in heaven would have no change without a commensurate change in one's nature on earth.

While much needs to be said about justification in these days when the historic, protestant understanding of that doctrine is under attack,[10] I want to focus primarily on regeneration. If justification is being assailed by formal refutations from the academy, regeneration is being undermined by practical neglect and reinterpretation in the church.

The Bible is neither silent nor confusing on this point. Jesus told Nicodemus that unless a person is born again he cannot enter, indeed he cannot even see, the kingdom of God (John 3:3,5). Of all the analogies available to our Lord to make His point, He chooses the analogy of birth. Watching the birth of a baby is an awesome experience. You know the baby is alive because he breathes, cries, moves, and eats. If he does not do these things, something is horribly wrong.

Paul wrote in 2 Cor 5:17 that "if anyone is in Christ, he is a new creation; old things have passed away; behold, all things have become new." The person who becomes a Christian is a new creation. He is powerfully and decisively changed. The apostle John made the same point in 1 John 3:8–10:

> Whoever makes a practice of sinning is of the devil, for the devil has been sinning from the beginning. The reason the Son of God appeared was to destroy the works of the devil. No one born of God makes a practice of sinning, for God's seed abides in him, and he cannot keep on sinning because he has been born of God. By this it is evident who are the children of God, and who are the children of the devil: whoever does not practice righteousness is not of God, nor is the one who does not love his brother (ESV).

---

[10] For a helpful, gracious defense of the historic Protestant view of justification see John Piper's *The Future of Justification: A Response to N. T. Wright* (Wheaton IL: Crossway, 2007).

To recover a biblical view of what a Christian is, we must also take seriously the many warnings the Bible gives about false conversions. There is such a thing as false faith. Many who clamored after Jesus "believed in His name" but Jesus "did not commit Himself to them" because they did not savingly believe in Him; that is, they did not trust in Him alone for salvation (John 2:23–25). Similarly, Simon Magus believed, but he was not saved because his faith was not saving faith (Acts 8:13,18–24). Jesus warned that the day of judgment will reveal that many who make professions of faith will be surprised that they are rejected by the Lord because their faith did not result in obedient lives. In other words, it was not saving faith (Matt 7:21–23).

Whereas Baptists, of all evangelicals, ought to be in the vanguard of protecting the biblical teaching on regeneration, (which is exactly where we have been historically) we have actually aided the public disfigurement of this doctrine over the last two generations. In fact, Southern Baptists are some of the worst offenders.

What do I mean? As I argue below, Baptists—including Southern Baptists—have historically called for a regenerate church membership. Yet in recent history our evangelistic and ecclesiological practices have resulted in gutting the biblical teaching on what it means to be a Christian. We have consistently failed to take seriously the radical nature of the new birth, as the Bible defines it, and, consequently, have allowed our shallow practice of evangelism to "dumb down" regeneration. The result is that we have subtly come to assume that being a Christian need not mean living in ways that are significantly different from unbelievers.[11]

Several years ago a NAMB "specialist in evangelistic follow-up" stated that, based on his observations, less than 10 percent of the people who make decisions as a result of typical Southern Baptist evangelism are active in Bible study one year later.[12] Less than one in 10! If General Motors had that kind of failure rate, they would be shut down and be forced either to reengineer their whole production process or to go out of business. The specialist's conclusion was that we need to do a better job of following up with newly converted people so that they will not go back into the world.

---

[11] This is not a uniquely Southern Baptist problem, as indicated by surveys that find little discernible difference between the lifestyles of those professing to be "born-again Christians" and those who are irreligious. See, for example, George Barna's research that found that "Born Again Christians [Are] Just as Likely to Divorce as Are Non-Christians," available at www.barna.org/FlexPage.aspx?Page=BarnaUpdate&BarnaUpdateID=170.

[12] James Dotson, "Neonatal intensive care critical to spiritual health of newborn Christians," Baptist Press article posted on July 2, 1999, available online at www.bpnews.net/bpnews.asp?id=507.

Intentional discipleship is crucial, but one cannot disciple a spiritual corpse. The undeniable reality is that much, arguably most, Southern Baptist evangelism results in spiritual stillbirths. Paige Patterson expressed agreement with this view when he wrote that three out of four of the converts that result from the evangelism of his "less Reformed" friends can be dismissed as being "not genuine."[13]

George Whitefield is reported to have preached more than 300 sermons on "ye must be born again." Once one of his hearers asked him, "Mr. Whitefield, why do you keep preaching, 'Ye must be born again; ye must be born again?'" The great evangelist responded, "Because ye must be born again!" We would do well to follow Whitefield's example.

If Southern Baptists are going to come together in order to make Christ known, we must recover a clear understanding of what it means to be a born-again Christian, and we must retool our evangelistic preaching to aim at nothing less. What is a biblical Christian, and how does a person become one? That is a vital question we must answer biblically.

If we fail to recover a biblical view of what constitutes a Christian, then we should not be surprised to see more and more thoughtful Southern Baptists opting out of denominational campaigns that perpetuate the failed evangelistic practices that result in a majority of our "converts" showing no signs of spiritual life shortly after their profession of faith.

What Is a Church?

The third question is, What is a church? The New Testament uses the word *church* in a universal, or catholic sense to refer to "the whole company of those who are saved by Christ."[14] Jesus had this in mind when He promised to build His church on the rock of apostolic testimony (Matt 16:18). Paul also was thinking this way when he called Christ the head of the church (Eph 1:22; 5:23).

The word pictures Scripture uses to describe the church emphasize our Lord's devotion to His people. The church is the bride of Christ for whom He willingly laid down His life (Eph 5:22–32). It is also His body (Eph 1:22–23) that lives in vital communion with Him. The intimacy Christ shares with His church is made evident in the way He framed His question to Saul, the persecutor of the church, "Why are you persecuting Me?" (Acts 9:4). Additionally, the church is also described as a house

[13] Tom J. Nettles and Russell D. Moore, eds., *Why I Am a Baptist* (Nashville: Broadman & Holman, 2001), 70.

[14] John L. Dagg, *Manual of Theology, Second Part, a Treatise on Church Order* (The Southern Baptist Publication Society, 1858; reprint edition, Harrisonburg, VA: Gano Books, 1982), 100.

or temple, comprised of living stones that are being built on Christ, the chief cornerstone (1 Pet 2:4–7).

If our Lord is passionate about the church, then how can His followers remain indifferent to it? We must love what He loves and be devoted to that which is the object of His devotion.

Though the church universal is a glorious concept, the emphasis in the New Testament is on the local church. Most of the letters in the New Testament were written to individual churches, and that is the focus of the question before us. What is a local church? Consider the answer given in article VI of the BFM 2000:

> A New Testament church of the Lord Jesus Christ is an autonomous local congregation of baptized believers, associated by covenant in the faith and fellowship of the gospel; observing the two ordinances of Christ, governed by His laws, exercising the gifts, rights, and privileges invested in them by His Word, and seeking to extend the gospel to the ends of the earth. Each congregation operates under the Lordship of Christ through democratic processes. In such a congregation each member is responsible and accountable to Christ as Lord. Its scriptural officers are pastors and deacons. While both men and women are gifted for service in the church, the office of pastor is limited to men as qualified by Scripture.

This statement wisely makes no issue of secondary matters, such as the plurality of pastors, the possibility of deaconesses, or whether "Baptist" must be in the name of a church. Those issues can be debated among us, but they must not detract from the essentials of what constitutes a local church of Jesus Christ. Such a church comprises baptized believers who are actively engaged in *associating* by virtue of a covenant commitment; *observing* the ordinances; *being governed* by the laws of Christ; *exercising* spiritual gifts, rights, and privileges; and seeking to evangelize the world.

The only way a church can honestly fit this description is by adhering to the principle of a regenerate church membership. This, of course, is precisely what Baptists have historically done. Recent years, however, have seen this principle widely forsaken throughout the SBC.

The historical record is overwhelmingly clear. From the earliest Baptist confessions of faith—of both Arminian and Calvinistic variety—in the seventeenth century to the minutes of associations and local congregations in the eighteenth and nineteenth centuries, Baptists have spoken with one voice on this subject.

Consider the testimony of the nineteenth-century Baptist E. T. Hiscox in his widely distributed *Directory for Baptist Churches*: "What class of persons should be admitted as members to the fellowship of Christian churches? Baptists say that godly persons, baptized on a profession of faith, are the only proper and suitable persons. That all others should be denied admission, and if already within the Church should be cast out."[15]

Commitment to a regenerate church membership requires that both formative and corrective discipline be practiced in a church. That is, on the one hand, care must be exercised in who is allowed into the membership; and those who do become covenant members are to be instructed and nurtured in the ways of Christ. On the other hand, when anyone who has become a member refuses to live in the ways of Christ, then he is to be lovingly corrected according to the directions of our Savior in Matt 18:15–18 and other passages that address this issue (1 Cor 5; Gal 6:1; 2 Thess 3:14–15; Titus 3:10; etc.).

Failure to reestablish and maintain this biblical and Baptist principle is the most glaring and damaging violation of God's Word among Southern Baptists today. The 2006 SBC Annual Church Profiles indicate that there are 16,306,246 members in Southern Baptist churches while only 6,138,776 people attend a primary worship service in those churches in a typical week. Of those that show up, Paige Patterson estimates that 30–40 percent are unconverted.[16] If he is anywhere near accurate, then less than 25 percent of our church members are Christians!

That could go a long way in explaining much of the godless activity that too often characterizes many churches. If a church is filled primarily with unconverted people, why should we be surprised when they act like it?

If we are going to work together to make Christ known, then we must be willing to get our own house in order by repenting of our widespread failure to honor Jesus Christ in our local churches. We must repent of our failure to work for a regenerate church membership and our neglect of our Lord's clear commands to practice loving discipline within our congregations.

I am not advocating any attempt to make wholesale changes in a church instantly. That would be disastrous. People must be taught. The Word of God must be allowed to speak to these issues. Pastors need to

---

[15] E. T. Hiscox, *The New Directory for Baptist Churches* (Judson Press, 1894), 17.

[16] "Interview with Paige Patterson," *FJ* (Fall 2000): available at www.founders.org/FJ42/article2.html.

exercise wisdom and patience as they lead churches to travel the path of recovery. We must have men of humility and courage who are willing to find that path and unflinchingly lead their churches to pursue it.

John Dagg made this sobering, searching comment in his *Treatise on Church Order*: "It has been remarked, that when disciplines leaves a church, Christ goes with it."[17] What if he is right?

So much for the three doctrinal points of the agenda. As we work toward establishing and maintaining a consensus on those questions, we must also commit ourselves to operating by two ethical principles. We must be committed to (1) obey the truth, and (2) live in love.

Obey the Truth

The Bible puts a premium on truth. God is the God of truth (Isa 65:16), and He calls us to buy the truth and never sell it (Prov 22:23). Jesus is truth personified, and He promised that we would know the truth and the truth would set us free (John 14:6; and 8:32). The third person of the Trinity is called the Spirit of truth, and Jesus promised His disciples that this Spirit would guide them into all the truth (John 14:17; 15:26; 16:13). By the truth we are sanctified (John 17:17,19).

Paul described the essence of sin as suppressing the truth and exchanging the truth of God for a lie (Rom 1:18,25). Those who will experience God's wrath would neither love the truth, nor believe it, nor obey it (2 Thess 2:10,13; Rom 2:8). The Galatian believers got driven off course by being hindered from obeying the truth (Gal 5:7). Heretics are described as those who have swerved from the truth (2 Tim 2:18), and Paul warned Timothy of days of apostasy when those in the church will turn away from the truth and start believing fables (2 Tim 4:4).

Being saved is equated with coming to the knowledge of the truth (2 Tim 1:4). Mature Christians are described as being of the truth and established in the truth (1 John 3:19; 2 Pet 1:12), and John spoke for all pastors when he said that he had no greater joy than to hear that his children were walking in the truth (3 John 4).

As followers of Christ, we must learn to honor truth not only by submitting to all that God has revealed in His Word but also by standing for truth in every area of life. That means we must be willing to speak the truth even when it is hard or might be offensive. It also means that when we are compelled to critique the views of another we will not hypocritically allow our zeal for the truth to become a justification for violating the ninth commandment.

---

[17] Dagg, *Treatise on Church Order*, 274.

For example, unconditional election and conditional election cannot both be true. Whichever position a person believes the Bible to teach, he should not be inhibited in asserting it and critiquing views that are contrary to it. Commitment to truth requires no less. Those who disagree with him should not lament his efforts but rather should applaud them, even as they in turn scrutinize his arguments in light of the Scripture they both affirm to be inerrant and infallible.

If truth matters and we are to be submissive to it, then we must be willing to defend it and argue for it. Working together does not prohibit that kind of engagement. In fact, working together for the sake of Christ actually requires that kind of allegiance to His revealed truth.

This attitude is missing in most ecumenical efforts. Too often truth gets sacrificed in the name of cooperation. The agenda I am proposing does not allow for such compromise. Truth must be valued and obeyed as authoritative. It must never be trumped by love.

In fact, genuine love would never allow that to happen because true love rejoices in the truth (1 Cor 13:6). Furthermore, Peter teaches that authentic submission to the truth leads to earnest love for the fellow believers. "Since you have purified your souls in obeying the truth through the Spirit in sincere love of the brethren, love one another fervently with a pure heart" (1 Pet 1:22).

That leads to my fifth and final point.

Live in Love

The God of love calls His children to live in love. All our relationships are to be characterized by love. We are to love our neighbors as we love ourselves (Matt 22:39) even if our neighbor is an enemy (Matt 5:44). As followers of Christ, we are called to live in love just as He also loved us and gave Himself for us (Eph 5:2). No servant is greater than his master; and if our Lord loved sinners sincerely and sacrificially, so should His disciples.

Beyond the love that Christians are to have for all people, we have a special responsibility to love one another. In fact, Jesus said that our love for one another will be the distinguishing mark that we are His disciples. "A new commandment I give to you, that you love one another; as I have loved you, that you also love one another. By this all will know that you are My disciples, if you have love for one another" (John 13:34–35).

Love is not an option for the Christian. It is our Lord's marching orders. When we fail to love one another, we become a hindrance to making Jesus Christ known to the watching, unbelieving world. Jesus did not say that the world will know we are His disciples by our theology, our good works, or our zeal for truth. Rather, they will know by the way we love one another. Francis Schaeffer called this "the final apologetic."[18]

When we find ourselves disagreeing with Christian brothers over points of theology, we need to reread the apostle Paul's description of the "more excellent way" in 1 Cor 13. In that chapter we are taught that both great gifts and great works are nothing without love. Verse 2 is particularly instructive for Christians who have doctrinal controversies with other believers. "And though I have the gift of prophecy, and understand all mysteries and all knowledge, and though I have all faith, so that I could remove mountains, but have not love, I am nothing."

Paul holds out a prospect that is every Calvinist's dream: to understand all mysteries and all knowledge! What lover of truth would not desire that ability? Think of the advantage you would gain in theological debates or the books that you would be able to write on vitally important topics! Yet such theological expertise is absolutely worthless without love.

Unless we come to believe this and remember it, our doctrinal differences will inevitably lead to acrimonious conflicts that are more concerned with winning arguments than helping brothers. And the world will listen and watch and have no basis on which to conclude that we are disciples of Jesus Christ.

All this is what Paul had in mind when he exhorted us to speak the truth in love to one another so that we might grow in spiritual maturity (Eph 5:15). We do not sacrifice truth on the altar of love and unity. Neither do we justify unloving attitudes, speech, and behavior in the name of truth. Rather, in love, we stand for and speak the truth.

What if we were to start relating to one another like this within the SBC? Would our doctrinal disagreements suddenly disappear or become unimportant? No, but there would be a greater opportunity for real unity to be kindled and for doctrinal issues to be openly discussed without insult and caricature.[19] Where brothers and sisters quit misrepresenting one another and begin speaking carefully, honestly, and humbly to and about one another, a culture will be cultivated that promotes trust and cooperation. We would give evidence of a willingness both to give and to receive helpful criticism—an art that, on both points, has been largely lost in our day. We would find genuine fellowship and a desire to see Jesus Christ glorified in and through all our efforts.

---

[18] Francis Schaeffer, *The Mark of the Christian* (2d ed.; Downers Grove, IL: InterVarsity, 2006), 25–28.

[19] Two helpful articles on this point are Roger Nicole, "Polemic Theology: How to Deal with Those Who Differ from Us," *FJ* 33 (Summer 1998) available at www.founders.org/FJ33/article3.html; and Timothy George, "Speaking the Truth in Love," *FJ* 4 (Spring 1991) available at www.founders.org/FJ04/article4.html.

Conclusion

The SBC is not ultimately important, nor is it in any sense vital in the march of Christ's kingdom through the world. But God has been pleased to bless and use the people and churches of the SBC over the course of the denomination's history. The original vision of the founders of this convention is worth fighting for. Wisdom remains in "eliciting, combining, and directing the energies of the Baptist denomination of Christians, for the propagation of the gospel."

If we are going to recapture this vision, we must become absolutely clear on the nature of the gospel we seek to propagate and be clear on what happens to a person who savingly believes it. We must recover the biblical and Baptist doctrine of the church and work to see our local congregations biblically reordered.

Nowhere in this proposal have I suggested that everyone must or should become a convinced Calvinist, though you will hear no complaints from me were that to happen! Rather, what I have tried to argue is that every Southern Baptist who wants to work together to make Christ known should be willing to work for a consensus on basic biblical truths and to relate truthfully and lovingly to others within the SBC family.

All of us want to see the gospel proclaimed in greater power in our churches, in our communities, and to the nations. Can we not do that better together than alone? If so, then is it not worth the effort to reach out to one another on the basis of the gospel, in the spirit of truth and love, and link arms in the great work of making our Savior known?

I am convinced it is worth it and that the time has come for us to press on in this great work together.

Glossary of Some Important Theological Terms
As Used by the Authors of
Calvinism: A Southern Baptist Dialogue

Shawn D. Wright

Amyraldianism

Named for Moise Amyraut (1596–1664), a French Reformed theologian, this is a version of Calvinistic doctrine often called "four-point Calvinism." It denies the doctrine of limited atonement, teaching instead that it is best to conceive of God's relationship to humanity as His having two wills. As the divine Mediator, Christ satisfies divine justice, and God calls each person to faith in Christ and offers everyone forgiveness of sins. This is God's universal will. Yet, the Lord foresaw that none would receive Christ because of their sin, so He has a specific will directed to just some. He decrees to give the elect faith in Christ so that they will be saved. Since Amyraut taught that Jesus had died for all persons indiscriminately and that God offered salvation to all persons on the *condition* of their repentance and faith (which he denied they could meet apart from divine intervention), this doctrine is sometimes referred to as "hypothetical universalism."

Arminianism

Named for Jacob, or James, Arminius (1560–1609), a Dutch Reformed theologian who questioned some of his church's teaching on the relationship between God's sovereignty and human free will in salvation. Arminians teach that God grants all humans free will and restores their ability spiritually, that Jesus died for all persons, that God's election of persons to salvation is conditioned upon His foreknowledge that they will trust in Christ and persevere in the faith, and that Christians can fall away from the faith and be damned eternally. Southern Baptists have never fallen into Arminianism because of their belief, shown in their confessions, that Christians cannot lose their salvation.

Augustinianism

Calvinism's teaching on the sovereignty of God as it works out in the doctrine of salvation. So called because the great church father Augustine (354–430) taught the same thing as Calvin and other Calvinistic theologians at the time of the sixteenth-century Reformation in upholding the sovereignty of God in salvation due to humankind's deadness in sin apart from the sovereign intervention of God.

Charleston Tradition

The Charleston, South Carolina, Baptist Church was the first Baptist church in the South, having been planted by the Philadelphia Baptist Association in 1758. The Charleston Association's theology was traditional five-point Calvinism. It greatly influenced southern Baptist life through the association's statement of church discipline, its confession, and its many prominent leaders.

See "Sandy Creek Tradition."

Classical Calvinism

Often used to refer to the Calvinistic doctrine of salvation as promulgated by the Synod of Dort.

See "Dort, Synod of" and "Five Points of Calvinism."

Consistent Calvinism

See "Five Points of Calvinism."

Decree(s) of God

This refers to the fact that from eternity past God determined everything that would happen in His creation. He has a comprehensive plan for the world. According to the Baptist Catechism, "The decrees of God are his eternal purpose according to the counsel of his will, whereby, for his own glory, he has foreordained whatsoever comes to pass." Scriptural proof includes Ps 115:6; Isa 46:10; Rom 11:36; and Eph 1:11.

Theologians sometimes speak of the "decrees" of God, but in reality there is one eternal decree. As A. A. Hodge argued, "We believe that the Decree of God is one single, eternal intention. There cannot be an order of succession in His purpose. The whole is one choice. . . . The question, therefore, as to the Order of Decrees is *not* a question as to the order of acts in God's decreeing, but it *is* a question as to the true relation sustained by the several parts of the system which He decrees to one another."

See "Infralapsarianism," "Sublapsarianism," and "Supralapsarianism."

Definite Atonement

The belief that Christ bore the wrath of God for God's elect alone. God the Father chose certain persons to be His children, and on the cross the Son died for those persons alone. This is the "L" of TULIP. It is often referred to as the fifth point of Calvinism; if one is a four-point Calvinist, or Amyraldian, this is the point that is denied.

See "Amyraldianism," "Five Points of Calvinism," and "Universal Atonement."

Doctrines of Grace

Usually shorthand for the "five points of Calvinism."

See "Five Points of Calvinism."

Dort, Synod of

Where Calvinism, as we normally call it, was formulated. An international synod of Reformed Protestants in Dort, Holland, in 1618–1619. It was called to respond to the followers of Arminius who had objected to the Reformed, or Calvinistic, Dutch national church's views in five areas. The canons that Dort decided upon in response are often referred to as the five points of Calvinism.

Double Predestination

The belief, held only by some five-point Calvinists, that God not only eternally predestined the elect to salvation but also decreed the damnation of the non-elect eternally, leaving them in their sins. The Canons of the Synod of Dort say that the Scripture "declares that not all men are elect but that certain ones have not been elected, or have been passed by in the eternal election of God. These God out of His most free, most just, blameless, and unchangeable good pleasure has decreed to leave in the common misery into which they have by their own fault plunged themselves, and not to give them saving faith and the grace of conversion" and "finally to condemn and punish them eternally" for all their sins (1.15).

See "Preterition" and "Reprobation."

Effectual Calling

The Calvinistic doctrine that the call of the gospel to all who hear it is effective for those whom God has chosen to salvation. It is "God's sovereign action in securing a response to his summons . . . the effective evocation of faith through the gospel by the secret operation of the Holy Spirit, who unites men to Christ according to God's gracious purpose in election."

Extent of Atonement

The answer to the question, For whom did Christ die? The two options are: (1) for the elect alone (five-point Calvinism); and (2) for all persons indiscriminately (other evangelicals).

See "Definite Atonement" and "Universal Atonement."

Five Points of Calvinism

Dort's response to the Arminian doctrines. Often remembered by the mnemonic "tulip": (1) T—the *total depravity* of fallen humankind in sin; (2) U—God's *unconditional election* of certain of these fallen persons to salvation due only to His will and not to any foreseen merit or faith in them; (3) L—Christ's *limited atonement* on the cross for God's elect; (4) I—God's *irresistible grace* in effectively calling His elect through the gospel and granting them new life through His Spirit; (5) P—the certain *perseverance of the saints* through the trials of life until they arrive in heaven.

See "Arminianism" and "Dort, Synod of."

Free Offer of the Gospel

The *bona fide* ("in good faith") offer of salvation to all who hear the gospel and will repent of their sins and trust in Christ for forgiveness. Some non-Calvinists do not think that Calvinists can freely offer the gospel to all persons since they believe in a definite atonement of Christ for the elect alone. Calvinists respond that the extent of the atonement does not come into play in the preaching of the gospel, for the call is to sinners to repent and trust in Christ; the evangelist need not preach that "Jesus died for you." The only group that denies the free offer to all sinners indiscriminately is hyper-Calvinism.

High Calvinism

A term usually used synonymously with "hyper-Calvinism." Sometimes, though, it refers to supralapsarian Calvinism.

See "Hyper-Calvinism" and "Supralapsarianism."

Hyper-Calvinism

An unbiblical extension of five-point Calvinism. It teaches God's eternal justification of the elect, antinomianism (that is, the non-obligation of Christians to obey God's law), and that the gospel should not be preached indiscriminately to all sinners, but only to those who are "sensible" of their spiritual need. Baptists have eschewed this view because of its refusal to preach the gospel to all sinners and its teaching that God does not have real love for all persons.

Infralapsarianism

Latin for "after the fall." A Calvinistic view of the logical (not the chronological) outworking of God's eternal decree. It teaches that only after God had decreed to create humans and to permit the fall did He choose His children to be His own and to leave the rest of fallen humankind in their sins. Thus God's election is of persons whom He viewed as already sinful. And the non-elect are condemned for their own sin and rebellion. Ephesians 1:3–7 is used as a support of this position.

See "Supralapsarianism."

Limited Atonement

See "Definite Atonement."

Moderate Calvinism

Four-point Calvinism.

See "Amyraldianism."

Particular Redemption

See "Definite Atonement."

Preterition

God's sovereign passing by of the non-elect, thus excluding them from His decree of salvation.

See "Double Predestination" and "Reprobation."

Regular Baptists

Baptists in the South who followed the Calvinism of the Philadelphia Baptist Association, usually adopting the Philadelphia Confession as their statement of faith.

Reprobation

From the Latin verb *reprobare*, to reprove. This is the belief that God has eternally condemned all non-elect persons to eternal condemnation for their sins. Calvin insisted "that this is not just a matter of God's 'passing over' the non-elect, but an actual hardening so that they are actually strengthened to resist the gospel," although he also taught that humans are unable to understand the full counsel of God on this issue and must humbly trust His goodness and justice in this.

See "Double Predestination" and "Preterition."

Sandy Creek Tradition

The Sandy Creek (N.C.) Association, founded in 1758, was started by Shubal Stearns, who came out of the Separate Baptists of Connecticut. It was marked by zealous evangelism and lively worship. Some historians think that this tradition is best seen as distinct from the Charleston Tradition, both of which, with their different emphases, fed into the founding of the Southern Baptist Convention in 1845.

See "Charleston Tradition" and "Separate Baptists."

Separate Baptists

Baptists in the South who traced their heritage to the Separate Congregationalists who separated from established Congregational churches as a result of the spiritual fervor that swept through New England in the First Great Awakening of the 1730s and 1740s. Some historians claim that this tradition was less Calvinistic, and more revivalistic, than the Regular Baptists. Others claim that it was generally as Calvinistic, although not willing to adopt the Philadelphia Confession because its churches thought there were doctrinal matters that churches should not specify but leave to individual conscience.

See "Sandy Creek Tradition."

Sublapsarianism

Usually used as a synonym for infralapsarianism.

See "Infralapsarianism."

Supralapsarianism

Latin for "beyond the fall." A Calvinistic view of the logical (not the chronological) outworking of God's eternal decree. It teaches that after God decreed to create all humanity He then decided to choose the elect to be His children and to condemn the non-elect eternally. And this took place logically before God allowed sin to enter the world, so those whom He elected and reprobated were not viewed as being sinful. Romans 9:6–24 is thought to support this position.

See "Infralapsarianism."

Unconditional Election

The Calvinistic doctrine that God eternally chooses the elect to salvation in Christ because of His sovereign and loving will alone. His choice of them is not due to any quality He sees in them or to the faith He foresaw they would have in Christ. They deserve only His just, eternal wrath; but He graciously gives them life instead.

Universal Atonement

The belief that Christ bore the wrath of God for all persons indiscriminately. It is held by all evangelicals except for five-point Calvinists. Not only is it thought to make sense of biblical passages like John 3:16 and 1 John 2:2, but it is also thought to warrant the free offer of the gospel to all persons.

See "Definite Atonement," "Arminianism," and "Amyraldianism."

Name Index

Subject Index

A

altar call   *93, 135, 165, 178–80, 181*

Anabaptists   *78, 187*

atonement, doctrine of   *117, 118, 119, 120, 121, 128, 129, 130, 131, 132, 134, 136*

atonement, limited   *122–26, 132*

atonement, substitutionary   *56, 121, 140–44*

B

baptism, believer's   *189*

Baptist Faith and Message   *38, 39, 79, 83, 91, 248, 252, 254*

Baptists, American   *35, 183*

Baptists, English   *181, 183, 187*

Baptists, General   *34, 78*

Baptists, Particular   *34, 48, 78, 187*

Baptists, Primitive   *181*

Baptists, Regular   *80*

Baptists, Separate   *48, 80*

Baptists, Southern   *171–72, 181, 183, 188, 190, 247*

Baptists, Texas   *73–75, 79, 82, 84, 94*

Baptists, American   *35*

Billy Graham School for Missions, Evangelism, and Church Growth   *177*

C

calling, effectual   *48, 186, 233–240, 242*

Calvinism, Baptist   *77–81, 84*

Calvinism, classical   *75–77, 79, 84*

Calvinism in the SBC (Lifeway 2006 Study)   *13, 14, 15, 16–17, 20–21, 22, 24–25, 26*

Christology   *85*

church, the   *272–75*

Church Growth Movement   *160, 167–68*

compatibilism   *53, 198*

conversion   *89, 179*

covenant   *147*

Cyprian   *30*

D

damnation   *200*

decision   *166–67*

determinism   *197*

E

ecclesiology   *91, 189*

elect, the   *198*

election, doctrine of   *131, 197, 269*

election, unconditional   *217–33, 239*

eternal security   *29*

Scripture Index